International and Development Education

The *International and Development Education Series* focuses on the complementary areas of comparative, international, and development education. Books emphasize a number of topics ranging from key international education issues, trends, and reforms to examinations of national education systems, social theories, and development education initiatives. Local, national, regional, and global volumes (single authored and edited collections) constitute the breadth of the series and offer potential contributors a great deal of latitude based on interests and cutting edge research. The series is supported by a strong network of international scholars and development professionals who serve on the International and Development Education Advisory Board and participate in the selection and review process for manuscript development.

SERIES EDITORS
John N. Hawkins
Professor Emeritus, University of California, Los Angeles
Senior Consultant, IFE 2020 East West Center

W. James Jacob
Assistant Professor, University of Pittsburgh
Director, Institute for International Studies in Education

PRODUCTION EDITOR
Heejin Park
Research Associate, Institute for International Studies in Education

INTERNATIONAL EDITORIAL ADVISORY BOARD
Clementina Acedo, *UNESCO's International Bureau of Education, Switzerland*
Ka-Ho Mok, *University of Hong Kong, China*
Christine Musselin, *Sciences Po, France*
Yusuf K. Nsubuga, *Ministry of Education and Sports, Uganda*
Val D. Rust, *University of California, Los Angeles*
John C. Weidman, *University of Pittsburgh*

Institute for International Studies in Education
School of Education, University of Pittsburgh
5714 Wesley W. Posvar Hall, Pittsburgh, PA 15260

Center for International and Development Education
Graduate School of Education & Information Studies, University of California, Los Angeles
Box 951521, Moore Hall, Los Angeles, CA 90095

Titles:
Higher Education in Asia/Pacific: Quality and the Public Good
Edited by Terance W. Bigalke and Deane E. Neubauer

Affirmative Action in China and the U.S.: A Dialogue on Inequality and Minority Education
Edited by Minglang Zhou and Ann Maxwell Hill

Critical Approaches to Comparative Education: Vertical Case Studies from Africa, Europe, the Middle East, and the Americas
Edited by Frances Vavrus and Lesley Bartlett

Curriculum Studies in South Africa: Intellectual Histories & Present Circumstances
Edited by William F. Pinar

Higher Education, Policy, and the Global Competition Phenomenon
Edited by Laura M. Portnoi, Val D. Rust, and Sylvia S. Bagley

The Search for New Governance of Higher Education in Asia
Edited by Ka-Ho Mok

International Students and Global Mobility in Higher Education: National Trends and New Directions
Edited by Rajika Bhandari and Peggy Blumenthal

Curriculum Studies in Brazil: Intellectual Histories, Present Circumstances
Edited by William F. Pinar

Forthcoming titles:

Policy Debates in Comparative, International, and Development Education
Edited by John N. Hawkins and William James Jacob

Increasing Effectiveness of the Community College Financial Model: A Global Perspective for the Global Economy
Edited by Stewart E. Sutin, Daniel Derrico, Rosalind Latiner Raby, and Edward J. Valeau

Access, Equity, and Capacity in Asia Pacific Higher Education
Edited by Deane Neubauer and Yoshiro Tanaka

CURRICULUM STUDIES IN BRAZIL

INTELLECTUAL HISTORIES, PRESENT CIRCUMSTANCES

EDITED BY
WILLIAM F. PINAR

palgrave
macmillan

CURRICULUM STUDIES IN BRAZIL

First published in 2011 by
PALGRAVE MACMILLAN®
in the United States—a division of St. Martin's Press LLC,
175 Fifth Avenue, New York, NY 10010.

Where this book is distributed in the UK, Europe and the rest of the world,
this is by Palgrave Macmillan, a division of Macmillan Publishers Limited,
registered in England, company number 785998, of Houndmills,
Basingstoke, Hampshire RG21 6XS.

Palgrave Macmillan is the global academic imprint of the above companies
and has companies and representatives throughout the world.

Palgrave® and Macmillan® are registered trademarks in the United States,
the United Kingdom, Europe and other countries.

ISBN: 978–0–230–104105

Library of Congress Cataloging-in-Publication Data is available from the
Library of Congress.

A catalogue record of the book is available from the British Library.

Design by Newgen Imaging Systems (P) Ltd., Chennai, India.

First edition: March 2011

10 9 8 7 6 5 4 3 2 1

Printed in the United States of America.

Contents

List of Figures

Acknowledgments

I thank Palgrave Macmillan's Burke Gerstenschlager, Professor W. James Jacob, and Professor John Hawkins for their support of this project.

I thank Ashwani Kumar, graduate assistant at the Centre for the Study of the Internationalization of Curriculum Studies—who helped in ways large and small, and whose synoptic essay on Brazilian curriculum studies appears here as chapter 1.

I thank Carole Wallace for making possible my daily life at UBC: she handles countless bureaucratic (especially, financial) details, welcomes visitors to the Centre, and is a talented webpage designer. On this occasion, she also edited the chapters composed by our Brazilian colleagues. What would I do without you, Carole?

I am grateful to Elizabeth Macedo for her help throughout the project.

Without the support of the Social Sciences and Humanities Research Council of Canada, this project could not have been undertaken.

Without the generosity of my Brazilian colleagues, this project would not have materialized. To each of you—Nilda Alves, Antonio Carlos Amorim, Elba Siqueira de Sá Barretto, Carlos Eduardo Ferraço, Alice Casimiro Lopes, Elizabeth Macedo, and Inês Barbosa de Oliveira—and to the members of the international panel—Tero Autio, Bernadette Baker, and Ursula Hoadley—I express my gratitude.

WILLIAM F. PINAR

Series Editors' Introduction

We welcome another contribution in William F. Pinar's credits of books and scholarly works on curriculum studies, which provides another country case study in *International and Development Education Book Series* by Palgrave Macmillan. *Curriculum Studies in Brazil: Intellectual Histories, Present Circumstances* builds on the historical underpinnings of curriculum studies in Brazil while introducing and challenging current education issues in one of the world's emerging economies. As in his first volume in our series on South Africa, Pinar assembles a unique team of local and international experts to thread together a tapestry of curriculum studies in Latin America's largest country, one significantly influenced by European, North American, and other Latin American education systems. Pinar links this volume to his previous works in the Introduction and adds two additional contributions critiquing Brazil's curriculum studies in chapters 9 and 10. The four concepts that Pinar identified as essential discursive movements in South African curriculum studies (see Pinar 2010) are also applicable in the Brazilian context: disciplinarity, dialogue, agency, and translation. But, circumstances differ in the two countries and thus Pinar identifies four different concepts that portray the current field of curriculum studies in Brazil: enunciation, eventfulness, the quotidian, and hybridity.

Seven Brazilian contributors were asked to compose essays, which provide an intellectual history, an account of the present circumstances, and an overview of curriculum studies in Brazil. They also bring in their own research agendas in their respective chapters. Chapter 1 by Ashwani Kumar summarizes these essays and serves in some aspects as a second introduction to the volume. To respond to the theoretical nature of Brazil's curriculum studies, Pinar included contributions from renowned theoreticians who could comment on the essays composed by the Brazilian scholars. These international scholars examine curriculum studies from various theoretical and regional perspectives. The concluding arguments are given in the volume's Epilogue by Brazilian scholars Antonio Carlos Amorim and Elizabeth Macedo.

As a critique of the often negative internationalization and neoliberal influences on education, *Curriculum Studies in Brazil* is the first comprehensive volume on this subject. It joins a growing body of literature in international education on curriculum studies and is a must read for those interested in Brazil's vast and dynamic education context.

John N. Hawkins
University of California, Los Angeles

W. James Jacob
University of Pittsburgh

REFERENCE

Pinar, William F., ed. 2010. *Curriculum Studies in South Africa*. New York: Palgrave Macmillan.

List of Acronyms and Abbreviations

ANFOPE	National Association for the Training of Education
ANPED	National Association of Graduate Studies and Research in Education
CIERS-ED	International Center for Studies of Social Representation and Subjectivity–Education and Teaching
CNPq	National Advisory Board for Scientific and Technological Development
FCC	Carlos Chagas Foundation
FINEP	Research-financing agency
IBE	International Bureau of Education
MSH	Laboratoire Européen de Psychologie Sociale de la Maison des Sciences de l'Homme
NGO	non-governmental organization
OHP	overhead projectors
PCN	National Curricular Parameter
PDE	Education Development Plan
PROPED/UERJ	Program Graduate Education/State University of Rio de Janerio
PT	Workers' Party
PUC/SP	Catholic University of São Paulo
UCLA	University of California at Los Angeles
UFRJ	Federal University of Rio de Janeiro
UK	United Kingdom
UNESCO	United Nations Educational, Scientific and Cultural Organization's
US	United States
USP	University of São Paulo

Introduction

William F. Pinar

Internationalization is the decisive claim for progress within educational discourse. As a precondition, we need to understand our own traditions, our own languages. That is why the history of any discipline is so important.

Daniel Tröhler (2003, 778)

Internationalization is, then, also a series of localizations, as it requires its practitioners to devise genealogies[1] of present circumstances both internal and external to our fields of study and expertise. Among the questions to ask are the following: What are our key concepts and from where do they originate? How have we redefined them to connote contextually specific meanings, situations structured by the legacies of the past, the problems of the present, and our aspirations for the future? To discern the historicity and emplacement of the present requires attunement to our articulations of these circumstances, as we ourselves comprise the means by which to discern what is "there."[2] It is, then, the subject—simultaneously in the sense of both the human subject[3] and the academic discipline—in which and through which internationalization occurs. We can glimpse these trajectories in this collection, as these seven scholars in Brazil grapple with local legacies and present situations through concepts imported from Europe as well as from North America and elsewhere in South America. Migrating concepts are at work in understanding curriculum not only in Brazil; these same if now locally inflected concepts stimulate understanding of curricular concerns in places far from Brazil, as international panel members from Finland, the United States, and South Africa question those very concepts, their genealogies, and the situations they depict. I underline the significance of subjectivity in this dialogical process of internationalization by introducing the Brazilian participants through summaries taken from my online interviews with each.

Localization is no first step to a future of universalization, as internationalization (in my sense) institutionalizes the endless effort to communicate across difference. Moreover, despite its primacy in my own intellectual formation (Pinar 2009a), I have no romance with the particular; uncritically coinciding with it affirms provincialism. But the route to cosmopolitanism lies through threading the needle of the particular, as it is the immanence[4] of historical reality that enables its reconstruction. Such cosmopolitanism is subjective and social, always situational, indeed worldly, never an instantiation of a "new *partisan universal*" (Sekyi-Otu 1996, 118).[5] Although "identity"—including national identity[6]—is prominent in the internationalization's conceptualization, it is no unchanging foundation but, rather, an ever-shifting site of subjective experience[7] and social meaning.

The Project

This is not the first time that readers of English have encountered curriculum studies in Brazil. In the *International Handbook of Curriculum Research*, we enjoyed opportunities to study the genesis of the field and the first decades of its development (Moreira 2003), including an explication of its shifts during the 1990s (Lopes and Macedo 2003) as well as a glimpse of the 1990s federal curriculum reform (Moraes 2003). In this present volume students can extend this knowledge into the decade just concluded by glimpsing the ongoing work of Nilda Alves, Antonio Carlos Amorim, Elba Siqueira de Sá Barretto, Carlos Eduardo Ferraço, Alice Casimiro Lopes, Elizabeth Macedo, and Inês Barbosa de Oliveira. Although each of these project participants would acknowledge that curriculum studies in Brazil is too vast for any one individual to convey, each scholar provides compelling compositions[8] of curriculum studies in Brazil. These are made even more vivid by exchanges with the international panel: Tero Autio, Bernadette Baker, and Ursula Hoadley.

Spanning the theoretic to the practical, the field of *curriculum studies* is the only academic specialization within education that develops as it labors to understand curriculum within and across the school subjects. Not confined to single subjects such as "science" or to single topics such as "teaching" or "learning," curriculum studies is, in simple terms, the "big picture" field, concerned with the panorama of educational experience, especially as it is represented in and/or associated with the curriculum. Educational experience cannot be understood unless we appreciate the relations between curriculum and subjectivity, society, history, and culture. The field's most animating question asks, "what knowledge is of most worth?"[9]

That question is an ongoing provocation to which one answer cannot suffice. Answers depend on historical moment, national culture, political situation, as well as the intellectual commitments and subjective investments of the individual scholar, teacher, and student. In the present historical period and political situation, that question tends to be answered by policymakers in economistic terms, as the globalization of national economies has provided politicians with opportunities to demand that the "market" provide the rationale and serve as the final destination of public schooling. Despite the uniformity of this answer, it becomes variegated as it comes under the influence of national history, culture, and politics. In Brazil, for instance, economistic considerations, conceived in the 1990s federal curricular guidelines as "work and consumption" (Moraes 2003, 215), were supplemented by concerns for the environment, for cultural pluralism (including sexual orientation), public health, as well as "local themes" articulated by states, municipalities, and schools. These "transversal themes" were not installed in the school curriculum "top-down" but juxtaposed to state and municipal guidelines, comprising a mélange of policy pressures that distinguishes the complexity of curriculum in Brazil. There will be allusions to these multiple sites of governance and curriculum development throughout this collection.

To understand and develop curriculum across these multiple sites—not the least of which is the school classroom—Brazilian scholars employ a wide range of intellectual traditions and tools.[10] Empiricism has become ethnography, as the obligation to understand education in schools acknowledges the situatedness—including the subjectivity—of the researcher. Ethnography is only as profound as its theoretical scaffolding; in Brazilian studies of school life, history has not been subsidiary to sight, with its risk of reiterating of what anyone can see. No neo-positivism here, but, rather, theoretically informed studies of what teachers and students accomplish despite the pressures of policy and the exigencies of daily life. Always historically informed, studies of the histories of school subjects are juxtaposed with theoretical engagements with "subjects"—historical actors as well as the academic disciplines and their archival organization, such as libraries.

Within nations and regions—Brazil is no exception—there are groupings of scholars that adhere to specific conceptions of curriculum studies. In her mapping of curriculum studies in South Africa, Ursula Hoadley (2010, 128) employs the concepts of "tribes" and "territory" to denote social characteristics and epistemological properties of various disciplinary communities. Within "tribes" (a term Macedo also invokes in her "final word") individual scholars inflect shared concepts with different, sometimes original, meanings: that is the case in Brazil. I prefer the concept of "citizen"—with its connotations of rights and responsibilities—to "tribesman." I acknowledge my citizenship in U.S. curriculum studies (Pinar 2008), a field that is at the moment in a phase of devolution.[11] While working in specific "territories"—autobiography, for instance—I continue to craft connections to the larger field, including, now, the worldwide field, an ongoing engagement with "internationalization" expressed intellectually in the present project (and its predecessor: Pinar 2010a) and institutionally through the International Association for the Advancement of Curriculum Studies.

I studied curriculum studies in Brazil by means of self-report and international dialogue.[12] In the first phase of the project I interviewed the participating Brazilian scholars regarding their intellectual life histories and subjective investments in their field; from these interviews I prepared introductions. Interesting and important in itself, this phase of the project—"situating-the-self" (Pinar 2010a, 231)—enables us to appreciate where the "other" is "coming from" (Simpson 2002). In the second phase participating scholars composed essays—the chapters comprising this collection—sketching the intellectual history and present circumstances of curriculum studies in Brazil while emphasizing their own engagement and research. Ashwani Kumar—PhD student at the University of British Columbia and my research assistant—introduces us to these essays in chapter 1. In the third phase members of the international panel questioned the participants regarding those essays; I summarize and comment on these exchanges in chapters 9 and 10.

Because the curriculum field in Brazil is so theoretically sophisticated, I selected theoreticians to engage the chapters the participating Brazilian scholars composed. An Australian trained in the United States, Bernadette Baker brings to the project an unmatched expertise in post-structuralism, especially the work of Foucault, which she used to rethink the history of education in the West (Baker 2001). Few bring the knowledge of north European *Didaktik* and North American curriculum studies as effectively as Tero Autio does; he explicates the interface of these traditions in his *Subjectivity, Curriculum, and Society* (2005). Students of *Curriculum Studies in South Africa* (2010a) have met Ursula Hoadley (2010) before; her chapter mapping that field brings a detective's sharp sense of tension expressed through theoretical differences.

The exchanges between panel members and participating Brazilian scholars occurred via the Internet over a two-year period. After two rounds of questions and replies I studied the exchanges for their discursive movements, including the concepts those movements conveyed. As was the case in South Africa, these were not necessarily the concepts the participating scholars themselves might have emphasized. Twice I invited participants to critique my commentary, the first time in draft form (so I might correct errors) and the second time publicly in the epilogue, a "final word" articulated by the participants themselves. That invitation and positioning will, I trust, counter their work's recontextualization into my own.

It is inevitable that my own singularity—including my intellectual life history as well as present preoccupations and commitments—provides the "apparatus" through which I discern the key concepts embedded in the exchanges I studied. As the Brazilian scholarship itself emphasizes, knowledge is always situated, always provisional, always open to reformulation. My summary of these exchanges (chapter 9) is simultaneously a knowledge claim and an assertion in an ongoing conversation that I hope will extend beyond the individuals engaged here. That "beyond" means attention not only to the "event" this collection documents but also to the provocation of a myriad exchanges, most of which will not occur in English or be published in North America but will be acknowledged in the disciplinary histories future curriculum studies scholars will be compelled to write. I expect curriculum studies in Brazil to play a prominent role in that future.

It is the disciplinarity—specifically the intellectual advancement—of nationally distinctive fields that the internationalization of curriculum studies can support. By pausing to explain our work to sometimes uncomprehending colleagues, one is provoked to reexamine assumptions as well as sharpen the coherence of and/or extend one's research into unanticipated areas, all discursive movements that can advance intellectually our understanding of curriculum in its internal complexity and external circumstances. It is this reciprocity between the foreign and the familiar, the global and the local, the abstract and the concrete that animates disciplinarity, encouraging us to construct the field its constituents in the schools deserve. That confidence derives from studying the scholarship of the colleagues I introduce now.

The Brazilian Scholars

Nilda Alves has been engaged in everyday life research for 25 years, examining the "varied networks"[13] through which we recreate knowledge through our daily, even routine, practices. No covert behaviorism, these "networks of knowledge" are "deeply" embedded within us and "lead us to action." How did she arrive at the everyday? Alves' "theoretical itinerary" passed through Lukács, Gramsci, Agnes Heller, and Henri Lefebvre to Michel de Certeau and "the invention of everyday life." In education, Freire and Stenhouse were important; more recently, the works of Deleuze, Foucault, and Boaventura de Sousa Santos have been influential. Social movements (including race and gender as well as the ecological movement) have also been key to Alves's intellectual formation. These three movements have also demonstrated ways of "interrogated society theoretically-methodologically," always stressing the significance of "social change" (underscored by Alves' academic training in geography and sociology). These intellectual and historical influences combined with her political activism—forefronting the centrality of "open conversation" to "the collective"—all contribute to Alves' sharp sense of what is at stake in research into everyday life.

Alves started teaching in 1961 as an elementary school teacher; she has also taught geography at the secondary school level. An activist in the student movement, she fled to France after the military coup d'etat in 1964. She was one of the 5,000 political exiles living in France during the dictatorship. After completing her doctorate there (from Université René Descarte-Paris V), Alves commenced her university teaching career in 1983. She continued her political activism, especially as larger political issues were linked to questions of research and to teacher associations (Alves served as president of two such associations: the National Association of Graduate Studies and Research in Education [ANPED] and National Association for the Training of Education [ANFOPE]). Policy has been a persistent concern, specifically that concerning the funding of research in education. Alves has also continued her association with France, enjoying an ongoing research relationship with colleagues at the Université de Rouen (where her colleague Inês Barbosa de Oliveira also took her doctorate). Alves' recent research focuses on the relations of teachers with technologies, and on photography and the communicative capacities of the image.

Antonio Carlos Rodrigues de Amorim locates his research in "postcritical" efforts to rethink the last decade of Brazilian curriculum studies. His own intellectual movement from sociology and structuralism to poststructuralism began while working with elementary schoolteachers in Campinas' public schools. Amorim concentrates upon "cultural representations" and "relations of power" because social reality in Latin America is characterized, he writes, by "the centrality of cultures" and "the political force" of power in history. From discipline-based to cultural and political provocations of his ongoing intellectual project, Amorim has focused on subjectivation. It has been the work of Gilles Deleuze—especially his concept of the *rhizome* and Amorim's invocation of it to comprehend the production of school knowledge (specifically biology)—that has left him in a state of "addiction to a type of writing which is many times... abusive and invasive." From "rhizome" he has been drawn to the concept of *event*. Inspired by Deleuze's work on art and literature, Amorim articulates "event" as structured simultaneously by perception and communication. Postmodernism, he argues, has the same referents as modernity, among them (1) the figure of the subject, (2) autonomy often associated with "transformation," (3) relations of power as structured by cultural (class, gender, ethnic) categories and ideological concepts such as hegemony, and (4) the "continuous unyielding effort" for what Amorim characterizes as "critical transcendental thought," which he defines as the formulation of "just ideas" that enable "understanding" of the world.

"My research," Amorim explains, "is placed in the *escape* from this set and in the necessary and disenchanted *encounter* with the emptiness derived from the disappearance of basis and structure." Because they aim at "*disfiguration*," his investigations are "dissonant" with mainstream curriculum studies in Brazil. The questions his work poses concern "new forms of living," the creation of "creative acts in a world grounded in *virtuality*, in *temporal comprehension*, in *nomadic* movements and, in many cases, on *barbarism*." To pursue this project, Amorim examines cinema and photography for "fragments of a history of Brazil." Among these various representations of "national identity," he finds a range of moods and dispositions, for example, identity as "globalized, uprooted and deformed; marked by violence, disillusion and by the excess of a presentism. Futureless." It is through art—specifically, cinema, photography, and literature—that Amorim encounters reality. It is through fiction, he suggests, that reality is rendered.

Amorim worries that the relation between education scholars and their intellectual projects has not always changed, despite the entrance of "postcritical" categories such as "culture, time and identity." Like the Marxist structures preceding them, these too reify transformation; many recapitulate the same static bifurcated relations between theory and practice, between social reproduction and social transformation. Amorim wonders whether certain terms have not become "hegemonic" in the Brazilian field. Concepts such "hybridism," the "in-between," "trace," and "boundaries" have become fashionable. They have degenerated into an uncritical vocabulary.

It was the concept of *rhizome*, defined by "heterogeneity, multiplicity and a-signification," that enabled Amorim to critically engage knowledge as it is organized in daily life in schools, and in ways that exceed reproduction theory. At present, he is focused on "the relations among "time, being and event" and among "time, image and duration" (especially as theorized in cinema studies), and on the relations among "time, sign and sense" (especially as theorized in literary studies). These concepts enable him to "compose the curriculum" as a "field of sensation," a concept of "education which frees itself from the humanist substance which saturates it," inaugurating a "search for alternatives to survival in a post-human state: somnambulistic, unconscious, action-less, uninhabited." Amorim appreciates the risks in this ambitious understanding—he discerns no "propitious horizon"—and despite its pluralist rhetoric of inclusion, he suspects he may "have to invent tactics of invisibility to resist."

For over 30 years *Elba Siqueira de Sá Barretto* has worked as a researcher at the Carlos Chagas Foundation (FCC), a renowned research institution. Since the 1990s, she has worked also as a curriculum studies professor at the University of São Paulo (USP), the same institution from which she graduated with a Bachelor of Arts degree in 1965. Licensed as a specialist in education, de Sá Barretto shared the hope of many of her generation, for example, that a socialist revolution could result in a more just and equal society. "I understood the political meaning of education and its potential to help change reality," she reflects. As a teacher in a public secondary school, de Sá Barretto participated in the student movement focused on adult education, inspired by the work of Paulo Freire. Like Freire, de Sá Barretto also spent time in Switzerland. After returning to Brazil, she took her masters and doctorate in sociology at the University of São Paulo.

At FCC, de Sá Baretto began her career as a research assistant in the 1970s, a time when scientific research was being emphasized. Under the supervision of senior colleagues, new researchers were encouraged to complete graduate degrees. Carlos Chagas research teams have been free to formulate their own proposals and projects, frequently resulting from previous research work. In addition to these internally directed investigations, she and her colleagues have also conducted research contracted by government and other institutions. After accepting a position at the foundation, de Sá Barretto joined a research team conducting performance assessments (based on Bloom's[14] categories) of MOBRAL students, the country's largest adult literacy program that was implemented in 1967 by the military regime. Later, she studied students (according to social origin and gender) in São Paulo's schools, with a special focus on how these students were being impacted by teachers' expectations. The source of de Sá Barretto's masters thesis research (funded by the Ford Foundation), her work was published in the FCC journal *Cadernos de Pesquisa*. Barretto worked with Bourdieu's concept of *habitus,* which she aligned with studies by Rist, Becker, Rosenthal, and Jacobson. She also drew upon the work of Basil Bernstein, influential in South African curriculum studies as well. That work was followed by a twelve-year comprehensive research program focused on education and social selectivity, employing various theoretical and methodological approaches. de Sá Barretto has served as coordinator of several of these studies on primary education.

Barretto's first significant curriculum experience occurred during 1984–1988, when she served as an advisor to the São Paulo State Secretariat of Education, an agency responsible for the education of over 4 million pupils. At that time, curriculum continued to be organized according to separate school subjects despite recommendations supporting curriculum integration. Controversy concerning the curriculum stemmed not only from debates within the academic disciplines but also among different political groups supporting the government's educational agenda. Not unlike the curricular recommendations[15] made in the United States during the mid-1990s, the new history curriculum became "the target of violent criticism by the mainstream media, which labeled the whole curricular reform as populist." As in the United States, the new curriculum was withdrawn and a revised version was published years later. This experience remains a source of important casebook material for the curriculum courses Barretto teaches at the University of São Paulo.

In 1995, the Ministry of Education asked the Carlos Chagas Foundation to conduct research on curricular proposals from several Brazilian states in order to define the National Curricular Parameters (PCN) for the primary school. Funded by UNESCO, this research assembled experts (from different parts of the country) who had studied the state curricular proposals made between 1985 and 1995 in the areas of Portuguese Language, Mathematics, History, Geography, and the Sciences. Curriculum proposals from three state capitals (São Paulo, Belo Horizonte, and Rio de Janeiro) were studied as well. de Sá Baretto served as the research coordinator. Although not "crucial" to the federal ministry's pronouncement of PCNs, the research did provide "legitimacy" to the guidelines, which were modeled after Spanish conceptions created by Professor César Coll at the University of Barcelona. In the controversy that followed, several academic groups opposed the very idea of a common curriculum; their critique was focused on the heterogenity of the nation and of knowledge itself; others worried that a common curriculum would be susceptible to neoliberal testing regimes. In 2006, de Sá Baretto concluded that there was insufficient evidence to claim that the school curricula adopted during these reforms had suffered any significant "homogenizing process," despite the fact that centralized authorities had increased their control over established curriculum. In 2009, de Sá Baretto again argued that school curricula had not been homogenized despite their association with national assessments.

Recently, de Sá Baretto has been at work on a research project aimed at *Understanding Teachers' Work from the Subjects' Own Perspectives.* This project brings together thirty-one groups of researchers in Brazil and abroad (from Argentina, Portugal, Greece, and France), conducting research on the *Social Representations of Students in Teacher Education Courses Concerning Teachers' Work*. This research is based on Moscovici's[16] theory of social representations, which enjoys the support of *Laboratoire Européen de Psychologie Sociale de la Maison des Sciences de l'Homme* (MSH, Paris, France) and of the Carlos Chagas Foundation, which created the International Center for Studies of Social Representation and Subjectivity, Education and Teaching (CIERS-ED) that hosts the program in São Paulo. de Sá Baretto asserts, "educational reforms have to pay more attention to the subjectivity of the subjects, if they really want to bring about effective changes."

Carlos Eduardo Ferraço studies aspects of daily life in schools, for example, "processes of production and sharing of curricular knowledge," including "networks" of knowledge, action, and power. Ferraço is focused on the relations between the content "taught" in the school disciplines and the "broader contexts" of students' lives. These concerns derive from Ferraço's fifteen-year experience as a teacher of mathematics in public elementary schools, an experience "marked by the search for a kind of knowledge that would break...with segmentation and linearity and broaden possibilities." His interest in the everyday and the lived has been "structured by historical and political events," specifically by the government's "carelessness" in its dealings with the public school. As a teacher of mathematics, Ferraço participated in several curriculum reforms designed to align instruction with policy directives. The instrumentalism of these "reforms" was imported from the United States; Bobbitt is acknowledged as an influence. As it does in the United States, such "reform" communicates the "feeling that we were working in a mistaken way in the schools." "Correcting the mistakes" made by the schools required "reform" focused on changing teachers' behavior. According to such "logic," Ferraço points out, "the concrete daily life of the schools does not matter," as what teachers and students do with academic knowledge is ignored by the officials making policy pronouncements.

Influenced by the research of Professor Nilda Alves, Ferraço has focused on the recontextualization of the curriculum as performed by teachers and students during daily life in schools. Ferraço asserts that his work in the field of curriculum is not independent. Rather, his work occurs in a larger movement of researchers[17] who focus on the daily life of schools both as a starting point and as a goal. That relationship "makes my work stronger." Studying everyday school life acknowledges the subjectivity of classroom practice, Ferraço points out, including the subjective situatedness of the researchers themselves: "every type of knowledge is a kind of self-knowledge." He continues: "The 'truths' we produce, because they are ours, are only partial and have to do to our processes of identification, our hybrid identities. They express who we are and what we want."

While studying for the master's degree at the Fluminense Federal University, Ferraço enjoyed access to a wide range of conceptions of educational practice, following from the work of Marx, Gramsci, Engels, Lefebvre, Goldman, Cheptulin, Kosik, Vázquez, Bronowski, and Freire. Inspired by Nilda Alves and Regina Leite Garcia, and drawing upon the works of Lefebvre (particularly his idea of networks of knowledge), Ferraço dedicated his studies to the processes of the production of knowledge in the daily life of schools. Although other theoretical influences have followed (among them the work of Michel de Certeau), especially during his doctoral and postdoctoral programs in education, Ferraço has remained committed to studying daily life in schools.

From Ferraço's point of view, the curriculum achieves actuality less by protocols of prescription than by "the knowledge, action and power networks that exist" in schools. Ferraço concludes that it is no longer sensible to speak of "the curriculum" but only of curricula "in networks, plural...and complex." The "mutant conditions of subjects" and "their relations of enunciation" embedded in various "networks" enable the creation of "hybrid" environments "in-between" existing cultural or political identities and those "official discourses" prescribing a single totalizing system. These lived "gaps" are sites of resistance, opportunities to challenge official directives. This insight constitutes, Ferraço suggests, "our contribution to the intellectual advancement of the field." This insight contributes not only to the advancement of the Brazilian field, but, I should think, also to that of the US field, long trapped by the binaries "resistance" and "reproduction" (Pinar 2010b).

Such a self-enclosed, finally imaginary system disappears in Ferraço's conception of curriculum grounded in the actuality of teachers' and students' practices that they themselves recontextualize historically, politically, and socially on a daily basis. These "networked curricula" reconstruct larger political events. It is the "emergency"—global warming, human rights, and poverty, among other ongoing crises—that contradicts conceptions of multiculturalism as primarily commemorative. Through these curricular practices, then, decolonization occurs through deconstruction. The intellectual advancement of the field, Ferraço concludes, rests not only upon the sophistication of our understanding of school practices but as well upon our capacity to influence official policy.

Alice Casimiro Lopes questioned my query concerning her intellectual life history, expressing skepticism concerning the very concept of "an active individuality" when viewed from "a broader historical and political context." Although her research has not been "determined by specific events,"

Lopes feels that "they are interrelated," especially as her research aspires to "interpret" events while "interact[ing] with them." It is this intersection of interpretation and events "that contributes toward forming my individuality in research." With this cautionary note in mind, Lopes narrated her history of intellectual engagement with events within and outside curriculum studies in Brazil.

A former secondary school chemistry teacher committed to the improvement of classroom teaching, Lopes appreciated that teaching was embedded in (but, she emphasized, not reducible to) sociopolitical reality. An "early interest" in Marx attuned Lopes to "emancipatory political struggles," assuring her "sympathy with the critical perspective of curriculum, with its neo-Marxist basis." That attunement was intensified by political events in Brazil during the 1980s while she was completing a teacher-training course and her master's degree in Education. "There were," she reports,

> heated debates between the Gramscian perspective of education, the perspectives of theorists of correspondence and the perspectives of popular educators due to different theoretical conceptions and policies. In that context, I came close to Gramscian theoretical positions and the political positions of the popular educators, the latter shapers of the Workers' Party (PT) project in Brazil.

Despite these political dispositions, perhaps due to her training in chemistry, Lopes found herself "more specifically concerned with epistemological matters." Due to these concerns, she studied (during her master's degree course) Bachelard and his "applied rationalism," focusing on "epistemological obstacles" in Brazilian chemistry textbooks published between 1931 and 1990.

During her doctoral studies (supervised by Professor Antonio Flavio Barbosa Moreira), Lopes came to feel that epistemology was insufficient for a comprehensive analysis of school knowledge. She drew closer to curriculum studies (especially the work of Michael Young, Basil Bernstein, and Ivor Goodson) and didactics (specifically Yves Chevallard), while continuing her study of a Bachelardian analysis of science. She came to understand school knowledge as constituted by the processes of *didactic transposition* (Chevallard) and *disciplinarization* (Goodson)—for example, the incorporation of scientific and social knowledge in school practices.

Toward the end of the 1990s Lopes became "mobilized" by the debates over proposals to centralize curriculum in Brazil. The president of Brazil (Fernando Henrique Cardoso) led this neoliberal project typified by "centralized curricular exams and proposals, textbook evaluation, models of teacher training by competencies." The public debate was "heated" and pitted Brazilian curriculum scholars against the government and its legal-regulatory apparatus; Lopes participated through publications and lectures. Her research focused on the incorporation of curricular guidelines through *recontextualization* (working from Bernstein) and *hybridization* (influenced by García Canclini), employing curricular discourses focused on the organization of school knowledge, especially those associated with *integration* and *disciplinarity*.

As Lopes continued her studies of culture and politics, she reconfigured those conceptions, "assuming more variegated and complex approaches" drawn from the work of Stephen Ball, Stuart Hall, and García Canclini. In her work—while the influence of cultural and postcolonial studies became stronger and that of neo-Marxist theory, of structuralism in general, weakened—Lopes retained neo-Marxist associations of knowledge with political emancipation. Now Lopes thinks about the curriculum as non-homogeneous, marked by hybridisms (influenced by Canclini, Bhabha, and Hall), and as unstructurable by epistemological certainties. Lopes is absorbed by study of those processes of signification by which culture, including the curriculum, is reconstructed. Such processes of *recontextualization* involve *deterritorializations, reterritorializations*, and the formation of "*impure*"[18] *genres*. Lopes points out that power relations—not necessarily institutionally stabilized—are "always generating possibilities of *resignification*, not necessarily more democratic and less hierarchized." For example, locating the genesis of the 1990s neoliberal reform proposals in demands of globalized capital fails to confront the facts of local recontextualizations of these proposals, indeed "to the point that many of their meanings have been appropriated by political and educational groups opposing the neoliberal project." Lopes has dedicated herself to studying the local "recontextualization of meanings of policies considered global." In particular, Lopes has investigated how proposals concerning competencies, curricular integration, and "learning to learn," among others, resignified in school subjects, specifically in secondary school science.[19]

Inspired by the work of Ernesto Laclau, Lopes theorizes *recontextualization* in order to understand (in a post-Marxist sense) the formation of hegemonies in curricular policies. She understands "articulation" after Laclau as "any practice established between elements in which the identities of those elements are modified as a result of articulatory practice." Such practice functions to "hegemonize" antagonism of the Brazilian curriculum to "the changing world." In this ongoing project Lopes is expressing her long-standing preoccupations with progressive political and economic change.

In reply to my question concerning the problem of proximity (for instance, between the ministry and education professors), Lopes asserted, "In Brazil, no researcher is *forced* into our Ministry's service." Working in government service or with labor unions or political parties is "not necessarily negative," she added, as long as one retains intellectual independence. Lopes pointed out that intellectual independence hardly means lack of influences, be it in intellectual debates "of our time," priorities of research-funding agencies, or in "*friendships*[20] and relationships that we construct in our academic life." (Lopes cited her collaboration with Elizabeth Macedo as an example of the latter and her engagement with the Workers Party as an instance of the former). The question is not whether there is influence, but what influence is at work and how it affects one's research. Also the willingness to analyze influence "critically" is "extremely important in intellectual work. To work intellectually, in my opinion, is exactly to be willing to understand the power relations and the conditionings around the actual knowledge produced." Here is an instance of "recontextualization" within curriculum research itself.

"The field of the curriculum in Brazil has advanced a great deal in recent years," Lopes concludes.[21] Until the late 1970s, Lopes reports, "administrative-scientific studies" dominated Brazilian curriculum studies; they were superseded by so-called "critical" approaches in the 1980s. These often Marxist-inspired studies peaked in the 1990s and then began to wane as post-structuralist and postmodern critiques took center-stage. There were throughlines, however, though not always welcomed ones: "At times, the critical approaches, and even the post-structuralist and postmodern approaches, did not overcome the somewhat prescriptive characteristic that marked works in the instrumental approach." Recall that Amorim makes a similar observation.

Despite this failure, Lopes judges that critical post-structuralist and postmodern research complicated the field's understanding of curriculum as well as broadened and diversified its range. Perhaps due to the intensity of present preoccupations, she speculates, the intellectual history of the field is understudied. Although it is "important to incorporate new theoretical contributions," Lopes observes, "it is similarly important to continue attuned to the history of curricular and pedagogic thinking." Although curriculum history has been a casualty of present circumstances, there are compensations. For instance, a new "hybridism"—one containing both critical and post-structuralist approaches—typifies research undertaken today. "At least," Lopes adds, "that is how I tend to position myself." In conversation with the field's history, as Lopes recommends, such hybridism portends continued intellectual advancement for the Brazilian field.

Elizabeth Macedo also questioned the concept of "life history" as capable of elaboration, at least as a "coherent whole." Macedo points to the complexity of psychic life—"irrational reasons, projections and unaccountable fantasies"—that inform "our intellectual preoccupations and define our research agendas." To identify the "genesis" of one's present projects invokes "an arbitrary moment" and "project[s] over the past a non-existent order" that renders intelligible "my present moment." Acknowledging these points, Macedo "eliminate[s] … the fact of being the daughter of an elementary school teacher and, therefore, of living surrounded by people who talked about school, prepared lessons and teaching materials, corrected work and complained about low salaries." Coming of age surrounded by such talk "created in me ambivalence about education…. That was how I graduated as an engineer (chemical) at the same time [how] I became a teacher."

There are other moments of "genesis," however misleading the concept can be. While studying at the Federal University of Rio de Janeiro (UFRJ), Macedo encountered the idea of competencies (as formulated by Eva Baker and James Popham). At the same time, however, she encountered scholarly literature on the Reconceptualization of U.S. curriculum studies (for a summary, see Pinar 2008). Macedo was also introduced to Stenhouse, Schon, and Levy. The internationalization of curriculum studies was, in Brazil, a fait accompli.

After the military regime ended, Marxism—including Freire's work—occupied center-stage in Macedo's study. She felt forced to choose among "a technocratic view of education, an excessively economics-based Marxism and a phenomenological orientation." She chose none of the three, fastening instead upon the Frankfurt School, which she understands now as "foundational" to her "research preoccupations." In particular, Habermas enabled Macedo to juxtapose scientific knowledge (her disciplinary background) with everyday school life, "making it possible to think of a concept of curriculum as dialogical space." Scientific knowledge could be thematized as also normative, situated in "communicative action" in curriculum "as an intersubjective space." Macedo's research shifted from politics to culture conceived in post-structuralist terms. During the mid-1990s Brazilian curriculum studies had undergone a major shift characterized by identity politics and postmodernism; Macedo comments, "Foucault became an important reference." Although the Frankfurt School no longer seemed sufficient, Macedo rejected Foucault, at least insofar as his early work (see Paras 2006) represented the "total effacement of that subject and the practices of freedom."

After 2000, Macedo's research began to focus on "cultural difference" while maintaining her earlier preoccupations with the recent history of Brazilian curricular thought and of school subjects. From cultural studies of difference she moved to postcolonial studies, noting that "culture" had replaced "knowledge" as the bedrock of curriculum thinking. Troubled by such reification of curriculum categories, Macedo engaged post-structuralism, specifically the work of Bhabha and Appadurai: "I began to define curriculum as cultural enunciation, considering it as text that cannot be fixed, except momentarily in the midst of hegemonic struggles." Devised in part to overcome the binary between a formal and a lived curriculum, Macedo's concept of curriculum as enunciation clashed with the everyday school life research.

Working from the theory of Laclau and Mouffe, Macedo was able to "abandon Habermasian universalism" without replacing these with those "more radical postmodern approaches" that embrace particularity but convert it into universality, as in the ethnic essentialisms characteristic of identity politics. (Macedo prefers to theorize difference as associated not only with identity.) Now Macedo understands curriculum policy as "a hegemonic struggle to fix the meanings of the curriculum, an impossible task because, as Derrida says, meaning is always deferred." A trace of her earlier engagement with the Frankfurt School is evident in Macedo's continuing concern for "agency" and its relationship with "structure," now theorized as structures never coinciding with themselves—indeed, "structures are displaced, so that there is always something resisting the symbolization." Given that perspective, Macedo cannot consider herself or her research as determined by structures, nor can she regard her undertakings as independent of those structures. There is, she reports, a "constant colloquy...with governmental education departments, schools and labor unions, through books and participation in meetings." In these venues theoretical formulations and research can be debated by the larger (and more varied) audiences constituting the public.

A preoccupation with culture—more specifically with cultural exchanges—constitutes a throughline in Macedo's intellectual life history, surfacing still in her present engagement with the postcolonial literature. She regards the postcolonial as "resistance to ... globalism" as it testifies to the neocolonial subjugation of minorities. Focused on cultural flows, Macedo bypasses the binaries of reproduction and resistance as domination can never be complete, in part because culture is always the enunciation of difference. Rejecting postmodern conceptions that favor fragmentation, inspired by Bhabha and Stuart Hall, Macedo theorizes negotiation as a form of subversion. This is complicated conversation animated by agency.

Inês Barbosa de Oliveira demands the inclusion of what is absent. Licensed to teach preschool and the initial elementary school grades, Oliveira worked in the mid-1980s with her colleagues to build a "progressive and democratic" school. This collaboration gradually transformed her from a "questioning" individual to a state of "militancy." Oliveira completed her doctorate in France; her dissertation focused on Habermas' theory of social transformation coupled with work developed by Jean Houssaye.[22] Oliveira's intellectual formation follows her life history—her schooling, her professional experiences, including her reflections and practices as a teacher and a researcher. It has also been influenced by coming of age during the military dictatorship (1964–1985), the conclusion of which was marked by an "intense social effervescence." The reciprocity of intellectual life history and political history is clear to Oliveira: "If my democratic preoccupation was shaped from the doubts and individual issues referring to relationship with immediate authority figures, its more political growth and consolidation are somehow inscribed in the context of the reemergence of social movements in the early 1980's."

Of late Brazil has been suffering from neoliberal ideas, featuring an intensifying mercantilism of life in general and that of the school in particular, as well as the corporatization of politics, including academic politics. Not only in Brazil, Olivera adds, but in Latin America as a whole, educational research has grappled with the theory of neoliberalism and its practice as politically enforced through governmental policies. The curriculum field has not escaped this crisis but, she adds, has not been limited to analyses of it, as other intellectual movements have been influential, among them cultural studies, postcolonial studies, and postmodernism in its multiple aspects: gender studies, race studies, and feminist theory.

Despite these pressures, Oliveira has never confined her research to specific policies, focusing instead on more fundamental epistemological questions, not without occasional resistance from colleagues. Such resistance provides provocations for further research, underscoring the importance of attending to intradisciplinary matters as well as to public policy issues. It is the lived convergence of such provocations—internal to the field, external in public policy senses, both supplemented by intellectual influences from associated fields—that can stimulate intellectual advancement.

Focused, in part, on the history of school subjects in Brazil, Oliveira and her research group colleagues study widening circles of relevant scholarship, including conceptions of knowledge, especially as these have been inflected by debates concerning modernity/postmodernity, social emancipation, citizenship, and everyday life. She affiliates herself with those colleagues who are committed not only to "the understanding of curricula themselves, but [also] to their potential contribution to social emancipation and construction of social democracy." The latter concept Oliveira situates not in U.S. progressivism but in European traditions: "anarchist theory would be its closest origin," she suggests, but it is always cosmopolitan in political practice.

Brazilian curriculum studies is, de Oliveira judges, "a field of immense potential," one "that has been advancing." She attributes this intellectual advancement to its incorporation of concepts from other fields as well as to its responsiveness to developments in the public sphere, all congealed within the discipline and reconstructed as new concepts and understandings: "Shocks among its different currents require a production of arguments by all those involved and, therefore, deepening of reflection." In reply to my question, de Oliveira describes "intellectual advancement" eloquently; it is characterized by

> dialogue between what we do, what we think and what we wish for, going beyond that which we already know, producing new and differentiated knowledge that not only takes existing reflections deeper, but also broadens the field in which they have been placed.

What field could aspire to more?

NOTES

1. As Paras (2006, 154) points out, Foucault's concept of "genealogy" was "committed not to experience but to an anonymous systematicity that generated meaning while avoiding the notion of an experience-laden subject." Internationalization's emphasis upon the local hardly excludes this Foucauldian concern for "episteme," but it is not limited to it. In my conceptualization, internationalization eschews Foucault's hostility to "progress" and his disposition to discern "domination" and "control" as primary (Flynn 1993, 280). Although "progress" is never free from domination and efforts at control, it is not condemned to succumb to them. True, generating genealogies entails preoccupation with language "as the prime vehicle through which 'practices'... are read. Change is thus tagged as movement or shifts in what language renders visible" (Baker 2001, 612). But "power"—even when defined vaguely by Foucault as "relations, a more-or-less organized, hierarchical, coordinated cluster of relations" (quoted in Baker 2001, 613)—is not my key concept, as I reject (as did Foucault; see Ransom 1997, 81) any a priori concept of organization and explanation.

2. Insightfully Schubert (2009a, 139) links my conception of disciplinarity— with its emphasis upon the specificity of nationally distinctive fields' intellectual histories and present circumstances—with my autobiographical theory of curriculum summarized in the concept of *currere*. However, he mistakes my call for a curriculum studies "canon" as reinstantiation of the past rather than its reconstruction (2009a, 140 n. 3). Like dialogical encounter, internationalization is crucial as it enables us to understand how to move from the provincial to the cosmopolitan, a move threaded through the particularity of our histories and present circumstances. These must be kept separate in order to see how they are simultaneously different and similar. Conflating the two— as Henderson and Kesson (2009, 134) do in their collapsing of verticality

(e.g., the past) and horizontality (e.g., the present) into "diagonality"—re-expresses the presentism that condemns us to the surface of things. Endorsing diagonality, Schubert (2009b, 142) fails to appreciate the canonical as crucial in the reconstruction of the past, a prerequisite to intellectual advancement in the present.

3. "Subjects" are simultaneously school subjects and the human subjects the school subjects enable us to become. In my terms, then, the "subject" is not the empirical fact of anatomical individuality, but the socially informed "site" of the inner self, for example, subjectivity, wherein the capability of becoming otherwise (including "oneself") can be enacted. Although in the passage quoted below Butler's language sometimes overstates the linguistic and spatial features of subjectivity, her elaboration of the "subject" does specify the relations between self-reflexivity (including self-knowledge) and subjective reconstruction. Although she employs none of these categories, her own choices address what is at stake in mine: Butler (1997, 10–11) writes,

> The "subject" is sometimes bandied about as if it were interchangeable with the "person" or the "individual." The genealogy of the subject as a critical category, however, suggests that the subject, rather than be identified strictly with the individual, ought to be designated as a linguistic category, a placeholder, a structure in formation. Individuals come to occupy the site of the subject (the subject simultaneously emerges as a "site"), and they enjoy intelligibility only to the extent that they are, as it were, first established in language. The subject is the linguistic occasion for the individual to achieve and reproduce intelligibility, the linguistic condition of its existence and agency. No individual becomes a subject without first becoming or undergoing "subjectivation" (a translation of the French *assujetissement*).

As you will see, curriculum studies in Brazil is very much interested in the achievement of agency through linguistic means, that is, through devising categories of understanding especially school "sites" that invoke as they represent action.

4. Immanence implies the presence of past and the foreshadowing of the future in the present, animating (as it destabilizes) "what is" with what might be but is not yet. Language, then, is no dead letter dripping with subjective and social meaning but a palimpsest that contains traces of the past and clues for the future (Radhakrishnan 2008, 68). For the U.S. poet Walt Whitman, objects became "incantations designed to help us see the world afresh and recognize the spirituality of the material" (Robertson 2008, 19). "Without the transcendental potential of actualization," Radhakrishnan (2008, 224) summarizes, "the immanence of possibility cannot be redeemed." And the "vehicle of immanence is," Gordon (1996, 248) reminds, "subjectivity."

5. For Sekyi-Otu (1996, 118), such a *partisan universal* encourages the "discredited discourse of race" to be "succeeded by the baffled and atavistic irrationalism of a violent ethnicity," a reference to postcolonial Africa, academic echoes of which can be discerned in contemporary identity politics in North America. Such "*mechanical antagonism*" is the "obverse side of the *mechanical solidarity*

to which the racial structure of power relations condemns all the colonized" (Sekyi-Otu 1996, 131). No such simplistic reinstantiation of binaries—racial or political—is evident in the Brazilian scholarship examined here.

6. Despite the skepticism of globalization theorists toward the utility of the "nation" as an organizing concept, I continue to employ it as the primary site wherein curriculum studies occurs. There is little risk of "essentialization" here, as the Brazilian scholarship never (as Baker rightly cautions) reduces "curriculum reform... [to] insular and immanentist views of countryhood" but, instead, acknowledges itself as "continuously interpenetrated by forces that seem to come from beyond the borders and belonging of a singular or specific national timespace" (Baker 2009, xxiii). In Macedo's terms, the "nation" is a "nodal point."

7. As these opening paragraphs testify, I will be employing, variously, concepts sometimes associated with antagonistic discourses, as this use of "experience" illustrates. Associated with American pragmatism and European existential phenomenology, the concept of "experience" has been an apparent casualty of post-structuralism. Although the early Foucault was determined to expel "experience" and other terms (such as the "subject") associated with the existentialism he was determined to repudiate (see Paras 2006, 20; Miller 1993, 44), later he became preoccupied with them (see Paras 2006, 123). Given its role in essentializing identity and reifying the subject, feminist historian Joan Scott was tempted to abandon "experience" altogether, but given its ubiquity in everyday language, she decided otherwise (see Jay 2005, 251). Although contemporary curriculum studies in Brazil seems almost entirely influenced by post-structuralism (even, I would say, gesturing toward a post-post-structuralism), the discerning reader will note traces of antecedent and even antagonistic discourses, among them Marxism, pragmatism, and phenomenology, accenting the "hybridity" of its discourses.

8. Memorably articulated by Jacques Daignault (in Pinar et al. 1995, 483–485), "composition" underlines the creativity of scholarly production, especially scholarship associated with the humanities. Curriculum studies in Brazil—as glimpsed here—derives primarily from the humanities (especially philosophy) and secondarily from the social sciences. Daignault invoked the concept's affiliation with music, even using the notion of "notes" to specify the auditory patterning of concepts that, like jazz (see Aoki 2005 [1990], 367ff.), reflect disciplined improvisation. Antonio Carlos Amorim employs this powerful concept as well.

9. Associated with a now discredited (Egan 2002, 23ff.; Popkewitz 2008, 97; Boyarin 1997, 50) but once "wildly popular" (Greenfeld 2002, 111; Goodlad 2002, 238) Herbert Spencer (who thought "science" was the answer; Mathur 2003, 140), the question "What knowledge is of most worth?" forces us to forefront academic knowledge in relation to history, culture, politics, society, and subjectivity, each of these as an element of situations to which the ongoing (my thanks to Elizabeth Macedo for stressing this point) question helps us to reconstruct our pedagogical replies. In the Brazilian scholarship presented here, the question does appear, albeit in different forms, most explicitly in

Macedo's conception of "enunciation" (what to articulate derives in part from one's knowledge of what the situation requires), in Lopes's analysis of libraries (knowledge that is of most worth is organized there), and in Barretto's emphasis upon "recontextualization" (wherein policy is reconfigured in light of local circumstances). In each instance, we are called upon to summon knowledge that addresses present circumstances.

10. In North America, the interdisciplinary character of curriculum studies has become a political vulnerability, as colleagues in single-field-focused specialties (such as educational psychology) demand definitions of curriculum studies. On two occasions in Canada, deans have posed to me this question of definition. Communicating no innocent interest in understanding, this question functioned as skepticism toward curriculum studies, questioning its coherence and legitimacy. In the United States, where forty years of school reform was supplemented by demands by the Bush (and now Obama) administration that education professors align teacher education with government's own objectives and conduct only quantitative research on "what works," external pressure upon education schools has evidently made predators of "colleagues" who decline to search for replacements of retiring curriculum studies scholars. "The field is no longer dedicated to school improvement," comes the explanation, but such a sentence only underscores the fact that curriculum studies scholars cannot be counted on to do whatever politicians demand. The explanation is primarily a pretext for reallocating funds to one's own specialty, including the so-called learning sciences (Taubman 2009, 160ff.).

11. Like individuals, academic fields exhibit periods of crisis, breakthrough, consolidation, expansion, and sometimes disintegration, in part due to external circumstances, in part due to internal dynamics (Axelrod 1979). (For autobiographical accounts of the devolution of philosophy of education, see Waks 2008.) After a period of paradigmatic crisis—the Tylerian protocol of institutional curriculum development was rendered irrelevant by the 1960s national curriculum reform—the U.S. field underwent a reconceptualization of its basic concepts, a decade-long event that my colleagues and I summarized in *Understanding Curriculum* (Pinar et al. 1995; see also Pinar 2008). That moment of disciplinary consolidation was incomplete, as several stakeholders resisted the new reality (see, for example, Wraga 1999). The field was then splintered by identity politics (see Pinar 2009b, 21–35; 2009c, 529), by the Bush and Obama administrations' emphasis upon "what works," and by opportunistic "colleagues" in colleges and faculties of education desperate to increase their budgets (see note 10). The very future of the U.S. field is now in question.

12. Relinquishing those utopic fantasies associated with "dialogue," the concept of "exchange" (for a definition, see Pinar 2010a, 239, n. 1) focuses our attention on the empirical reality of whatever transpires. As you will see (in chapter 9), information was exchanged as concepts were challenged, explained, and defended, but little "dialogue"—in the sense of open-ended encounter among equals—occurred. As critics of the concept complain (see Pinar 2004,

198), such conditions are rarely met, certainly not in many classrooms, let alone, I would add, among scholars working in very different national (or even regional) circumstances.

13. All quoted passages derive from personal communication with the participants.

14. An educational psychologist, Benjamin Bloom (1913–1999) developed a classification scheme for educational objectives in the so-called cognitive domain, contributing to the theory of "mastery-learning."

15. I am thinking of the University of California, Los Angeles (UCLA) historian Gary Nash's secondary school history curriculum revision project that conservatives successfully repudiated. Led by Lynne Cheney, former head of the National Endowment for the Humanities (and wife of Vice President [during 2001–2009] Richard Cheney), conservatives maligned the National History Standards that she had funded (along with the Department of Education) as a "grim and gloomy" monument to political correctness. She pronounced the standards project a disaster for giving insufficient attention to the Confederate General Robert E. Lee and to the Wright brothers (credited with creating aviation) and far too much to "obscure" figures (such as Harriet Tubman) or to patriotically embarrassing episodes (such as the Ku Klux Klan and McCarthyism). Available online at: http://hnn.us…

16. Serge Moscovici (born 1925) is a Romanian-born French social psychologist.

17. Ferraço works in two research groups (1) "School routine and curriculum" housed at PROPED/UERJ (Program Graduate Education/State University of Rio de Janerio) and coordinated by Professors Nilda Alves and Inês Barbosa de Oliveira and (2) "Curriculum, Routines, Cultures, and Knowledge Networks," coordinated by Professor Janete Magalhães Carvalho, housed at PPGE/CE/UFES.

18. Lopes's use of Canclini's notion of "impure genres" resonates with "contamination," a key concept for Pasolini that specifies hybridity and transference (Pinar 2009b, 185, n. 32)

19. In response to my comment concerning the intersections of gender and militarism in explaining the centrality of science in the U.S. secondary curriculum, Lopes replied that militarism is less important in Brazil. Regarding gender, she commented that "we have many women in science, but we don't have a feminist science."

20. That term proves important in curriculum studies in South Africa. See Waghid 2010.

21. How many curriculum studies scholars worldwide can claim such progress in their own nationally distinctive fields? The U.S. field, as noted, seems to have been in a tailspin since the late 1960s, despite efforts (such as Pinar et al. 1995) to stabilize it. South African scholars were also critical of their field's present state (Pinar 2010a).

22. In his model of pedagogical understanding, Houssaye defines any act of teaching according to the three vertices of a triangle: the teacher, the student, and knowledge. Behind lies the knowledge content of the training material. Available online at http://translate.google.com.

REFERENCES

Aoki, Ted. 2005 (1990). "*Sonare* and *Videre*: A Story, Three Echoes and a Lingering Note." In *Curriculum in a New Key: The Collected Works of Ted T. Aoki*, ed. William F. Pinar and Rita L. Irwin (pp. 367–376). Mahwah, NJ: Lawrence Erlbaum.

Autio, Tero. 2005. *Subjectivity, Curriculum, and Society: Between and Beyond German Didaktik and Anglo-American Curriculum Studies*. Mahwah, NJ: Lawrence Erlbaum.

Axelrod, Charles David. 1979. *Studies in Intellectual Breakthrough: Freud, Simmel, Buber*. Amherst: University of Massachusetts Press.

Baker, Bernadette M. 2001. *In Perpetual Motion: Theories of Power, Educational History, and the Child*. New York: Peter Lang.

Baker, Bernadette. M. 2009. "Introduction." In *New Curriculum History*, ed. Bernadette Baker. Rotterdam, Boston, and Taipei: Sense Publishers.

Boyarin, Daniel. 1997. *Unheroic Conduct: The Rise of Heterosexuality and the Invention of the Jewish Man*. Berkeley: University of California Press.

Egan, Kieran. 2002. *Getting It Wrong from the Beginning: Our Progressivist Inheritance from Herbert Spencer, John Dewey, and Jean Piaget*. New Haven, CT: Yale University Press.

Gordon, Robert S. C. (1996). *Pasolini: Forms of Subjectivity*. Oxford: Clarendon Press.

Goodlad, Lauren M. E. 2002. "Character and Pastorship in Two British 'Sociological' Traditions: Organized Charity, Fabian Socialism, and the Invention of New Liberalism." In *Disciplinarity at the Fin de Siècle*, ed. Amanda Anderson and Joseph Valente (pp. 235–260). Princeton, NJ: Princeton University Press.

Greenfeld, Liah. 2002. "How Economics Became a Science: The Surprising Career of a Model Discipline." In *Disciplinarity at the Fin de Siècle*, ed. Amanda Anderson and Joseph Valente (pp. 87–125). Princeton, NJ: Princeton University Press.

Henderson, James G., and Kathleen R. Kesson. 2009. "Curriculum Disciplinarity and Education Research: Advancing a Scholarly and Professional Agenda." *Educational Researcher* 38 (2): 132–136.

Hoadley, Ursula. 2010. "Tribes and Territory: Contestation Around Curriculum in South Africa." In *Curriculum Studies in South Africa*, ed. W. F. Pinar. New York: Palgrave Macmillan.

Lopes, Alice Casimiro, and de Elizabeth Fernandes Macedo. 2003. "The Curriculum Field in Brazil in the 1990s." In *International Handbook of Curriculum Research*, ed. William F. Pinar,(pp. 185–203). Mahwah, NJ: Lawrence Erlbaum.

Mathur, Ajeet, Hongyu Wang, William E. Doll, Jr., William F. Pinar. 2003. "What Knowledge is of Most Worth?" In *The Internationalization of Curriculum Studies*, ed. Donna Trueit et al. (pp. 137–177). New York: Peter Lang.

Moraes, Silvia Elizabeth. 2003. "In Search of a Vision: How Brazil is Struggling to Envision Citizenship for its Public Schools." In *International Handbook of Curriculum Research*, ed. William F. Pinar (pp. 205–219). Mahwah, NJ: Lawrence Erlbaum.

Moreira, Antonio Flavio Barbosa. 2003. "The Curriculum Field in Brazil: Emergence and Consolidation." In *International Handbook of Curriculum Research*, ed. William F. Pinar (pp. 171–184). Mahwah, NJ: Lawrence Erlbaum.

Paras, Eric. 2006. *Foucault 2.0: Beyond Power and Knowledge.* New York: Other Press.

Pinar, William F. 2007. *Intellectual Advancement Through Disciplinarity: Verticality and Horizontality in Curriculum Studies.* Rotterdam and Taipei: Sense Publishers.

Pinar, William F. 2008. "Curriculum Theory Since 1950: Crisis, Reconceptualization, Internationalization." In *The Sage Handbook of Curriculum and Instruction*, ed. F. Michael Connelly, Ming Fang He, and JoAnn Phillion (pp. 491–513). Los Angeles: Sage.

Pinar, William F. 2009a. "The Primacy of the Particular." In *Leaders in Curriculum Studies: Intellectual Self-Portraits*, ed. Leonard Waks and Edmund C. Short (pp. 143–152). Rotterdam and Tapei: Sense Publishers.

Pinar, William F. 2009b. *The Worldliness of a Cosmopolitan Education: Passionate Lives in Public Service.* New York: Routledge.

Pinar, William F. 2009c. "The Next Moment." In *Curriculum Studies: The Next Moment*, ed. Erik Malewski (pp. 528–533). New York: Routledge.

Pinar, William F. 2010a. *Curriculum Studies in South Africa.* New York: Palgrave Macmillan.

Pinar, William F., ed. 2010b. "The Unaddressed 'I' of Ideology Critique." *Power and Education* 1 (2): 189–200. Available online at: http:// www.wwwords. co.uk.

Pinar, William F., William M. Reynolds, Patrick Slattery, and Peter M. Taubman. 1995. *Understanding Curriculum: An Introduction to Historical and Contemporary Curriculum Discourses.* New York: Peter Lang.

Popkewitz, Thomas S. 2008. *Cosmopolitanism and the Age of School Reform: Science, Education, and Making Society by Making the Child.* New York: Routledge.

Radhakrishnan, R. 2008. *History, the Human, and the World Between.* Durham, NC: Duke University Press.

Ransom, John S. 1997. *Foucault's Discipline: The Politics of Subjectivity.* Durham, NC: Duke University Press.

Schubert, William H. 2009a. "*Currere* and Disciplinarity in Curriculum Studies: Possibilities for Education Research." *Educational Researcher* 38 (2): 136–140.

Schubert, William H. 2009b. "A Response to 'Curriculum Work at the Intersection of Pragmatic Inquiry, Deliberation, and Fidelity,' by James G. Henderson and Kathleen R. Kesson." *Educational Researcher* 38 (2): 142–143.

Sekyi-Otu, Ato. 1996. *Fanon's Dialectic of Experience.* Cambridge, MA: Harvard University Press.

Simpson, David. 2002. *Situatedness, Or, Why We Keep Saying Where We're Coming From*. Durham, NC: Duke University Press.

Taubman, Peter M. 2009. *Teaching by Numbers: Deconstructing the Discourse of Standards and Accountability in Education*. New York: Routledge.

Tröhler, Daniel. 2003. "The Discourse of German *Geisteswissenschaftliche Padagogik*—A Contextual Reconstruction." *Paedagogica Historica* 39 (6): 759–778.

Waghid, Yusef. 2010. "Toward Authentic Teaching and Learning in Post-Apartheid South Africa: In Defense of Freedom, Friendship, and Democratic Citizenship." In *Curriculum Studies in South Africa*, ed. William F. Pinar (pp. 201–220). New York: Palgrave Macmillan.

Waks, Leonard. ed. 2008. *Leaders in Philosophy of Education: Intellectual Self-Portraits*. Rotterdam and Tapei: Sense Publishers.

Wraga, William G. 1999. "'Extracting Sun-Beams Out of Cucumbers': The Retreat from Practice in Reconceptualized Curriculum Studies." *Educational Researcher* 28 (1): 4–13.

Chapter 1

Curriculum Studies in Brazil: An Overview

Ashwani Kumar

Introduction

Brazilian curriculum studies can be roughly divided into three phases: Pre-Marxist (1950s–1970s); Marxist (1980s–mid-1990s); and Post-Marxist (mid-1990s–present). The pre-Marxist phase is not discussed but referenced in the chapters that follow; it was dominated by a Tylerian instrumentalism variously depicted as positivist, behaviorist, technocratic, administrative, and/or scientific (see Macedo's chapter 7 of this volume[1]). The Marxist phase focused on school-society relationship employing concepts such as power, ideology, hegemony, and reproduction. Marxism—characterized by emphases upon subjectivity, everyday life, hybridity, and multiculturalism—dominated the Brazilian field until the mid-1990s when postmodern, poststructural, and postcolonial discourses replaced it.

In the following sections I turn to discuss in detail the nature of curriculum discourses in Brazil during the Marxist and the Post-Marxist periods. I must point it out here that by no means these are sharp divisions; indeed, there is a coexistence of various discourses (positivist, Marxist, and post-Marxist). But such periodization does reflect general trends. Moreover, as an outsider to Brazilian curriculum theory and guided by Elba Siqueira de Sá Barretto's (chapter 4 of this volume) remark pinpointing "the lack of research on the historical perspective of the curriculum [in Brazil]," such an organization helped me organize the intellectual history of the field.

Marxism (1980s–mid-1990s)

The New Sociology of Education, and the critical theories on curriculum as a whole shifted the discussions, until then prevailing in the psycho-pedagogy field, to issues of power, ideology and culture...
Elba Siqueira de Sá Barretto (chapter 4 of this volume)

During the 1960s and 1970s Brazil was in a great political turmoil characterized by underdevelopment, imperialism, and the widely felt need for structural reforms. There was as well intense hope that a socialist revolution would create a more just and equal society in the country (chapter 4). This period was also characterized by debates on the relations between education and social development. Notably, the links between education and social development had already been the subject of attention of sociologists, among them Florestan Fernandes, Otávio Ianni, Fernando Henrique Cardoso, and Luiz Pereira, who focused especially on urbanization and industrialization. The importation of sociological perspectives represented a new focus in the educational field, which had been marked by "psycho-pedagogical studies" (chapter 4).

During the late 1970s and early 1980s scholarly production in curriculum studies was not extensive. An article by José Luis Domingues, based on the ideas of Habermas, was one of the first works articulating the main curriculum categories of technical-linear, circular-consensual, and dynamic-dialogical. At that time, only the texts by Michael Apple and Henry Giroux had been published in Brazil. Abraham Magendzo's *Curriculum e Cultura na América Latina* [Curriculum and Culture in Latin America] was also an important reference for the first courses introduced in Brazil (chapter 4). Antonio Flávio Barbosa Moreira's *Currículos e programas no Brasil* [Curricula and Programs in Brazil] became a key, indeed, canonical text.

During the first half of the 1990s, articles on the New Sociology of Education, then a subject little known to Brazilians, began to circulate, introduced by Brazilian scholars who had obtained their doctoral degrees in the United Kingdom, among them Antônio Flávio and Lucíola Licínio dos Santos (chapter 4). Such critical scholarship focused on the selection and distribution of school knowledge, an attempt "to understand relationships between the processes of selection, distribution and organization and teaching of school contents and the strategies of power inside the inclusive social context" (chapter 4). In their *Currículo, cultura e sociedade*, Moreira and Silva defined curriculum as school content; they also identified ideology, power, and culture as the main themes of the curriculum theory.

The New Sociology of Education and the critical theories on curriculum shifted discussion from psycho-pedagogical themes to issues of power, ideology, and culture. Moreira and Silva and others have played important roles as disseminators of studies conducted by scholars working primarily in the United States and United Kingdom.[2] The concept of "class *habitus*," theorized by Bourdieu; studies by Rist, Howard Becker, Rosenthal, and Jacobson; as well as contributions of Basil Bernstein and his frame of "invisible pedagogy" provided a conceptual framework for many in this period (chapter 4). Scholars questioned instrumentalist conceptualizations of curriculum as a set of psychological or epistemological principles concerned with the developmental order of the contents, adapted to the students' age, according to methods of curricular integration. In such an analysis investigations were carried out problematizing the organization of knowledge that constitutes the dominant forms of curriculum (see Alice Casimiro Lopes' chapter 6). However, the domination of Marxism gave way to the postmodernism.

Post-Marxist Phase (Mid-1990s to the Present)

By the mid-1990s Marxism came under serious criticism due to its devaluation of everyday life. Such criticisms, rooted as they were in the so-called post-discourses, allowed a fundamental and epistemologically remarkable step leading to the "deterritorialization"[3]—a passage of flux, change, or transition in the existing models, theories, and paradigms—of curriculum, which has resulted in the exhaustion of macro-analyses and the territorializing tendencies typical of Marxist scholarship. Brazilian curriculum studies is now preoccupied with everyday school life, hybridization of curricular policies, cultural studies, and the emphasis on differences, the latter marked by the identity politics of postmodernism (see Antonio Carlos Amorim's chapter 3). I turn first to studies of everyday life in schools.

Curriculum as Everyday Life

Research that is concerned with educative everyday lives and with different practices, knowledge and significations...originate...from the idea that it is in multiple and complex processes that we learn and teach.

Nilda Alves (chapter 2 of the volume)

In each quotidian[4] reality, the struggle [for social emancipation] happens in different forms, and the better we understand our reality, the better are the chances of entering in this struggle in an efficient way. That explains the need [of] plunging into the quotidian. It is not possible to fight in the abstract field!

Inês Barbosa de Oliveira (chapter 8 of the volume)

[Everyday life research] conceive[s] the curriculum as articulated around social practice for the purpose of inverting the hierarchical relationship between theory and practice.

Elizabeth Macedo (chapter 7 of the volume)

"Research into/on/with everyday life" (see Alves' chapter 2) conceives the curriculum as social practice (Macedo's chapter 7), often focused on the network of relationships between practitioners and the "routines" of public schools (Ferraço's chapter 5). The major everyday life researchers in Brazil include Nilda Alves, Regina Leite Garcia, and Inês Barbosa Oliveira, whose work questions the linear organizations of knowledge and views knowledge as the situated consequence of networks of subjectivities in everyday life (chapter 6), problematizing the view that the official prescriptions are directly translated into the curriculum as practiced. In this research, curriculum as an official document becomes curriculum as articulated in action and power networks, woven in the school's daily life, whose threads, with its Deleuzian "knots" and "lines of flight," are discernible not only in daily life but also beyond them, reaching into various settings where participants live (chapter 5). What matters for understanding curriculum is not only formal documents but also what is practiced in schools and related contexts (chapter 7). Everyday life researchers ask two specific questions: What narratives and images are produced and shared in school routines in the processes of "negotiation," "translation," "mimicry," and "uses"? How do those processes empower practices of "resistance" and "invention" in relation to the homogenizing mechanisms of the official prescriptions? (chapter 5).

Everyday life research emerged in Brazil in response to criticism of technocratic conceptions of school life, conceptions imported from the United States. Abstracting students and teachers as variables, technocratic studies disregarded subjectivity, assuming the "impossibility" of knowing what goes on inside the school. Technocratic studies seemed to assume that what happens inside is not important, even frequently wrong. Everyday life research also derived from the Marxist overemphasis upon reproduction and hegemony; it found that students and teachers not only reproduce what is, they also create, every day, new forms of being, making, and knowing. Macro-changes in history are woven into people's day-to-day lives, if in ways not often detectable at the moment when such changes occur, but in incidents that people do not foresee (chapter 2).

In everyday life, subjects practice different ways of "experimenting-problematizing" the official curriculum, sometimes "transgressing" it in "powerful" and "inventive" ways, constituting networks of "antidisciplines." Everyday life researchers have discovered that when participating in the daily curricular experience, even if following pre-established curricular materials, teachers and students weave "practical alternatives" with the threads provided by the networks they are part of, in and outside school. Thus, it can be said that there are multiple curricula in action in schools, in spite of the different "homogenizing mechanisms" (chapter 5).

Everyday knowledge has been dismissed as mere "common sense," to be replaced by scientific knowledge assumed to be superior to that discovered in the quotidian (chapter 8). Such a social science pays no attention to the multiple "meanings and uses" the "common senses" have for practitioners. Interacting with the complexity of the daily life in schools structured by various networks and sharing the "action-knowledge" of teachers and students produce appreciation of the complexity of curriculum. Everyday life researchers realize the impossibility of control over the diversity of the curricular practice by means of categories that purport to measure them (chapter 5). In addition, such a social science assumes that it is possible to study an object by itself, without understanding the multiple processes, contexts, and interrelationships in which it is inserted (chapter 2). Everyday life researchers labor to understand events invisible to the quantitative-scientific methods of research models intent on generalizing the singular. For everyday life researchers, the curriculum is constituted in networks of significations and, thus, is performed by people incarnated in specific social, historical, cultural, political, and economical settings that are interconnected and that influence each other mutually (see chapters 5 and 8). In opposition to the "interposition" and the "censorship" that science imposes on narrative knowledge, everyday life research is dedicated to listening to the common, affording attention to the daily practices of the subjects in schools. Such an aspiration requires a research methodology sufficiently open and flexible to describe the daily communicative interactions through situating the subjects in their own world (chapter 5), thereby acknowledging all the experiences that schools have neglected in the name of scientific knowledge and Western white bourgeoisie culture (chapter 8).

In addition, everyday researchers question the idealist and utopian visions of state curriculum proposals. They argue that although people may have idealist and utopian visions and believe in a promising future for education, there is no possibility of an instituted consensus, of a common ideal prescribed to be reached with the same intensity and by everybody, as implied by the official curriculum policies. The complexity of daily life diffuses any utopian intentions. That realization construes education as lived in the present, not something to be achieved in the future. Curriculum is what actually happens in schools, in the concrete conditions and contexts where the students and teachers act. Finally, everyday life research constitutes a rejection of the increasing dominance of common/ universal/standardized curricula and the installation of global systems of evaluations—which define what to teach and when to teach, thereby, reducing the freedom of schools and local systems to adapt to different realities. Given such market-driven homogenizing educational policies, everyday life researchers, such as Oliveira, endorse struggles against economistic thinking and speak for social emancipation in the quotidian contexts of school lives. In each quotidian reality, Oliveira argues, this struggle is undertaken in different forms, and the more fully subjects (researchers and the researched) understand their reality, the greater are the chances of smart struggle for emancipation. Present conditions, Oliveira argues, provide the need for plunging into the quotidian.

What have been the major theoretical positions behind the development of everyday life research in Brazil? The first major theoretical influence came from Gramsci and the Frankfurt School, particularly Habermas, an influence that greatly impacted the works of Ana Maria Saul and José Luiz Domingues, who exercised a decisive influence on research into everyday life. For these researchers, introducing the concept of the quotidian into curriculum studies was necessary in order to understand school life and its relationships with the broader social reality. Methodologically, everyday life researchers felt that the subjects' active participation was indispensable and developed a process called "participant research" (similar to action research in North America). Notably, it was due to their methodological approach that such studies made a strong relationship with the social movements based on the thinking of Paulo Freire (chapter 2). The second major influence on everyday life research was related to the works of Robert Stake, who recognized the need to observe what happens daily in the school with the impossibility of generalizing conclusions. Stake emphasized the "multiplicity" and "complexity" of everyday school life. The representatives of this tendency in Brazil are Menga Lüdke and Marli André, whose works are a necessary reference in everyday life studies (chapter 2). Also influential in Brazil is research conducted by Justa Ezpeleta and Elsie Rockwell (chapter 2) underscoring the importance of studying schools as they are, seeking to understand what is created by teachers and students. Also influential is the great English curriculum specialist Stenhouse and his idea of "teacher-researcher," as well as his followers, such as Elliot, who also underlined teachers' reconstruction of official proposals, especially as they participate in research regarding those same daily practices of reconstruction (chapter 2).

Finally, the research on everyday life, to understand the roles of cultural artifacts with which the practitioners weave networks of relationships, was influenced by Cultural Studies, including the work of Lefebvre, Certeau, Boaventura de Souza Santos,[5] Humberto Maturana, and Bhabha (chapter 5).[6] Moreover, the dialogue with postmodernity, especially with Deleuze, in the 1990s, brought the metaphors "tree" and "rhizome," and the networked curriculum, marked by a conception of "rhizomatic"[7] knowledge (chapter 7).

Curriculum as Postmodern and Post-structural Text

> These [postmodern] studies seek a methodological way out of the totalizations and metanarratives, and look out for possibilities of analyzing the singular, the local and the partial.
>
> Elba Siqueira de Sá Barretto (chapter 4)

During the 1990s post-structuralist and postmodern perspectives began to be more widely disseminated in Brazil, but it is primarily curriculum scholars who have most contributed to debates regarding the significance of postmodernism for educational theory (chapter 4). An important article by Moreira and Silva went beyond the New Sociology to acknowledge the so-called linguistic turn, for example, postmodernism. Later, while A. F. Moreira began to advocate an association between modernity and postmodernity, the work of Tomaz Tadeu da Silva underwent a strong change in the direction of post-structuralism (chapter 7). His published collection of essays, *Teoria educacional crítica em tempos pós-modernos* (Critical Educational Theory in Postmodern Times), which critically reviewed Foucault, Deleuze, Derrida, Rorty, and others, is a landmark publication, addressing the central issues of postmodernism as well as establishing continuities and ruptures with the existing curriculum discourses in Brazil (chapters 4). The work of Silva gave centrality to the curriculum as a "practice of meaning," altering the prevailing conception of culture as the primary source of content to be taught. He worked as a supervisor of many researchers in the field. A study of the dissertations defended between 1996 and 2002 showed that A. F. Moreira, N. Alves, and T. T. Silva (specifically his work incorporating critical perspective) were the principal Brazilian references in those studies.[8]

Research conducted according to postmodern perspectives occurred mainly in the University of Rio Grande do Sul, influenced by Tomaz Tadeu da Silva, Alfredo Veiga-Neto, Rosa Maria Fischer, Guacira Lopes Louro, Sandra Corazza, and Marisa Vorraber.

According to the survey conducted by Paraíso on the postmodern research literature, the studies emanating from the University of Rio Grande do Sul have primarily focused upon (1) relations of power and subjected identities (inspired by cultural, feminist, postcolonial, ethnic, and queer studies); (2) subjectivation, challenging the assumptions about the "subject" based on critical and traditional theories; and (3) the problematization of the "educational truths," of curriculum knowledge considered as "legitimate," evidencing the constructed and contested nature of knowledge production in education. These studies attempt to seek a methodological way out of totalizations and metanarratives, looking for possibilities of analyzing the singular, the local, and the partial (chapter 4). Key in this development was the work of Antonio Flávio Moreira, Alice Casimiro Lopes, Elizabeth Macedo, and Lucíola Licínio Santos, which sought to understand both the theoretical assumptions that have influenced the Brazilian curricular thinking and hybridizations of the current curricular discourses, as well as the proposed perspectives for action (chapter 4).

Influenced by the post-structural critique of "disciplinarity," Alfredo Veiga-Neto has developed a Foucault-based research program to argue in favor of interdisciplinary studies centered on a "humanist-essentialist" perspective. In view of a "humanist-essentialist" perspective, the "pathology of the knowledge," resulting from the separation of knowledge from the complex environment, leads to an instrumental approach subservient to the interests of capitalist development. Veiga-Neto questioned the conception of "disciplinarity" based on a unitary vision of reason that disregards the knowledge-power relations that engender the disciplinary knowledge. For Veiga-Nato, the school has its rituals of space and time marked by the "disciplinarization of the knowledge" that maintain relationships with the processes of "governmentability" (chapter 6).

For Veiga-Neto, the curriculum is an artifact of school culture centered on order, representation, and transcendence. As a consequence, school subjects exhibit specificities similar to scientific knowledge. In such a scenario, the knowledge-power relations that form subjects are not part of school knowledge. Thus, such a "scientific" school subject does not reflect institutional specificities of the subjects, nor does it aim to consider the trajectories of various communities. As a consequence of this critique of school subjects the Brazilian field has undertaken research into the history of school subjects in Brazil (chapter 6). Such research is being conducted under the coordination of Antonio Flavio Moreira,

Elizabeth Macedo, and Alice Lopes. Based especially on the works of Ivor Goodson, Thomas Popkewitz, and Stephen Ball, these researchers investigate the transformation of scientific knowledge into school knowledge. This research helps understand how social hierarchies and divisions of culture—erudite culture, popular culture, systematized knowledge, and commonsense knowledge—are maintained at the same time cultural hybrids are produced (chapter 6). As well, this sociohistorical research focuses on the stability of the subject-centered curriculum as an organizational technology of school control. It is with this understanding that Macedo maintains that the subject-centered organization does not prevent curricular integration movements, but he submits them to its logic. To question the social goals implied by school curricula, whether disciplinary, integrated, or even simultaneously disciplinary and integrated, becomes criticism of the power relations embedded in the curricular organizations (chapter 6).

Currently, curriculum theory is also being developed based on concepts of Deleuze's philosophy, namely, the relations among time, being, and event; the relations among time, image, and duration, of cinema studies; and the relations among time, sign, and sense. Amorim views curriculum as a "sensation field" that frees itself from the humanist substance that saturates it while searching for survival in a post-human state: "somnambulistic, unconscious, actionless, uninhabited." In the process of visualizing the curriculum as a "disfiguration context," cinema studies are influential. In this view, the curriculum field anticipates new forms of living, generating creative acts in a world grounded in virtuality, on temporal comprehension, on nomadic movements and, provocatively, on "barbarism." Despite the postmodern emphasis of his research, Amorim criticizes postmodernist scholarship for exhibiting the same bases and the same referents as modernist scholarship does, among them: (1) the figure of the subject, specifically his/her conscience, autonomy, and power of transformation; (2) the relations of power structured on a plane subject to interpretation by cultural (class, gender, ethnic) and ideological categories as well as those of hegemony; (3) the continuous unyielding effort for the elaboration of "just ideas" (involving interpretation, analysis, judgment) connected to claims of representation of understanding the world; and (4) the "re-effort" toward critical transcendental thought. Moreover, Amorim observes a strong analytic tendency among postmodernists to reduce registers to text. Efforts to understand the relations between cultures and languages are collapsed into "discourse" as a metanarrative of cultural curriculum studies. Such centrality of identities and the subjectvist substance represent a tendency, Amorim argues, similar to structuralism.

Curriculum as Hybrid and Multicultural Text

> [O]nly a conservative identity, closed on itself, could experience hybrid-
> ization as a loss.
>
> Ernesto Laclau (cited in chapter 6)

In recent times hybridism has characterized a major theoretical tendency
in Brazilian curricular thinking. Hybridism signifies the ways in which
diverse curricular traditions struggle for representation in the form of distinct curricular choice and organization and have their meanings reconfigured in that struggle. Such hybrid identities in no way mean to disregard
the history of existing traditions, the negotiations that are made with such
traditions, and their multiple libraries—of books, theories, films, theater
plays, images and memories. Hybridism has, without doubt, greatly contributed to the complexity of the understanding of curriculum in Brazil,
a contribution that is evidenced in the production of articles, books, theses, and dissertations. New theories from philosophy, politics, sociology,
and cultural studies are being incorporated, creating a hybridism that, at
times, renders the curriculum so multifaceted that it risks losing resonance
with the history of curricular thinking (chapter 6). Nevertheless, hybridism is important for opening up new perspectives. For the field to advance
hybridism must be critically embraced as an opportunity, not as a loss. As
Laclau notes, only a conservative identity, closed on itself, could experience
hybridization as a loss. Hybridism does not always lead to overcoming the
somewhat prescriptive nature that marks research as instrumentalism. It is
still a common practice to consider research as a means for constructing
proposals for schools to guide practice. Relationships among proposals/
guidelines/theories and practices are treated in a "verticalized manner,"
which assumes that it is up to theory, even one of post-structuralist inspiration, to illuminate the paths of practice (chapter 6).

Hybridism in curriculum research has also been accompanied by multiculturalism. The turnaround of the field of curriculum in the direction
of multiculturalism coincided with the greater consolidation of democracy
in Brazil and with the expansion of the political space won by the cultural
minorities, especially the Black Movement (*Movimento Negro*). The racial
equality law, the recognition of Zumbi dos Palmares as a national hero,
the implementation of affirmative actions in the universities and in the
public sector, and the inclusion of Afro-Brazilian history and culture in
the curricula of all Brazilian schools by a presidential decree in 2003 are all
indices of multiculturalism's curricular importance (see chapters 4 and 7).
With the promulgation of the new Constitution in 1988, native languages

were to be the medium of instruction for indigenous peoples in the first grades of compulsory school. A movement to rescue native languages and cultures has emerged. In 2008, the federal government made indigenous studies compulsory at all levels of education. Cultural organizations, ethnic movements, nongovernmental organizations (NGOs), universities and other research institutions have produced studies and curriculum materials to enhance multicultural education. At the same time, teacher education initiatives addressing multiculturalism have also started to appear. In the field of curriculum, scholars such as Vera Candau, Ana Canen, and Antonio Flávio B. Moreira are known for conducting multicultural studies (chapter 4).

Influenced by postmodern perspectives, multiculturalism has played a central role in the transition from the Marxist emphasis on "social classes" to the forefronting, indeed celebration, of "difference." This emphasis upon "cultural differences" has overlooked those who struggle to obtain basic social goods. The discourse on "differences," some contend, has functioned to obscure the issue of inequalities as they become relevant only as they affect certain discriminated groups. Barretto thinks that the "racialization" of certain identity movements deserves a more profound reflection in the field of curriculum. Ferraço maintains that multiculturalism risks conceiving the school as a museum of different cultures, as if it could exhibit these by means of commemorative dates, characters, habits, and other categories of curricular prescription. In this multicultural perspective the Other is "visited" from a "tourist perspective," which stimulates a superficial and voyeuristic approach to "exotic" cultures. A postcolonial perspective would demand a "multicultural curriculum" that would not separate issues of knowledge, culture, and aesthetics from those of power, politics, and interpretation. It fundamentally demands a "decolonized curriculum." The "museum" of multiculturalism has also been criticized as controlling the dynamic processes of "cultural difference" as it administers a false consensus structured by "cultural diversity." Although the idea of cultural diversity is welcome, minoritarian cultures become located in their own self-enclosed circuits (chapter 5).

Curriculum as Cultural Enunciation

I feel it is necessary to radicalize the possibilities of overcoming those binarisms [formal and experienced curriculum; scholastic culture and culture of the school; scientific and everyday knowledge]... it is necessary to deconstruct the logic in which they [binarisms] can be thought, which in the case of the curriculum I imagine could be done [by] treating it as cultural enunciation.

Elizabeth Macedo (chapter 7)

The fundamental shift in the field—from the Marxism of the 1980s to the "post" discourses of the 1990s—constituted a moment of transition from a "political concept of curriculum" to the "centrality of culture" in curriculum. In the political conception, curriculum (school knowledge) is a shared repertory of cultural meanings as well as a means of cultural reproduction. The primacy of cultural reproduction dissipated as cultural production and "practices of meaning" underscored teachers' and students' agency. These binary pairs persisted between formal and experienced curriculum; scholastic culture and culture of the school; scientific and everyday knowledge. To overcome such binaries, Macedo and Ferraço began to view curriculum and culture as sites of enunciation.

Studies of curriculum policies make such distinctions very clear both in critiques of the "top/down models" (which argues that curriculum documents are imposed by the government schools) and in the proposition of "down/top models" (which argues that curriculum should develop from the everyday life situations of the schools). The former focus was associated with the new sociology of education and critical theory with their emphasis on the notions of "official curriculum" and the idea of "reproduction." Although fewer in number, policy studies focused on curricular alternatives present in the everyday life of schools were also there. These studies emphasized the creative dimension of everyday life while minimizing its reproductive function and criticizing the inflation of the importance accorded to "official" curricula in Marxist models. In both approaches (Marxist and everyday life studies), a distinction can be seen between "production" and "implementation" of the curriculum that accentuates the dichotomies outlined above. These dichotomies, Macedo argues, can be surmounted by theorizing curriculum as the space of cultural enunciation. The process of enunciation is dialogical as it tracks dislocations and realignments resulting from cultural antagonisms and articulations, thus subverting the "hegemonic moment" and replacing it with hybrid, alternative places of "cultural negotiation" (chapter 5).

The devaluation of the "experienced" vis-à-vis the "official" curriculum expresses the fantasy of verisimilitude in representation. The written nature of the "official" curriculum effaces the effects of the mediation of language in everyday life. Studies of the experienced curriculum can seem to assume a self-evident, even "natural" relationship between representation and meaning. It is as if the official or formal curriculum were disassociated from the thinking that produced it, as if it were a distortion of the lived experience in relation to which it was presumably written. The formal curriculum (this reasoning goes) cannot produce resonance, because it is the "illegitimate expression" of the reality, a stance assumed by some works in the down/top model used in analyses of curriculum policies in Brazil. The majority of the studies, however, insist on the authority of the curricular documents produced by the state. Ferraço rejects any contraposition between "official curricular prescriptions" and "performed curricula." In fact, he argues that in the routine of the schools, the "curricula performed" or "curricula practiced" or "networked curricula" is expressed as a potential possibility for the problematization and/or broadening of the official curriculum. Ferraço considers schools, teachers, and students as hybrid subjects in culture's in-between, who use the curricula without being imprisoned by political or cultural, original or fixed identities and indeed threaten the official discourse of the whole system. Given this analysis, Ferraço argues that it is imperative to have a political perspective based on unequal, negotiated, and translated but neither fixed nor uniform political identities that are able to act in the gaps. Political identities must be multiple and inventive, as the uses and translations of the curriculum in schools take the forms of different logics, ethics, and aesthetics. This "knowledge-action" of the school subjects is ambivalent, even slippery, dislocating the instituted and creating unforeseen possibilities at the same time as it conserves what is given as official reference.

Curriculum theory, Macedo and Ferraço argue, must deconstruct binary distinctions between formal and experienced, reproduction and production, and school knowledge and scientific knowledge. Derrida's notion of "supplement," Macedo suggests, is useful for overcoming such binaries, functioning like a non-essential increase to something that is already complete but paradoxically lacks something. The supplement provides the incompleteness that it identifies in the supplement. It is impossible, Macedo emphasizes, to conceive "experienced curricula" or "cultural production" inside schools without historically shared meanings, without the iterability that characterizes signs and that allows signification (in this case formal curriculum). Consequently, the experienced curriculum would share with the written curriculum a past understood as "instituted outlines." Experienced curriculum, to which the fantasy of the perfect representation attributes the possibility of referring to something concrete, is like the official or written curriculum, only infinite deferments that do not reference any origin (chapter 7).

If there are only deferments, Macedo continues, distinctions such as those between formal and experienced as well as between reproduction and production become unsustainable. Such distinctions support a scheme in which creation exists only as resistance to past impositions.

In a situation of infinite deferments, the movements among past, present, and future meanings necessitate articulation and antagonistic negotiation. The curricular document only interrupts the flow of meanings created by the infinite deferment, fixing them momentarily. Without such a "fixing" there would be no text or meaning, but at the same time these interrupt the actual fluidity of the creation. This is something that could be roughly named as an "impossible fixing" and, in the same movement, necessary (chapter 7).

The idea that textual structure is decentered, without limits, but momentarily fixed around a provisional center every time a text is produced, opens up new possibilities of meanings. Derrida's concept of "brisure," Macedo notes, articulates this idea. Curricular texts, like open structures, are overdetermined and, thus, closed, constructing modes of address that in themselves have a "provisional quality." In the perspective of the curriculum as cultural enunciation, dichotomies no longer make sense because the curriculum as enunciation emphasizes dialogues with traditions, thereby, spawning a "zone of ambivalence," an "in-between space" that is neither past nor future, but both and neither of them (chapter 7). In this "frontier zone" all that exists are "cultural flows" that represent the complexity of the social and the human. According to Ferraço, such an understanding allows curricularists to become researchers of daily life in multiple networks of ongoing negotiations permeated by ambiguities—ambivalences of the possibilities that are presented in interstices but are never fixed or immutable.

The idea of curriculum as enunciation has been criticized as neglecting the operations of power. Macedo counters by pointing out that such a concept enables curriculum theorists to work in a more rigorous way with the power and, specifically, with the agency of subjects, thereby providing a way out of the doomed struggle against an absolutely hegemonic power that Marxist theories, including the New Sociology of Education, have devised. Such a possibility, however, Macedo urges, demands politicization of concepts such as "brisure" and "hybridism," which may lead to a "theory of hegemony" on post-Marxist bases. Such a "discursive theory of hegemony" can provide tools for understanding the overdetermination of the curricular texts and the discursive closings they allow, at the same time countering criticisms of relativism associated with post-structural and postcolonial curriculum theory.

Conclusion

In recent decades curriculum studies in Brazil has undergone significant shifts—first a positivist movement, then a Marxist ideology, and now a post-Marxist philosophy. Curriculum studies in Brazil is an intellectually vibrant and impressive field, one that will exhibit a strong presence worldwide. What can contribute to the continued intellectual advancement of the field? Research on the intellectual history of Brazilian curriculum studies is key, Barretto acknowledges. While focused on the "next moment" that is attentive to theoretical, social, and political developments in Brazil and worldwide, curriculum studies must remain attentive to the past, constantly reevaluating the significance and meaning of work conducted earlier. Such historicity includes ongoing attention to institutional politics that influence graduate education of future scholars (chapter 6). Through a critical reconsideration of the "canon," curriculum theorists return to their libraries to reconstruct their understanding and their identities. This ongoing reconstruction of knowledge that is of most worth is animated by the ongoing negotiation of meanings that a complicated conversation implies. Emphasizing everyday life and enunciation as event, each represented as duration in images that reconfigure the very meaning of representation, curriculum studies in Brazil provides key concepts that contribute creatively to the ongoing formation of the worldwide field.

NOTES

1. Note that most references in this chapter refer to other chapters within this volume.
2. The major theorists whose works have been disseminated widely in Brazil include Michael Young, Basil Bernstein, Michael Apple, Philip Wexler, Henry Giroux, Stephen Ball, Peter McLaren, John Willinsky, and Stuart Hall, among others.
3. "In Gilles Deleuze and Félix Guattari's *A Thousand Plateaus* (1980), a territoriality is depicted as any entity or institution that restricts the free flow of desire. The family and the state count as prime examples of territorialities, and they conspire to produce the modern subject—the controlled and, as Deleuze and Guattari see it, inhibited subject of liberal humanism and the Enlightenment project: 'there is no fixed subject unless there is repression,' they insist. They argue that desire itself needs to be 'deterritorialized,' and treat nomadic existence as some kind of ideal of deterritorialization" (Stuart 2001, 370).
4. Oliveira employs the term "quotidian" for everyday life.
5. See Oliveira's chapter 8 for a discussion on the implications of Boaventura de Sousa Santos's ideas of "sociology of absences" and "sociology of emergences" for everyday life research. According to Oliveira, the concepts of "sociology of absences" and "sociology of emergences" allow the quotidian researcher to think concretely about the emancipating potential registered in everyday

curricular practices and to think of the possibilities to diffuse these practices on a larger scale as an inspiration for others to develop them, respectively.

6. Ferraço's chapter 5 in this volume represents an important example of the influence of cultural studies in the conceptualization of everyday life research in Brazil.

7. "In *A Thousand Plateaus*, Deleuze and Guattari put forward the notion of the rhizome as a model for how systems should work in a postmodern world. Prime examples of rhizomes in the natural world would be tubers or mosses, and it is characteristic of a rhizomatic system that, as Deleuze and Guattari put it, any point on it can be connected up to any other (as in the intertwining of mosses). Rhizomes are contrasted to trees and roots, which, in Deleuze and Guattari's opinion, 'fix an order,' and are thus implicitly restrictive and authoritarian. The implication is that since rhizomes do not feature the linear development pattern of trees and roots, they are more democratic and creative, thus forming a better basis for systems in a postmodern world than the tree-like hierarchies most Western societies tend to favor instead. In common with their poststructuralist and postmodernist peers, Deleuze and Guattari are firmly opposed to hierarchy and authority, and concerned to find alternative methods of constructing networks. Something like the rhizome idea can be found in the Internet, which similarly allows for connections to be established between any two points of the system, as well as having no clearly identifiable 'centre,' or central authority" (Stuart 2001, 350).

8. Notably, the studies that adopted a Marxist perspective during this period found theoretical support in the works of Antonio Gramsci, Dermeval Saviani, and Gaudêncio Frigotto (Lopes, 2010).

REFERENCES

Deleuze, Gilles, and Felix Guattari. 1980. *A Thousand Plateaus*. Paris: Les Editions de Minuit.

Lopes, Alice Casimiro. 2010. Email correspondence.

Stuart, Sim. 2001. *Routledge Companion to Postmodernism*. London and New York: Routledge, Taylor & Francis.

Chapter 2

Everyday Life in Schools
Nilda Alves

This story[1] refers to my experience during 25 years of research dedicated to understanding the everyday lives in educative networks. It will be told logically and according to thematics that emerged during that research and involved the author of this text. This story, however, as in every human experience, did not happen all at once, with all the understanding I have today, nor in the linearity of the explanation with which it is told here. However, although told in the first person, it must be made clear that it results as much from this author's individual contribution as from a collective effort, because we are—and the whole story shows this—an accumulation of everyday actions and events, insignificant but necessary shapers of our humanity, the fruit of the labor of many. When describing these processes, I hope to show our permanent and everyday discovery that leads us to understand our daily need to create different ways of doing things, in knowledge networks and in multiple and complex significations.

The Beginning of My Story

My story begins by indicating how research on/into/with everyday lives began in Brazil, aware that the way in which I identify myself is only one of those existing lives, which leads me to affirm that it would be possible to write other stories about that particular relationship and call it *cultures and everyday lives*.

The first tendency of studies *on* everyday life originated from and was predominant in studies developed from a technicist view of everyday school life, supported by ways of thinking that arrived in Brazil with technicians from the United States, under "agreements" signed by the two countries. In those studies, everyday life—in the singular and treated as an abstraction, without considering the subjects involved—is identified as a "black box." From the viewpoint of official proposals on education for the educative, scholastic, and other *spacetimes*,[2] I can say that the idea of "black box" is still hegemonic throughout the world, although it is mentioned little in this study.

Those who use this "black box" metaphor seek to indicate the "impossibility" of knowing what, in fact, goes on inside the school, sustaining, at the same time, the idea that certain possible approximations are not necessary or that "what happens inside is not important," and even "frequently wrong." Consequently, without caring about what is happening inside the "black box," those in that tendency feel that intervention in the *system* should focus on *input,* based on *feedback* using possible data obtained upon completion of the earlier process, possible, they believe, by evaluating the *output.* The application of the final exams of cycles and courses, as done in our country and many others, materializes that "model."

A second tendency of research *into* everyday lives—now pluralized and involving the subjects—appears, in this story, when research processes are developed around two concepts that are based on the understanding that the hegemonic conceptions of everyday school life as well as its relations with culture are insufficient and even wrongly used for grasping what is happening in these everyday lives with their subjects and the problems they face and the solutions they find for them.

The first of these concepts shows a tendency that, when related to an important discussion on the new curriculum paradigms, refers to the theoretical-epistemological referential of Gramsci and of the philosophers of the so-called Frankfurt School, particularly Habermas.[3] For that tendency, introducing the everyday dimension into curriculum studies was necessary to understand the school at its different levels and the relationships it had with the broader social reality. Methodologically, its researchers felt that, above all, the subjects' active participation was indispensable, through meetings organized for that purpose and in a process called *participant research.* Due to this, the studies made have a strong relationship also with the social movements organized around that methodology, especially those based on the thinking of Paulo Freire.

The start of the second of these movements was related to the research of the American thinker Robert Stake (1983a, 1983b). He mentions, on one hand, the need to cross sources by observing what happens daily in the school and, on the other, the impossibility of generalizing the conclusions in those studies, initiating with those two methodological proposals a way of "thinking" about the school's everyday life. His work will allow important research to be done in Brazil, creating theoretical-methodological possibilities for researching everyday life.[4] That research is considered necessary, with the study of that dimension, to incorporate the ideas of multiplicity and complexity in the processes of everyday school life.

After having read the works of Stenhouse (1991), who developed the idea of *teacher-researcher* in England, and that of his followers, such as Elliot (1990), we can understand that knowing of so many schools existing in the same educative system is possible only insofar as we must incorporate the multiple subjects of everyday school life in processes necessary for that knowledge. This had already been immediately indicated to us, in a sense, by the two above-mentioned tendencies. Stenhouse shows that teachers, as they go about questioning their various practices (as identified, known, and analyzed through research processes), are those who can intervene in the daily processes of schools, developing alternatives to official proposals. Stenhouse and his followers perceived that possibility/necessity when they understood the cultural differences in our society. Therefore, in Brazil it is with their studies that we begin to relate educative everyday lives with cultures.

The research tradition with which I am associated as well as the critical dialogue it establishes with the traditions mentioned earlier began to be identified and be better defined after the publication in Brazil of research conducted in Mexico, especially that by Justa Ezpeleta and Elsie Rockwell (1986). What we have come to understand is that hegemonic educational research restricts attention to those aspects of school life that match its analytic models, thereby failing to discern what goes on in schools outside those models. What we have come to understand is that it is important to study schools in their reality, for example, how they are, without judging the worth of what we discover, and, principally, to seek to understand what is done and created in schools as understood by those *practitioners* (Certeau 1994) who work and study in them and take their children to them.[5]

With the introduction of authors associated with Cultural Studies into Brazil and the creation of groups researching the issues faced by them, it was possible to broaden the research *on/into/with the everyday lives* by understanding the relationships that maintain among them the multiple everyday lives in which each one lives, especially considering the cultural artifacts with which the practitioners of those everyday lives weave their relationships.

The translation in 1994 of Certeau's book *A invenção do cotidiano* (*The Invention of Everyday Life*) was decisive in expanding our research and for the research groups united around his ideas.

As a result of these multiple influences and the research currently being done, we understand that we have established ourselves as a network of subjectivities in the everyday lives in which we live (Santos 1995). This insight is also articulated as a criticism of the model of modern science, which for it to be "constructed" needed to consider everyday knowledge as "common sense" surpassed by scientific knowledge. This meant, in the history of the sciences, understanding them as lesser and even mistaken, without comprehending the multiple meanings and uses they had for the practitioners of the everyday lives that were woven among them because they were necessary for humans to live.

In order to go beyond that modern opinion, a series of reflections is being developed that will enable us to advance our understanding of what the research *on/into/with everyday lives* can represent for broadening our understanding of those social processes that were neglected by scientific practice in modernity. Among these processes is the necessary understanding of the actual meaning of *process* (Foester 1998), because modern science was "constructed" applying the dichotomized vision of the relationship between subject and object, indicating that it is possible to study an object itself without understanding the multiple processes in which it is inserted, especially without considering the context formed by that relationship and how each term is deeply influenced by the other—the *dichotomy,*[6] a process necessary for scientific practice, in its history, does not help research on/into/with everyday lives, because it means *limits* on the possibilities that have to be developed.

We question those methods used by modern science that require considering everyday knowledge as being worthless for what was necessary to do and create at that moment. This leads to the understanding that *everything* (from methods to concepts, arriving at the truths produced) that was created by modern science represents *limits* on the understanding of contexts to be analyzed and understood with the cultures and knowledges created there. It has been calling for arduous work of theoretical-epistemological-methodological *weaving*[7] to understand the everyday lives in the multiplicity of relationships with the complex cultural processes, inside which the creation takes place of our everyday networks of knowledges and significations.

Note, therefore, that the research that we call "research on/into/with everyday lives" was created and has developed in the midst of disputes as much with other tendencies that analyzed the same *spacetime* as with tendencies that work with macro structures and visions.

Happenings and Everyday Life

Foucault tells us explicitly when assuming that "actual" history makes the "happening" come to life in what it has that is singular and acute, which is understood by *happening*, saying,

it is necessary to understand it not as a decision, a treaty, a reign or a battle, but as a relationship of forces that is inverted, a confiscated power, a vocabulary resumed and turned against its users, a domination that is weakened, distends, poisons itself, and another that enters, disguised. The forces at play in history do not obey either a destiny or a mechanics, but effectively the unforeseen outcome of the struggle. They are not manifested as successive forms of a primordial intention; nor do they assume the appearance of a result. They appear always in the singular uncertainty of the happening. (Foucault 1971, 146)

Changes in history are, therefore, woven into our day-to-day lives in ways not detectable even at the moment when they occur, but in incidents that we do not foresee, nor are we aware of at the moment when and where they occur, but they go on "happening" in so many knowledge networks and everyday life significations and go on *incarnating* in us habits, beliefs, values, and other such attributes. Research that is concerned with educative everyday lives and with different practices, knowledges, and significations present there originates from the idea that it is in multiple and complex processes that we learn and teach: "to read, to write and to count"; to speak, to dialogue, to argue, and to criticize; to put questions to the social world and to nature; to understand the ways in which human beings relate to each other; to poeticize life and to love the Other. In other words, at the same time that we reproduce what we learn from other generations and with determinant social lines of the hegemonic power, we are creating, every day, new forms of being, making, knowing, and signifying that they are integrating themselves, "in disguise," into our various contexts of life and into our bodies, before being appropriated and offered for consumption, and even that they end up changing society in varying processes of accumulation in all its relationships (Simmel 2006). It is in this way, then, that we learn to find solutions for the new problems created by earlier solutions. Nonetheless, one must be permanently alert, because attempts to "imprison" these processes are always violent and moralistic. However, all the time, there also appear ways of circumventing what they want "established" or "instituted" forever.

Movements Necessary for Research
on/into/with Everyday Life

The creation *processes* in research on/into/with everyday lives require an understanding of the *methods* that we devised to discern them in an attempt to go beyond the marks of science with which we had been trained. With these, we began to understand, in individual and collective processes, the ways in which knowledge and meanings are created in everyday lives, seeking to understand the different logics with which they are articulated. First, we feel that these processes include inseparably the *to do/to think* as much as the *practice/theory/practice,* in synchronous movements that blend, always, to act, to say, to create, to remember, to feel.

Consequently, in that research, it was necessary to create, incorporate, and develop the ideas of *knowledge networks* and the *weaving of knowledge networks,* knowing that we were being entirely "plunged" (Oliveira and Alves 2001) into the *space/times* that we researched—going beyond the lessons learned, struggling against what was *incarnate* in us: the blindness that had instilled in us the training received; the idea of separating subject from object; the idea that we worked with objects and not with processes; the movements that generalize, abstract, synthesize, and globalize—in short, to work with a permanent doubt and with uncertainty always present, learning to look into the eyes of others to discover our blind spots (Foester 1998).

My 2001 article "Deciphering the Parchment," which begins by explaining this process using a metaphor I learned with Certeau (1994) when explaining the process of researching everyday lives, says that in everyday lives, like stories that are permanently inscribed over others, it was necessary for us to dedicate ourselves to discovering what was happening beneath each layer, like in the parchments of the Middle Ages. That is what was demanded from each of the researchers on/into/with everyday lives.

In this article, prepared over a ten-year period, I discussed four movements that characterize the processes necessary for doing research on/into/with everyday lives.

The first refers to a necessary discussion with the dominant mode of "to see" what was called "the reality" by the moderns and referred to, as Latour (1994) warned, the world that today we would call "particular" of the workshop or of "abstract creations" such as Hobbes' *Leviathan.* The trajectory of research into everyday lives needs to go beyond what was learned with these particularities and abstracts of modernity, in which the *sense of vision* was extolled. It is necessary, for that reason, to plunge into this research with a complete sense of what we want to study. I called that movement, asking permission of the Brazilian poet Carlos Drummond de Andrade, "the sentiment of the world."

The second movement discussed in this article is what leads us to understand that the group of theories, categories, concepts, and notions we inherited from the sciences created and developed in modernity, a group that continues to be an indispensable resource for developing those sciences, is not only a support and a guide along the route to be followed, but also, and increasingly so, a *limit* on what needs to be woven for us to understand the logics of *weaving knowledges* in everyday lives. To name the process that leads us to understand as a limit what we are accustomed to seeing as support, appealing to historian Hill (1987), I used the idea of turning upside down.

In the third movement studied, I indicated the need for broadening what is understood as a source, discussing ways of dealing with the diversity, difference, and heterogeneity of everyday lives and of their practitioners, as much as exploring their multiple and different relationships. In the article, I gave that movement the name of "drinking from all fountains," discussing the importance for such research of incorporating varied sources, seen earlier as dispensable and even suspect: the voice that tells a story; the ordinary writings of the *practitioners* (Certeau 1994) of everyday lives; photographs taken in *space/times* without special meaning; archives of secretariats of ordinary schools in which papers are gathered that are not bureaucratic as they are usually considered (Alves 2003); and more.

Lastly, in this article, I assumed as the fourth movement that which needs to happen for conveying new preoccupations, new problems, new facts, and new findings that *happenings* bring us. A new manner of writing is indispensable for us to reach all those with whom we need to speak, especially the actual *practitioners* of the everyday lives, to tell them what we are going to understand when studying with them their actions and their knowledges, in a movement that Santos called "second epistemological rupture." I called this movement, with some doubts, "to narrate life and to literaturize science."

A fifth movement was added, some years later, based on many dialogues established with the researchers of that strand/tradition and with others, about the mentioned text and about a critique I made of it by asking, "Why didn't I see this before?"

I noticed, gradually, that while concerning myself with the movements I needed to do as a researcher—to understand all the *happenings* that my many senses enabled me to feel—I forgot what William Blake poeticizes: "how can one know if each bird that crosses the paths of the air is not an immense world of pleasure, forbidden by our five senses?" (Manguel 2001, 22).

However, secondly and especially, in all the *happenings* narrated, I did not question the defining existence of the *practitioners* of those everyday lives. It was not just that I, as a researcher, plunged into them to satisfy the need to work and to feel. It was also, and especially, to work with the feelings of all the practitioners with whom I worked and researched.

In the first article published, why then did I not try to work on a fifth movement that I could—perhaps, in a tribute to Nietzsche and Foucault, who were so preoccupied with it—call *Ecce homo* or perhaps *Ecce femina*, more appropriate for our educative everyday lives in which women are the principal educators? Perhaps because I am not so wise as the authors mentioned or perhaps because I am a woman in a society in which it is the man who has ideas, or else, because I am leaving my footprints on little-known terrain, roaming through *space/times* not yet revealed or difficult to reveal, I did not manage to formulate that which was virtually written in the text: what, in fact, is interesting in the research on/into/with everyday lives is the people, the *practitioners*, as Certeau (1994) calls them because he sees them in actions all the time. The question is why, when talking about it the whole time, did I not notice it; and why can I do that now.

The concept of the *happening* is not restricted to what happens but denotes as well that which is but is not yet. In that sense, therefore, when we document what transpires in schools we acknowledge that which is not yet, as well as that which cannot be entirely explained, including that which we cannot fully understand. In so doing, we are testifying to those realities that may be "disguised" or exist "virtually" but will be read later. If, for instance, as Deleuze and Guattari (1995) teach us, what exists is to be transformed into reality without any creation, then the virtual has to update what presupposes that creation. That is why Sousa Dias (1995) indicates that "the virtual happening has the structure of a problem to be solved and is persistent, in its problematical conditions" (92).

As a problem in action the *ecce femina* would appear only if the creation were to update the virtual, if the criticism made in the blending of all the dialogues established after the publication, in the chaos with which they are always presented, were to create, through repetition, differentiation such as music that becomes special for us only after being heard many times.

It was possible to create the *ecce femina* only because it was infinitely repeated— in a chaotic way, in the networks woven, in the different ways of speaking, and in so many possible senses—finally differentiating itself from what was written earlier, what is already in the past.

Accordingly, if the 2001 article I signed was assumed, when issued, to be a collective work sent to the various research groups I coordinated (Alves 2001,13), the second article appeared only because, in the same way, dialogues had been established in many research networks. That is because

> with the events of a life, things, peoples, books, ideas and experiences…consubstantiated in us, imperceptibly even with our uninterrupted movements and…outline our true individuality. And with all that not as subjective experiences, perceptions, affections and opinions of an I, but as pre-individual singularities, supra-personal infinitives and, as such, shareable, 'communicable', transmissible life currents. We write, paint and compose always with the multiplicity there is in us, that each one of us is—the creator subject is always collective, the author's name always the signature of an anonymous society. (Sousa Dias 1995, 104–105)

That is how things happen in the everyday lives experienced, as well as in the research *on/into/with everyday lives*.

With this work/example I hope to have in some way helped people to better understand our research, and that includes what we could call our mistakes. We are consoled by the thought that we sometimes succeed in doing things right.

NOTES

1. I work with the idea that narratives and images are *conceptual personages* as Deleuze (1991) understands. He says that "conceptual personages are the 'heteronyms' of the philosopher, and the name of the philosopher, the simple pseudonym of his personages" (62). Sousa Dias (1995), on that idea, says that "conceptual personages…designate…intimate elements of the philosophical activity, conditions of that activity, the 'intercessors' of the thinker, the ideal figures of intercession without which there is no thinking, philosophy or creation of concepts" (61–62).
2. To add together the terms, pluralize them, sometimes invert them, at other times duplicate them, was the way in which we have managed, up to now, to show how the dichotomies necessary in the invention of modern science have shown themselves to be limiting regarding what we need to create for researching *on/into/with everyday lives*. That way of writing was found necessary, therefore, to overcome the dichotomization inherited from that period. In that text other terms thus joined will appear.
3. That tendency was developed in the curriculum area, especially by Ana Maria Saul of PUC/São Paulo and José Luiz Domingues of the Federal University of

Goiás, who had at that moment a decisive influence on research into everyday life as well as in other areas.

4. The representatives of that tendency in Brazil are Menga Lüdke and Marli André, who formed a school of researchers of everyday life and are a necessary reference for those studies.

5. Reading Lefebvre's (1992) book about everyday life opened the door for better articulation of this discussion.

6. Many were the dichotomies necessary for scientific practice: the first of them between the "divine knowledges" and the "human knowledges" (Darnton 1986); but an infinity of others was sought in Augustinian formal logic: theory/practice; concrete/abstract; internal/external, among others.

7. This term has its origin in music, with its necessary "repetitions" and its possible "variations," so close to our everyday ways of living.

REFERENCES

Alves, Nilda. 2000. "Os Romances das Aulas." *Movimento: Revista da Faculdade de Educação da UFF, Rio de Janeiro*, n° 2, September: 7–32.

Alves, Nilda. 2001. "Decifrando o Pergaminho—O Cotidiano das Escolas nas Lógicas das Redes Cotidianas." In *Pesquisa no/do Cotidiano das Escolas*, ed. Inês Barbosa de Oliveira and Nilda Alves (pp. 13–38), Rio de Janeiro: DP&A.

Alves, Nilda. 2003. "Diário de Classe, Espaço de Diversidade." In *Prática da Memória Docente*, ed. Ana Chrystina Mignot and Maria Teresa Santos Cunha. São Paulo: Cortez.

Certeau, Michel de. 1994. *A Invenção do Cotidiano*: Artes de Fazer. Petrópolis: Vozes.

Comenius, João Amós. 1984. *Didactica Magna: Tratado da Arte Universal de Ensinar Tudo a Todos*. Lisbon: Fundação Calouste Gulbenkian.

Coutinho, Eduardo. 1991. A astúcia. In *Rede imaginária: televisão e democracia*, ed. Adauto Novaes. São Paulo: SMC/SP & Companhia das Letras.

Coutinho, Eduardo. 1997. "O Cinema Documentário e a Escuta Sensível da Auteridade." In *Projeto História—Etica e História Oral v. 15*, ed. Maria Antonieta Antonacci and Daisy Perelmutter (pp. 279–285). São Paulo: PUC/SP.

Darnton, Robert. 1986. "Os Filósofos Podam a Árvore do Conhecimento: a Estratégia Epistemológica da 'Encyclopédie.'" In *O Grande Massacre dos Gatos*, ed. Robert Darnton (page number missing). Rio de Janeiro: Graal.

Deleuze, Gilles, and Félix Guattari. 1991. *Qu'est-ce Que la Philosophie?* Paris: Ed. Minuit.

Deleuze, Gilles, and Félix Guattari. 1995. *Mil Platôs, vol 1*. Rio de Janeiro: Editora 34.

Elliot, John. 1990. *Investigación-acción en Educación*. Madrid: Morata.

Ezpeleta, Justa, and Elsie Rockwell. 1986. *Pesquisa Participante*. São Paulo: Cortez.

Foester, Heinz von. 1998. "Visión y Conocimiento: Disfunciones de Segundo Orden." In *Nuevos Paradigmas, Cultura y Subjetividad,* ed. Dora Fried Schinitman (pp. 91–113). 2nd ed. Buenos Aires: Paidós.

Foucault, Michel. 1971. "Nietzsche, la Généalogie, L'histoire." In *Hommage à Jean Hyppolite,* ed. Michel Foucault (pp. 145–172). Paris: PUF.

Foucault, Michel. 1999. *As Palavras e as Coisas*. São Paulo: Martins Fontes.

Ginzburg, Carlo. 1989. *Mitos, Emblemas e Sinais: Morfologia e História*. São Paulo: Companhia das Letras.

Hill, Christopher. 1987. *O Mundo de Ponta Cabeça*. São Paulo: Cia das Letras.

Julien, Marie-Pierre, and Jean-Pierre Warnier, eds. 1999. *Approches da la Culture Matérielle: Corps à Corps Avec L'objet*. Paris: L'Harmattan.

Latour, Bruno. 1994. *Jamais Fomos Modernos*. Rio de Janeiro: Editora 34.

Leite, Míriam Lifchitz Moreira. 2001. "Texto Visual e Texto Verbal." In *Desafios da Imagem: Fotografia, Iconografia e Vídeo nas Ciências Sociais,* ed. Bela Feldman-Bianco, Míriam L. Moreira Leite (pp. 37–49). 2nd ed. Campinas: Papirus.

Lefebvre, Henri. 1992. *A Vida Cotidiana no Mundo Moderno*. São Paulo: Ática.

Manguel, Alberto. 2001. *Lendo Imagens*. São Paulo: Companhia das Letras.

Oliveira, Inês Barbosa de, and Alves, Nilda. 2001. *Pesquisa no/do Cotidiano das Escolas—Sobre Redes de Saberes*. Rio de Janeiro: D, P&A.

Santos, Boaventura de Sousa. 1995. *Pela Mão de Alice: o Social e o Político na Pósmodernidade*. São Paulo: Cortez.

Simmel, Georg. 2006. "Cultura feminina." In *Filosofia do Amor*. São Paulo: Martins Fontes, (original de 1902).

Sousa Dias. 1995. *Lógica do Acontecimento—Deleuze e a Filosofia*. Porto: Afrontamento.

Stake, Robert. 1983a. "Estudo de Caso em Pesquisa Educacional." *Educação e Seleção,* São Paulo, Fundação Carlos Chagas, 4 (7): 5–14.

Stake, Robert. 1983b. "Pesquisa Qualitativa/Naturalista: Problemas Epistemológicos." *Educação e Seleção,* São Paulo, Fundação Carlos Chagas 4 (7): 19–27

Stenhouse, Lawrence. 1991. *Investigación y Desarrollo del Curriculum*. 3rd ed. Madrid: Morata.

Chapter 3

Curriculum Disfiguration

Antonio Carlos Amorim

The 1980s allowed the theoretical overcoming of curricular thought associated with technicism and, very soon, in Brazil, we went through discussions on sociology, the critical, postcritical, and post-structuralist theories (for further details see Lopes and Macedo 2002). At the center of many discussions and multiple debates, a great interest in school was recovered, as were perspectives of understanding the school curriculum in its interactions with knowledge, identities, values, moralities, and politics. A new force of argumentation is established by the selection of the discourse categories as relevant to think about the future of school. While this restructuring was internal to the curriculum field (as we can learn from many papers by Antonio Flávio Barbosa Moreira), it is also influenced by the prominence of curriculum during the 1990s in public debates in Brazil—specifically the formulation of National Curricular Directives to Elementary School and Tertiary Education, and to the National Curricular Parameters—it was also influenced by developments external to the academic field.

A set of traditions is created,[1] with new concepts and practices that, despite having a postmodernist view, in my judgment have the same basis and the same referents of modernity, since they insist on thinking with (1) the figure of the subject—and his/her conscience, autonomy, and power of transformation; (2) the relations of power structured on a plane interpreted by categories of culture (class, gender, ethnics) and ideology as well as those of hegemony; (3) the continuous unyielding effort for the elaboration of "just ideas" (through processes of interpretation, analysis, and judgment) connected to representational practices as a way of understanding the world; and (4) the effort toward establishing critical transcendental thought.

My recent research projects are efforts to escape from this set and in the consequent disenchanted encounter with the emptiness that follows the disappearance of the foundational structures. My investigations become dissonant with what can be identified precisely as the curricular field, because they aim at a disfiguration, and they propose to think the curriculum into "disfiguration." And while or when imagining disfiguration, the dialogue and interconnection with cinema image studies are potentially interesting, especially from postmodern perspectives.

Postmodern perspectives are not out of sync with institutional circumstances or with broader policies in Brazil, once they are shown as one set of "alternatives" among others, as long as they are characterized as strategies for survival in a, yes, postmodern world. The question to the curriculum field that I propose invokes approaches and discussions of new forms of living creatively in a world characterized by virtuality, temporality, nomadicity, and, in many cases, barbarism. This kind of questioning asks what kind of attitude or disposition scholars will take toward these "new forms of living." So although I am only suggesting new ways of looking and comprehending these subjects, in doing so I engender a kind of subject forgetfulness.

Certain contemporary artistic works, particularly the audiovisual productions I have examined in my research, express (in an exemplary manner) the circumstances of a certain *currentness*. Studying the aesthetics of these artistic productions, understanding their implications for a people and for representations of the world as structured by the look and its narrativization, is one of the major points of my research on curriculum. I wager on discussing politics and art in different ways from the ones that currently characterize the curricular field in Brazil, the limitations of which I have indentified earlier.

Analyses of national cinema, as well as of Brazilian photography, raise recurring questions concerning the Brazilian national identity. This is an identity that for many is globalized, unrooted, and deformed; it is marked by violence, disillusion, and presentism. It is futureless. Cinema, photography and literature are syntonic, often critically aligned, in varied intensities, with global developments. This is different from the theorizations of education and/or of our possibilities of "understanding reality." Rather than representing reality, educational theorization creates realities apart from the real. Our notions of fiction, truth, and imagination are conceptual forces for *another world* that I shall attempt to weave into my research.

When I started my incursion into Gilles Deleuze's concepts, using the idea of *rhizome* and associating it to the production of school knowledge, I was awakened by a taste, which to some extent became an addiction, for a type of writing that is at times nonsensical, abusive, and even invasive. If in my doctoral thesis I was able to circumscribe the *rhizome* in its potency of unstructuring biology teaching and the school curriculum as practice in action, in the years following that work I moved toward the present encounter with the very concept of "event."

Initially I want to clarify that, although my main dialogue is with Gilles Deleuze, to whom philosophy's main activity is the creation of concepts, I do not start my thinking *from concepts,* not even *curriculum concepts.* I seek some form of displacement from them, in order to underscore the questions of *what* the curriculum *wants* or what curricular statements create verbal actions, what scholars are wagering when they write what they assume is a *concept a priori.* Such displacement casts the curriculum onto planes of thought wherein styles/lines of writing, possibilities and inter-crossings of French philosophical concepts, and, especially, the movement of tracing connections between the work of Gilles Deleuze (and also of Michel Foucault)—affirming them as post-structuralist—and the field of curriculum in Brazil are all associated with important contributions made by Sandra Corazza, Tomaz Tadeu and Alfredo Veiga-Neto.

In my research, the relationship between curriculum and knowledge is not central, nor does the idea of transmission make any sense. Such argumentation is in accordance with post-structuralist critiques, opting instead for the centrality of language in the significance of cultural practices. The interactions between curriculum and identities, moralities and ethics become intense; however, in tracing connections between Deleuze and culture, especially in cultural studies—as identities, difference, and discourse—I move from an emphasis on the "context" to a discussion of politics organized around relations of power.

The research I have developed during the last three years articulates the potencies of concepts proposed by Deleuze in imagining writings that *differ* and, indeed, *differentiate* being a teacher in the intervals, the in-between spaces, for example, of students' initial university studies (Amorim 2007, 2008). The concepts of "event" and "composition" have been supported by my studies of literature. Currently, I associate writing with images and sounds, aiming at the composition of planes enabling the articulation of "event" with concepts of perception and communication, following Deleuze's studies of art and literature (Amorim 2006, 2008, 2009).

It seems to me that these research pursuits are not so associated with macrosocial events. In my latest project I try to learn (from interviews) about the interest shown by Brazilian researchers (from various disciplinary fields) in Deleuze's concepts, looking to see whether there are any connections among their concepts, interests, and their engagement in politics, culture, and everyday life. Perhaps, by such indirect means I may find experiences—for example, social and political events—that will be aligned with my attitude toward life, my hope and belief in the world.

In the other papers (Amorim 2006, 2007, 2008, 2009) I composed a plane of thought for *curriculum as a sensation* working with the images from Brazilian movies (Banco do Brasil's TV series *Values of Brazil*, the movies *Dois perdidos numa noite suja* and *Ônibus 174*: see Amorim 2009) and with undergraduate students' productions in "School and Culture" teacher education courses at the Education Faculty of the University of Campinas (Amorim 2007, 2008).

Cinema Images and the Figure

I work, first, with Gilles Deleuze's strategy of deterritorialization and how it can be used in an analysis that challenges the context of the narratives and the essential roles of subjects. At a second theoretical step, Deleuze's studies of Francis Bacon become references for visualizing the recent Brazilian cinema as revealing aspects of *disfiguration*. I focus on concepts such as "space," "nation," and "people" in discussions regarding cultures and identities among scholars working in the field of curriculum in Brazil. I consider these concepts as *forms* of immanence that cannot be expelled onto a plane of thinking. Perforating these is desire. Having them as company with which to think and compose other creations is fundamental.

I contest the centrality of culture in curriculum studies in Brazil and seek to replace ideas of identities, difference, body, and representation with two key concepts: *planes of sensation* and *composition*. Composing a *plane*, a geography of sensations, is the challenge of thinking without representation. Facing the power of words, images, and objects becomes for me a political commitment. I articulate images of cinema and literature and thereby registers of the school curriculum.

Although criticizing representation, I am choosing images from cinema (they could also be from photography and painting). I shall continue to wager on the centrality of the look. To do so, I will engage in the discussion of representation through Deleuze's theorization of language. In doing so I affirm the possibility of difference without identity. I also detach myself from the concepts of "conscience" and "subjectivation." In the Brazilian movies I analyzed, there was "figuration" but not "representation," as the films' montage disclosed gaps in which difference exists (Amorim

2009). These disfigurations vitiate the form-function distinction, rendering meaningless concepts of transformation, change, and formation. We are confronted with lines of force to which violence is fundamental. Learning, I assert, is a violent act of thought. The sign is the violence in/of language.

In the following pages I will trace explicit withdrawals from expressions that imply any determinism, for example, the substitution of the expressed for the silence that screams. That is, I want to think without the structuring relations of power and to find ways—with images and words—of escaping from representation and thereby free the *subject* from the *man*. This vexed relationship between representation and event, understood after Deleuze, has been important to me in seeking alternatives to representational thinking, despite it being a very intense and strong structuring force in the field of curriculum studies, especially when connected to concepts such as critique and politics.

The common thread we can use to associate Deleuze and education is crossed by the concept of event. With it we can compose the plane of language-event-difference-world. So, to wager on the doubled presence of the event (*time* + *image* = *world*), specifically, to "potentialize" its political import, has been made possible for me by Deleuze's theories of sign and sense, as well as by theorizations of literature, the plastic arts, and cinema.

The possible—that which intensifies desire—is created by the event. The future does not follow formatting. The images, the sounds, the words of literature "effectuate" the event, sometimes producing a version of vertigo, sometimes that of somnambulism, as if in a dream: a plane of composition. Such composition demands the deconstruction of the conceptual substance of "education." I present this deconstruction as art, on a plane of composition, wherein the objects "themselves" are not so important, but their shapes, colors, and sensations are. I work with images from Brazilian cinema, juxtaposing them with concepts and images Deleuze produced on/for Francis Bacon (Amorim 2009).

I work with the relationships between sensation and disfigurations, occasionally entering spaces of affiguration: for example, figureless figuration, subjects without representation. I did so via the intensity, the energy, that emits from the work of art. *Affiguration* centralizes not the subject, but rather the body; in so doing, it emphasizes the concept of becoming as affect, as sensation, incarnate in bodies. On this plane, concepts of identity no longer agglutinate structures of becoming in networks of power. Escaping from this plane of identity politics constitutes an event of curriculum *disfiguration*, composing lines of flight toward encounter with sensation. The concept of disfiguration keeps the figuration of the subject as the substrate on which forces operate.

Figure 3.1 Collection of Disfigured Images
Source: Amorim (2006, 1367).

According to Deleuze and Guattari, in *What Is Philosophy?* (*O que é a filosofia?*), we paint, write, sculpt, and compose with sensations.

Sensations, as percepts, are not perceptions which would relate to an object (reference). If they resemble something, it is a resemblance produced by their own means, and the smile on the screen is only made of colors, traces, shadows and light. If resemblance can impregnate the work of art, it is because sensation only relates to its material: it is the percept or the affect of the material itself, the smile of the oil, the gesture of the baked clay, the élan of the metal, the squatting of the Roman stone and the relief of the gothic stone. And the material is so diverse in any case, that it is difficult to say where the sensation begins or ends. How sensation could be preserved without a durable material and, short as the time may be, this time is considered as duration. What is preserved, as a right, is not the material, which constitutes solely the factual condition; but as this condition is preserved (while the screen, the color or the stone have not turned into dust), what is preserved in itself is the percept or the affect. Even if the material only lasted for seconds, it would give sensation the power of existing and of being preserved in itself, *in the eternity which coexists with this duration*. (216)

Cinema, photography, and memory perpetuate ephemeral duration. The smoothing of territories rhythmizing Deleuze's concepts of art and cinema by means of sensation and duration are potent in my thought flow.

It is not the transformation of an image that the fragment potentializes; it is its deformation, the creation of a zone in several forms, that is not identified: what is common to them is their indiscernability. Their sharpness is marked by the lines of force that grant the deforming incision. The sensation of colors and shadows requires the emptiness of clichés, of the "just" ideas, and of the words of "order" inscribed over the whole painting-world-reality. The white and dark shadows are the elements of space in the image, the fabric of which dreams are made. They are images-films of the ephemeral, diagrammatic machines.

> In the act of painting, as well as in the act of writing, there will be that which must be presented—although very inadequately—as a series of subtractions, of erasures. The need for cleaning the screen. Would this be then the role, at least the negative role of the diagram: the need for cleaning the screen so as to prevent the clichés to take it? (Deleuze 2007a, 54)

The release of images in the chaos of "national identity" has in its disfiguration the possibility of an "outside" eye, of a diagram that is the potency of the hand, the overthrow of the visual coordination. The diagram—*disfiguration*—is a revolt of the hand, according to Deleuze, a violence against the eye.

In this form of light, colors, and lines, the diagram—with its tracing and shades of gray as varied as possible and tending to disappear—also invokes the totalitarian sense of wishing to fill the whole screen, the whole space, and claims the absence of cliché. This diagram looks like and takes the paths (chaos-germ-trace-figure) of the hand, of the curriculum, of education. Ah, melancholy and nostalgia! A symbolic order of transcendence. How to think of it in another way? The diagram either turns into a code and has a position on the screen that could be considered minimalist, or it occupies the whole screen, avoiding chaos and disallowing the minor lines to germinate and what the hand manages to do "blindly." It is in the study of Francis Bacon's *oeuvre* that Gilles Deleuze finds a possibility of the diagram becoming something other than the maximum and the minimum of intensity. It is its presence that allows something to come out of it. "And that which comes out of the diagram is not a resemblance or a figuration. It is not something figurative, but what can claim a figure? A non-figurative figure, that is, which does not resemble something. A figure comes out of the diagram" (Deleuze 2007b, 108). This idea of the effect of the diagram as something that breaks up what a code wishes to mean, or gives meaning to, splits into intense lines of thought for pragmatics (and its set of signs) that retain the value of the icons' relationships but is not founded on a concept of similarity. Deleuze suggests a path that converses with algebra and linguistics but escapes these two fields, intersecting instead with art. He chooses painting since he finds in it a problematic field to continue choices among code-meaning-significance-sense. What can be achieved, perhaps, is to think through a diagrammatic exercise toward difference made visible. Difference, a qualitative impression produced through the contraction of sensible impressions that are repeated in experience, is the production of the new from an encounter with a natural sign that provokes in imagination forces unknown before, forces that surpass imagination and experience.

Becoming-Post

In the movies I presented and discussed, the existence of Brazilian identity could be thought through in terms of Deleuze and Guattari's concept of becoming. The curriculum *disfiguration* bears this potency; affiguration includes events released by/in this potency of curriculum creation. I will extend the plane of sensation so that *curriculum* associates the idea of becoming with affects as a politics of the figure (in its actualization of the body) in the modernity-postmodernity transition.

> The reality of becoming has little to do with a relation to real women, but everything to do with a relation with the incorporeal body of a woman as it figures in the social imaginary.... Deleuze and Guattari argue that there is a sense in which becoming-woman is primary in relation to the other kinds of social and political becoming-minoritarian. (Patton 2000, 81)

Deleuze's *oeuvre* on image and literature allows encounters with the concept of difference as *pure* intensity. With this concept we withdraw from a plane of representation to the plane of sensation. Focused on Brazilian movies, I have been producing relationships between the surfaces of events and the differences of images, indicating their potency as *becomings* that would release difference but not subordinate it to its metaphysical essence. The emphasis remains on subjectivities without subjects, questioning cultural and political categories such as territory, nation, and memory, very important to modernity's constitution of thought.

Exploring the relationships between the images from the movie *Nome Próprio* [*Proper Name*], (http://www.murilosalles.com/film/fotos.htm) directed by Murilo Salles (2007), and Deleuze and Guattari's concept of *becoming*, I can see, as Paul Patton (2000) comments, that *becoming* is metamorphosis, particularly when it is defined as a "becoming-minoritarian" (which affects only elements of the majority). The assemblages that institute and sustain such becomings are also of the war-machine type.

The movie is an adaptation based on the books *Máquina de Pinball* and *Vida de Gato* by Clara Averbuck and her texts published on the site and on her personal blog.

"Camila JAM" tries to represent the subject of abandonment in its complexity. It seeks a character without history. Therefore what happens doesn't really matter. Capturing Camila in her movement is what really matters. Living her time, taking responsibility for her choices, suffering her distress, her contradictions, giving herself. It's a movie about what there is. A direct movie.

The movie tells the story of a character who builds a worthy individuality on the daily struggles of her being, a narrative that will make her life worthy. Worthy, not as a heroic journey, but worthy in its ethical, aesthetic and existential decisions. Worthy enough to be written about.

To create bonds, Camila must announce a time when subjectivity no longer exists—it doesn't matter who she is—the family no longer exists, nothing that guarantees the existence of a human being beyond the bonds he or she creates to survive. With Camila, we want to look at a brave and complex female, capable of throwing herself from a cliff and developing from this journey the support she needs to exist. We want to subtract any epic meaning from existence, therefore we remove any of its traces from the film narrative. Creating a time in which the moral content doesn't matter. Moral is impregnated in the being [not in the narrative]. Moral blossoms from the scars originated in her process of giving herself absolutely and vertiginously.

"Camila JAM" is also the story of self-confinement. Camila cloisters herself to become a writer. Writing compulsively a personal BLOG of her experiences. But what kind of world is on the other side of the line?

Figure 3.2 Camila
Source: Murilo Salles (http://www.murilosalles.com/film/fotos.htm)

She confines herself to be connected, this is the paradox. Taking everything to the limit: a maximum exposition in an environment of absolute confinement, lonely people in front of their computers "plugged in" with a world of people who don't know each other, who promote "blind date," who gather by "identities," by the search for an identity. Camila is radical and consciously alone. She has no past and doesn't want to know her future. The only thing that matters is her path. The act of writing her identity. Completely alone.

"Camila JAM" is a movie about Camila's quest for redemption. Obsessive. Building herself and destroying herself. Lonely. Her unconditional quest for affection, for fondness. This existential experience incarnates her body.

In the end, we realize that "Camila JAM" is a movie that seeks its own Proper Name. A movie about a movement. A body-movie. (http://www.murilosalles.com/film/n_proprio_english.htm)

A *metamorphosis machine* would then be one that does not simply support the repetition of the same but rather engenders the production of something altogether different. In the discussions of cinema, we can imagine this *metamorphosis machine* operating in a range of directions, which indicates a kind of suppression of the subjects or their sensation. Particularly in this movie, the presence of images and writings at the same time on the screen implies the metamorphosis machine.

Figure 3.3   Camila's Blog and Body's Word
Source: Murilo Salles (http://www.murilosalles.com/film/fotos.htm)

Nowadays, perhaps in what is called postmodernity, we find images whose force is disturbed, existing between melancholy and cyclic narrative. *The real simply survives*, it is only watched, but there is no re-elaboration of reality—it continues in its raw condition—since it is not a matter of reconstituting the world, but rather of watching it. In the movie *Nome Próprio*, the sensation that the world is lost is very strong, and it is not representable! One can affirm the *subject* in this condition as a *being* that "effectuates" itself in its resurrection with the *real*, as a glorious, reconciling body in-between the world and reality. The look as a social practice or phenomenological affirmation of interpretation of the real is forgotten; another education through the images process "capillarizes" the transformation of what seeks the *survival* of a world without representation.

Why control or predict if later the world will not let itself be retained? The main character's body diagrams and disfigures itself. Losing sight of the real is indispensable in a melancholic dissolution of the world, in which reality is incomprehensible. There is loss of contact, loss of meaning, whose effects are felt through a montage juxtaposing images that multiply the actions and disperse them. "The possible encounters are in the intervals *between* images, in the *void* and in *silence*" (Amorim 2009, 186). Like the experimental cinema and the force-images it creates, this is an example of the frustrated encounter: *I feel, but I don't see.* The image will not return; the eyes of the spectator will remain closed. However, the images of the movie *Nome Próprio* persist in generating sensation, the desire to continue playing, even with nonsense, with abstraction at its maximum. There are images that struggle politically for the development and the preservation of the subject, of the human, in a "post-human" or "in-human" world. Becoming-human in *post*-human time is becoming-*post*, a result of the return to human in the images of *Nome Próprio*.

From the perspective of power, becomings may be regarded as process enhancement of the power of one's body, carried out in relation to the power of another but without involving appropriation of those powers. According to Patton (2000), one way in which bodies can increase their power is by entering into alliances with other bodies that enhance their own powers. The symbiotic relationship among images, words, and blog style is shown on the screen. We see a complex body, not social but individual, alone, in a kind of virtual alliance with other bodies or states of being—another diagram. In *Nome Próprio,* are these *becomings* also (after Deleuze and Guattari) *minoritarian becomings*?

"Only minorities can function as agents of media of becoming, but they can do so only on the condition that they cease to be a definable aggregate in relation to the majority" (Patton 2000, 81). The body is defined in terms of the affects associated either with the nurture and protection of others or with a dependent social status (such as the capacity for dissimulation or for cultivating the affection of others, and delight in appearances and role-play).

Figure 3.4   Becoming the Writing

Source: Murilo Salles (http://www.murilosalles.com/film/fotos.htm)

Curriculum?

Now I will propose questions for rethinking curriculum studies. I will do so in a plan for the composition of *curriculum*. My research is located in the post-Marxist moment in Brazilian curriculum studies. What I have been researching, therefore, confronts post-critical categories such as culture, time, and identity that have sometimes reified transformation and proposition. In other words, despite the new concepts, we still remain within the same relations between theories and practices, entombed between social reproduction and social transformation.

Such concepts grew more complex once the centrality of "culture" resignified concepts such as politics, subject, and reality. In addition to pluralizing the internal unities of these concepts—a fundamental and epistemologically remarkable step (policies, subjects and realities, in the plural, are the way we think now)—this centrality of "culture" triggered the deterritorialization of the sociology of curriculum, engendering the post-Marxist moment characterized by the exhaustion of macroanalyses, reterritorializing curricularists as practitioners of field research, almost equating them to culturalists. I am suggesting that "curriculum" has devolved into "culture," growing so vague as to be meaningless.

Currently in Brazil there is a deterritorialization of the curricular field into everyday life studies, underlining the hybridity of curricular policies and practices. Everyday life research is aligned with cultural studies, emphasizing language and the philosophy of differences as marked by discourses of postmodernity. Culture enables the curricular field to keep its pragmatic commitment as a force for change and criticism. Cultural policy, multiculturalism, and the very primacy of images and culture typified in cultural studies establish "culture" as hegemonic in curriculum studies in Brazil. Concepts such as *hybridity*, the space of the *in-between*, *trace,* and *borders* denote this state of affairs. With minimal attention to their theoretical origins (often in Foucault), they have been appropriated as the vocabulary of curriculum studies in Brazil. In methodological terms, they function to forefront historicism. The relationship between culture and language is disregarded in favor of discourses as a metanarrative of the cultural curriculum. Besides the persistence of centrality in identity and the illusion of the substance of subject, this means that "discourse" becomes a new albeit disguised form of structuralism. Time is chronological, marked by facts and events, which are evident in studies in Brazilian curriculum history as well .

The curriculum research that I am currently conducting derives from Deleuze's conception of time, emphasizing relations between time, being, and event; between time, image, and duration (especially as discussed in cinema studies); between time, sign, and sense of literary studies. I am composing the curriculum as a field of sensation, associating time with event. I am wagering on an education that frees itself from the humanist substance currently saturating it. This is a search for survival in a post-human state: somnambulistic, unconscious, actionless, uninhabited. Such a search means moving to a plane of composition of images for *curriculum*. It means thinking of education as a sign in the middle of a field of forces, among vectors of art (especially through the images of cinema and literature).

To think *what if* is to constitute a thought without a subject, a thought of time and spatial effectuation:

(a) Language is not representation but an escape from the dynamics of Who, What, With Whom, and When.

(b) It affirms the intensity of encounters and sensation.

(c) It is no longer subordinate to experience or subjectivation, once the lines of connection of singularity to the universal are conceptualized but never achieved, thus remaining a fantasy of transcendence, of idealization.

The point is to compose "realities" (letters, words, literature) that are so fascinating that they overcome representation as the field of possibilities in a future, a "how it could be." What is possible is created by the event, not by its formatting. Images, sound, and words are effectuated by the event and can be thought of as vertigo, in somnambulism, in dream—a plane of composition.

Such a thought position requires the destruction of the *substance* of education. The relationship between education and art becomes extended as the potentiality of agency in the body, in the object, in time, in sensations that did not occur before: *what matters is the duration of the work of art and of education.* Duration exists between things. To think (with Deleuze and Bergson) between things is an immanent force of movement-duration, a source from which created potencies emerge, and the potentiality of thoughts become associative and stratigraphic movements, not structured by habit. With attentive perceptions of what emerges, rather than automatized perceptions, a disjunctive synthesis appears, sensible and intelligible. In such an in-between, in the interval, we can settle down, at least for the duration.

In-between images can help us to live in the duration through gaps in time, in-between (non-artistic) images that have the power of affection. Power comes from these in-between images capable of accumulating time and producing indeterminacy, delays, and gaps. According to Maurizio Lazzarato, it is this capacity that gives a kind of power to our in-between images, a power of creation, a power of thought. And dealing with the concept of duration, we can talk about power. Movement opens gaps into the creation of sensation, to invention, to fabulations, to intensities—planes of composition and sensation.

NOTE

1. Available online at http://www.fe.unicamp.br. As potencialidades da centralidade da(s) cultura(s) para as investigações no campo do currículo / Antonio Carlos Rodrigues de Amorim, Eurize Pessanha (organizadores)—Campinas, SP: FE/UNICAMP, GT Currículo da ANPEd 2007.

REFERENCES

Amorim, Antonio Carlos Rodrigues de. 2006. "Invisible and not Discursive: Brazilian Cinema and the Amnesia of Identities." *Educação e Sociedade* 27 (97): 1367–1372.

Amorim, Antonio Carlos Rodrigues de. 2007. "Photography, Sound and Cinemas Affects and Percepts in the School Knowledge at School." *Teias* 8: 1–12.

Antonio Carlos Rodrigues de. 2008. "Curriculum, Lost Time." *Anais [Recurso Eletrônico]: currículo, teorias, métodos/ IV Colóquio Luso-Brasileiro sobre Questões Curriculares e VIII Colóquio sobre Questões Curriculares,* ed. Eneida Shiroma, Patrícia Laura Torriglia (pp. 1–20). Florianópolis: UFSC: FAPESC.

Antonio Carlos Rodrigues de. 2009. "Non-Figurative Narratives or Life Without Subjects." In *Exploring Selfhood: Finding Ourselves, Finding our Stories in Life Narratives,* ed. Gill Scherto (pp. 167–190). Brighton: University of Brighton and Guerand Hermès Foundation.

Deleuze, Gilles. 2007a. *Pintura, el concepto del diagrama.* Buenos Aires: Cactus.

Deleuze, Gilles. 2007b. *Francis Bacon, Lógica da Sensação* (Trad. Roberto Machado e colaboradores). Rio de Janeiro: Jorge Zahar.

Deleuze, Gilles, and Félix Guattari. 2004. *A Thousand Plateaus: Capitalism and Schizophrenia.* (translation and foreword by Brian Massumi). London: Continuum.

Deleuze, Gilles, and Félix Guattari. 1992. *O que é a filosofia?* (tradução de Bento Prado Jr. e Alberto Alonso Muno). São Paulo: Ed. 34.

Lopes, Alice Casimiro, and Elizabeth Macedo. 2002. "O pensamento curricular no Brasil." In *Currículo: Debates Contemporâneos,* ed. Alice Lopes and Elizabeth Macedo (pp. 13–54). São Paulo: Cortez.

Patton, Paul. 2000. *Deleuze and the Political.* London: Routledge.

Chapter 4

Curriculum Research in Brazil

Elba Siqueira de Sá Barretto

In order to address the imbrications of my research, my personal history, and historical and political events in Brazil and abroad, I will begin by briefly summarizing my career trajectory. For over thirty years I have been a researcher at the Carlos Chagas Foundation (FCC), a renowned Brazilian research institution in the field of education. Since the 1990s, I have also been performing academic activities at the School of Education at the University of São Paulo (USP), as a part-time professor responsible for the courses *Curricula and Programs* and *Curriculum Present Issues*.

I received my undergraduate degree from the School of Education, USP, in 1965, having attended college during a time of great political turmoil. It was then that I became aware of the situation of underdevelopment in Brazil, the issue of imperialism, and the need for structural reforms, and I nurtured the hope, as did many young people of my generation, that a socialist revolution, which was supposedly being planned, would create a more just and equal society in this country. I understood the political meaning of education and its potential to help change reality.

I first met Paulo Freire in 1965 and, after graduation, in between my activities as a teacher in a public teacher education program, I participated in the Education Movement (Movimento de Educação), which was training groups linked to social movements to work with adult education from Freire's perspective.

Owing to my husband's political problems during the Brazilian military regime, I spent a year and a half in Switzerland, between 1970 and 1971. In Switzerland, Pierre Furter—a UNESCO expert I had met in Brazil

—invited me to pursue my doctoral degree and offered to serve as my mentor, but I could not get my college diploma equivalence because I was not fluent in the French language. I also had problems getting a job, and, little by little, I learned the meaning of exclusion. Even regarding my basic skills, such as household chores, I felt inadequate while living among the Swiss, who consider their way of doing and understanding things always the best of all.

When excluded, we are invaded by a sense of total ineptitude and inadequacy, and our reaction is to reject the culture of the other. How can you not despise the Calvinist habits of a people accustomed to watch and punish on a daily basis? How can you not be suspicious of the narrow-mindedness and male chauvinism of the average Swiss when you have come from a cosmopolitan city? What can one say about the humanitarian action characterized by a paternalism that makes those it should care for feel subordinate? These feelings were shared to a certain extent by all Brazilians who were in the country for similar reasons: Paulo Freire and his family, Claudius Ceccon, and Rosiska and Miguel Darci de Oliveira. This experience allowed me to better understand the reasons for school failure in Brazil.

When I returned to Brazil I obtained my master's degree and doctorate in sociology from the USP, considered the most important Brazilian university.My career as a researcher was basically developed at the FCC, where I was first hired as a research assistant in 1973. Its Department of Educational Research, established in the early 1970s, provided the necessary infrastructure and environment for theoretical-methodological discussion, so essential to the development of educational research, at a time when scientific investigation in Brazil was starting to advance. Also one of the goals of the institution was to train new researchers by involving them in research activities.

My colleagues and I, who were beginners in research work, were under the supervision of senior researchers and completed our theoretical education in graduate programs, which were also being developed at that time. We attended classes in Psychology, Education, and Social Sciences at USP or at the Catholic University of São Paulo (PUC/SP).

By working with both researchers who had studied abroad and visiting researchers, the FCC research team grew and the institution became a reference center in the area. The research team was free to make proposals and to develop their own projects, which were frequently not only a result of the researchers' own academic interests arising from previous research work but also a response to the demand of governmental bodies and other institutions. Flexible teams with varied backgrounds contributed to expand the scope of the objectives and the set of studied data as well as to facilitate the emergence of new research topics and the adoption of an interdisciplinary approach to the problems at hand. The institution was known for its ongoing dialogue with universities, scientific associations, and research-fostering agencies. Many of our researchers have worked as directors or members of technical-scientific committees and were responsible for making decisions to determine areas of research and to identify sources of financial support for it. Furthermore, we have been connected to governmental bodies in charge of creating and implementing public policies on different levels of action, thus involving basic education teachers, teachers' associations, and other institutions of the civil society. Since its early days, the foundation has also shown concern for publishing research in the area, and its academic journals have played an important role among the vehicles of information it has created.

The main areas of research conducted at FCC are the education of children from birth up to six years of age; basic education policies (which include early childhood education as well as primary and secondary school); the education and practices of basic school teachers; educational assessment; and studies on gender, race, and education. FCC has conducted pioneering research in many of these areas, such as early childhood education, gender studies, and educational assessment. Especially in the case of gender studies, the production and action of its researchers, since the mid-1970s, was decisive in endowing the subject with academic legitimacy in Brazil.

Since its creation, the research conducted by the FCC has also been aligned with the debate on the access of the population to different levels of education, an issue that was part of a more comprehensive debate on the relations between education and social development in the 1960s and 1970s. This kind of approach had already come to the attention of researchers in the sociological field, such as Florestan Fernandes, Otávio Ianni, Fernando Henrique Cardoso, and Luiz Pereira, whose concerns were focused on educational issues generated by the processes of urbanization and industrialization in Brazil. Such an approach represented a new focus in the educational field, which so far has been marked by psycho-pedagogical studies (Weber 2004).

When I entered FCC, I became part of a team in charge of developing an important performance-assessment project of MOBRAL students, the country's largest adult literacy program, implemented by the military regime. As my experience with adult education had been highly politicized, the research design was frustrating to me, since the social dimensions of the project were, in my opinion, minimized in the face of the proposed highly pedagogical focus based on Bloom's categories. It was argued that it was the only possible approach in a period of increased repression by the military regime, but, in fact, even such an approach was not allowed, because the government broke off the agreement before data collection. I was probably mistaken about the impact that such an assessment could have had on the legitimacy of government policies.

Afterward, I carried out a brief study on critical incidents reported by teachers of urban school pupils in the city of São Paulo. The study, conducted from the socio-anthropological perspective I was dealing with in my graduate course, had a great impact and was published in an FCC scientific journal and as a chapter in a book (Barretto 1975). It gave birth to my master's thesis research, wherein I analyzed the expectancies of basic school teachers concerning pupils' learning difficulties and behavior problems in view of their social origins and gender. I used the concept of "class *habitus*" coined by Bourdieu; the approach presented in the studies of Rist and Howard Becker; the self-realizing prophecies of Rosenthal and Jacobson; and the contributions of Basil Bernstein, whose study on invisible pedagogy I had become familiar with.

In the late 1970s, when the military regime was already showing signs of softening and opening up politically, FCC was invited by a research-financing agency (FINEP) to make project proposals on education. A comprehensive research program under the topic Education and Social Selectivity, with different theoretical and methodological approaches, was conducted over 12 years (I was involved as coordinator of several studies on primary education). In this program, whose objectives were commitment to democratization of education and quality education for all, many dimensions involving access to different levels of schooling were examined.

In this area of research, later continued by studies on educational policies, I worked from different perspectives on investigations of selectivity problems, school failure and exclusion, and school dynamics. These included conflicts between the culture of the school/teachers, on the one hand, and that of the students, the majority of whom came from the lower classes, on the other. The analysis was conducted from the perspective of new methods of organizing the work in schools as a way to face the severe culture of school retention that punishes elementary education students.

In other research, I reviewed the reforms compulsory education had undergone; their genesis in the public policy agenda; and issues of management and implementation of school systems, decentralization, assessment in school, and evaluation of the school. Then I came to study those processes of subjectivation that lead to the construction and reconstruction of the meanings that different social actors and groups assign to the proposed changes. There were also investigations on rural education in the extremely poor regions of the northeast of Brazil; adult education, now focusing on the limited opportunities provided by the public and private sectors to this excluded segment of the population; and curricular reforms (which I will further discuss).

My PhD thesis was on compulsory education reforms and the relationship between the federal, state, and municipal levels in providing education; it focused mainly on the participation of local governments and had the empirical support of two studies conducted at FCC during the 1980s.

Among other things, the study made the regressive character of public policies more evident, since the assignment of responsibilities and resources to provide education services in the public sphere in Brazil has been historically marked by a differential strategy of service to the social groups at which they are aimed; these services tend to become more precarious when the power to exert social pressure on these groups is reduced. Up to the 1980s the basic references of the Social Science Program at USP revolved around the Marxist matrix. My analysis has mostly benefited from Claus Offe's reflections on the dynamics of the expansion of state social policies. The contributions of Poulantzas, Carnoy, and Borja were also important, and regarding national issues, the work of Fernando Henrique Cardoso and Sonia Draibe were particularly significant.

Because of my extensive experience in research work at the FCC, I became a senior researcher long before obtaining my PhD. In 1987, when I still had one year of study to complete my doctorate, I chose to participate intensely in the National Constitutional Assembly, as the president of a national entity. We created an education forum comprising 18 national entities that had a very important role in the expansion of educational rights as per the Federal Constitution enacted in 1988, a milestone in the return to the rule of law. My doctoral program was, therefore, postponed, and it was not until 1991 that I defended my thesis. Nevertheless, many articles containing partial data from the study I was conducting for my PhD research were published before I finished my thesis, since they offered inputs to the national debate on the right to education and the decentralization of the education system.

The efforts to investigate contemporary Brazilian education problems have been constant in the work we have conducted at FCC. It somehow corresponds to what has also been noticed in other research conducted on specific subjects in Brazil. Yet we have to admit that, to a certain extent, just responding to certain urgencies caused either by government demands or by the more encompassing educational reality does not necessarily contribute to the creation of lasting knowledge to support outreach policies. The fact that public policy nurtures the work of researchers whose critical analysis can serve as input to such policies—either to reshape them or to ratify them—does not conceal, however, the complex and potentially conflicting relationship between academic forums and educational policy

(Weber 2004). Their timing and priorities are not the same, and the appropriation of research findings by government leaders is subject to other factors outside the academic field.

My Experiences in Curriculum Studies

Based on what has been shown, it is clear that I am not only a researcher in the area of curriculum.

Curricular Reform in São Paulo Schools

My first significant experience in dealing with curriculum issues was not exactly academic. Between 1984 and 1988, as a researcher at the FCC, I was invited to work as an advisor to the São Paulo State Secretariat of Education, an agency responsible for the education of over 4 million pupils from primary and secondary schools. Direct election of the São Paulo state governor and other opposition governors in important southern and southeastern states was a decisive point in the transition process to democracy. Changes in policy guidelines were urgently needed.

The first challenge I faced was contributing to the implementation of the literacy learning cycle, which was centered on promotion by age. It was introduced by the government with the purpose of reversing school failure. I was part of the group that formulated the political and educational reasons for the introduction of promotion by age. I joined the efforts to understand the possibilities of curriculum flexibilization opened by these learning cycles, with the purpose of better handling the differences in learning styles of students coming from various segments of the population; it included reviewing the literacy approach based on the recent findings of Emília Ferreiro. These findings have had great influence in Spanish-speaking Latin America and Brazil.[1]

I also actively joined the effort to review the concept of assessment in the school system in view of the widespread debate between schools concerning the introduction of learning cycles. In the 1980s, the schools and the educational system transferred their focus from the isolated aspect of student performance to the variables of the school context that affected educational development, thus joining the efforts to find joint solutions to guarantee learning for all. As a decision maker, I discussed this with large teacher audiences and sometimes even with audiences who looked at the introduction of learning cycles with deep hostility, which was because of the culture of retention that is deeply ingrained in our school systems. It was my close involvement with the proposal of teaching in learning cycles of promotion by age that would make me look at the issue from an academic point of view years later.

My second challenge in the work I did at the Secretariat of Education was to participate in the more general process of curriculum reform of primary and secondary schools. The team to which I belonged was under the strong influence of the "critical-social pedagogy of contents," a Brazilian trend that became hegemonic in the curricular reforms triggered by the states and implemented by state governments opposing the federal government.

The dominant arguments were close to those developed by Synders in France and by Lawton in England; they also resorted to Gramsci, for whom the cultural experiences of children coming from popular classes should be taken as a point of departure, and not exactly as suppliers of teaching contents. The very nature of the social choice of curricular contents was not questioned, and its main purpose was to make the knowledge created with the contribution of the whole society accessible to all, and not only to the minorities that benefited from it to achieve prestigious positions (Barretto 1998).

My team outlined some very general guidelines based primarily on the intention of making school contents socially relevant to students from all population groups.

Consultants from three public universities from the state of São Paulo were hired to support the technical staff of the Secretariat of Education. Curriculum organization continued to be centered on the subject matrix, despite general recommendations that the approach to the areas of study should be integrated. The curricular proposals were made through a long process of consulting schools, with teachers as the main interlocutors. Students and the community as a whole have not been involved, although it is known that their interests and expectations on these issues are not always the same as those of teachers. But, considering the time period when this happened, consulting with schools was viewed as a practice that inaugurated a new era by ending the tradition of proposals made in closed government cabinets to be carried out by the schools.

However, the struggle for hegemony in the selection of curricular content was not with the schools. It reflected not only the great tensions emerging in the configuration of the disciplinary fields themselves, but also the divergences between the different political groups supporting the government on the wide front of the democratic left-wing parties.

As to some curricular components such as Portuguese and Mathematics, there was a general consensus on the orientations that expressed contemporary trends of approach. But there were many difficulties in the field of humanities, whose ideological component was more evident, as also reported by studies from other countries, such as the ones from Laville (1998) on the reform of History programs in Québec.

Discussions with History and Geography staff soon made it clear that an integrated approach to those domains of knowledge was impossible. History and Geography teacher associations were fighting against the loss of content from their respective disciplines as a result of the introduction of Social Studies during the military regime, which had transformed the two fields of study into notions of commonsense as a result of the loss of reference to approaches specific to the two disciplines.

Geography's efforts to forge its own identity and its desire to make the curriculum a tool of political struggle ended up covering a great amount of political economy. However, History that focused on the "winners" was criticized; the new History curricula spoke from the point of view of the "losers" instead, finding inspiration mainly in a reductionist review of Thompson's ideas, according to which social movements began to be seen as the most important propelling force of social change, and the state almost disappeared.

Even at the Secretariat of Education and the universities, the History program enjoyed no consensus. When it was made public, it became the target of violent criticism by the mainstream media, which labeled the whole curricular reform as populist. The material was withdrawn and the new version published years later. I did not follow the process from beginning to end, since I had already left the Secretariat of Education. But the subsequent state school administration did not make any special effort to implement the new curricular proposals.

As a result of the succeeding democratic governments, this has happened very often. The process of participatory curricular programming is slow and the effort made by one management group to renew curricular guidelines is not always followed by the succeeding management teams with the same determination to implement them, even when the same political party remains in power.

The National Curriculum and the Resulting Issues

When I applied to teach the discipline *Theories of Curriculum* at the School of Education at USP, at the turn of the 1990s, my previous experience with curricular reform was of great value to me. However, for a long time I was hired by the university on a temporary basis because I was not willing to accept a full-time agreement. This restricted my chances of being a mentor to graduate research students.

In 1995, the Ministry of Education asked FCC to begin research oriented toward the analysis of curricular proposals from different Brazilian states to help define National Curricular Parameters (PCNs) for the primary school. I was the research coordinator and the project was funded by UNESCO. A team of experts from different parts of the country studied the state curricular proposals made between 1985 and 1995. The analysis centered on the general elements making up the proposals, on their theoretical premises, and on the areas of study that composed the compulsory core curriculum: Portuguese Language, Mathematics, History, Geography, and the Sciences.

Curricular orientations from three capital cities were also included in the research for their innovative character. With a more democratic society as a reference, in the first half of the 1990s, the concern about "difference" emerged as the distinctive feature of certain proposals from some capital cities, such as São Paulo, Belo Horizonte, and Rio de Janeiro, which incorporated a significant number of university professors in their management staff in this period. Taking into consideration the proliferation of metropolitan areas, among which some of the world's largest population aggregates are included, the diverse and plural character of our cities—which reflects the character of the Brazilian society in a peculiar way—has offered fertile ground for tests in the educational area. The changes proposed to overcome the fragmentation of school curriculum had been focused on the disciplines, so São Paulo, Belo Horizonte, and Rio de Janeiro tried to reshape curriculum with a multireferential character, to be guided by supposedly more integrative principles that would enable differentiated groups of the school population to have a more successful learning experience.

Research results obtained on demand, like this one about national curricula, must be returned to the entity requesting them. In this case, the diagnosis pointing to trends, innovations, and weaknesses produced by 21 states and some capital cities was not crucial for the Ministry of Education to build National Curricular Parameters (PCNs). It was used, however, to give legitimacy to the government proposal. The construction of PCNs occurred under the strong influence of the Spanish curriculum model and had César Coll, besides some of his collaborators from the University of Barcelona, as its main mentor.

The academic community reacted to the national curriculum in many ways. A significant number of educational researchers were in the forefront opposing the government's efforts, questioning the possibility of a common curriculum itself, since there were difficulties in overcoming "homogenizing consensus" and in taking the differences between the Brazilian states into proper account. They were also fearing that the national curriculum would become subject to the national assessment system—created under the pressure of multilateral organizations in Brazil and in other Latin American countries in the 1990s—and thus end up having the public sector conforming to the logic of the market, as had been happening in England, Chile, and other countries.

Other researchers, although they recognize the risks involved in subjecting the national curriculum to the assessment system and thus narrowing the scope of education, were more cautious, steering clear of conclusions that did not take into account the specificities of the Brazilian situation. Those favorable to a common national curriculum, however, showed their disagreement with the restrictive consulting processes used in crafting the PCN and with the fact that the Brazilian experience in accumulated research on curriculum and education was not duly considered.

The proposition of national curricular parameters for elementary education, in the second half of the 1990s, followed the overall trend of educational reforms in this period concerning the integrated and continuous treatment of educational projects on the different education levels that became part of basic education, to which the whole population should be granted access.

Many Brazilian authors published essays oriented mainly toward the analysis of the theoretical-ideological premises concerning the orientation given by the federal government to the national curriculum. Some studies about curricular reforms in other countries, especially in England, Spain, and, to a lesser degree, in Argentina, were also published. Much on curriculum discussions by researchers from various countries was published by Brazilian publishing houses, especially as regards publications from Spain, which included work not only by authors proposing critical curriculum theories (such as Gimeno Sacristán, Perez Gomes, Enguita, Torres Santomé) but also by those having other theoretical orientations (such as Cesar Coll and his collaborators). New schoolbooks have been edited according to the new curricular guidelines, some of which were designed through the participation of consultants of the Spanish curriculum, which indicates that an internationalization process of textbooks was underway. This phenomenon should not be left unnoticed, since Brazil, having over 55 million students in basic education, is one of the most competitive editorial markets worldwide, particularly for schoolbooks.

However, there are very few studies to help us work at a higher level of performance, closer to reality, on the potential impacts of a curriculum that is declared national. In a regional seminar on curriculum development in the Southern Cone countries, promoted by UNESCO, International Bureau of Education (IBE), held in Buenos Aires, in 2006, I had the opportunity to argue[2] that there was not sufficient evidence to declare that the curriculum adopted in schools after the 1990s reform had undergone a homogenizing process, although it was evident that the central powers had increased their control over the established curriculum.

However, after the launching of the Education Development Plan (PDE) by the Ministry of Education in 2007, which linked governmental actions to basic education improvement indicators of student performance, obtained through the Brazilian Basic School Assessment System, the scope of school curricula is likely to be restricted in view of the practices of preparing students to do better in tests.

At the University

At the university, I have oriented several research projects in which the curriculum issue appears as an important focus in studies analyzing the educational reforms that implemented the learning cycles. By bringing tension to the educational and social project upon which the compulsory school system is mainly based, learning cycles lead to a confrontation with prevailing values, among them the one that accepts inequalities as resulting from individual differences. As non-retention measures, they break with the fragmentation resulting from the graded education system—the most common in Brazil—and lead to changes in the conception of time, space, and school content, as well as of the school culture itself, aimed at ensuring that the large pool of students, until recently excluded from the education system, may be able to stay in it and acquire relevant knowledge.

After I conducted, with my research groups at the USP, two critical state of arts on the policies responsible for the implementation of the learning cycles in several school systems in Brazil (Barretto and Mitrulis 2001; Barretto and Sousa 2005), I supervised studies on the cycle proposals adopted in three Brazilian capital cities, using methodologies that strive to approach the subject from a new perspective, aiming to better understand one of the country's most controversial policies in the field of primary education.

One of the studies (Campos 2007) proposed to examine the terms in which the interdisciplinary conception of the curriculum, suggested in the learning cycles by the local government, has been dealing with the transversal themes introduced by the National Curricular Parameters and with traditional disciplinary school practices, taking into account their different presuppositions and the processes of recontextualization they have gone through in a municipality of central Brazil. This research was also concerned with identifying curricular content that was most often selected for on-the-job teacher education during the eight years of implementation of the learning cycles proposal. Ivor Goodson, Gimeno Sacristán, and Maurice Tardif provided the basic theoretical support.

Another study dealt with the implementation of the learning cycles in Belo Horizonte, a capital that had been developing for 12 years a radical proposal for reversing school-excluding structures. The research consisted of a trajectory analysis of students who were not able to read and write during the nine primary school years (Mendonça 2007) and was mainly based on François Dubet and Bernard Lahire.

In the third study, made in São Paulo, I was unwilling to take for granted the argument of teachers' resistance to learning cycles—which is often cited by the Brazilian literature—in order to explain the difficulties in implementing reforms. I tried to demonstrate, based on participatory observation, that although teachers tend to disagree with the measures related to promotion by age, they are led to change their practices to comply with the new situations created by the presence of students with learning mismatched with that of their same-aged classmates (Cunha 2007). Tardif, Tardif and Lessard, and Gimeno Sacristán are important references.

I am also the advisor of a research study that proposes to analyze the circumstances in which systematic activities on the Afro-Brazilian culture have been introduced in a public school with a differentiated educational project. My advisee proposed to examine the effects of these practices on the different social actors involved and the tensions caused on the set of curricular practices. She focuses on issues of empowerment of African-descendant populations and also on the processes of reconversion of the practices of socialization of these groups into leisure when "consumed" by people from other social segments. The works of Apple, Giroux, MacLaren, and Garcia Canclini are fundamental references for this research.

I am now starting a research project aimed at understanding the conceptions of teachers' work from their subjects' own perspective. This project is part of a program that brings together 31 groups of researchers in Brazil and abroad (Argentina, Portugal, Greece, France) around a nuclear research on *Social Representations of Students from Teacher Education Courses for Basic Education Concerning Teachers' Work,* which is based on Moscovici's theory of social representations. It has the support of *Laboratoire Européen de Psychologie Sociale de la Maison des Sciences de l'Homme* (MSH, Paris, France) and of the FCC, which created the conditions for the installation and operation of an International Center for Studies of Social

Representation and Subjectivity—Education and Teaching (CIERS-ED) that hosts the program in São Paulo.

My research team at the USP is part of this program and is now proposing an outgrowth of research on the representations of teachers' work through multireferential approaches. Besides data related to the students of teacher education programs of the university itself (Pedagogy, Liberal Arts, and Mathematics)[3] at USP, the group intends to identify and analyze knowledge, values, and attitudes that are designed to build teachers' professionalism, according to the university professors educating these students, and taking into account the established and the active curricula being developed in these programs and their social and institutional contexts.

The need for intensified teacher education that arose in the last several decades in Western countries is now felt in Brazil as well, imposing compulsory higher education programs for teachers of young children. One of the consequences was that the number of higher teacher education programs have increased fivefold, especially those that prepare teachers for daycare centers, preschools, and initial grades of the primary school.

As to what programs for the education of teachers are to be recommended, there are conflicting models in Brazil, each one fighting for hegemony in the field of educational policies. Analyzing teacher education, one sees a great imbalance in terms of priority between pedagogical knowledge and knowledge of specific domains. In Pedagogy programs knowledge relating to the fundamentals of education, including education in society and instrumentalization of knowledge, is emphasized, but in other teacher education programs, the relationship is reversed, the prevailing knowledge is that of specific disciplinary areas.

The value of this knowledge, anchored in different conceptions of education and the social role of teaching, is expressed in curricular guidelines at the national and regional levels, as well as in curricula and programs designed by each educational institution. It is also found in the representations of the subjects involved in the educational process, regardless of the decisions taken at other levels, giving the programs a characteristic feature different from that described in the established curricula.

We admit, as do Tedesco and Fanfani (2004), that the tension between the foundational components of representations on teachers' work, which refers to the roles historically assigned to teaching systems, is on the basis of the teacher education paradigms: that of vocation/apostleship and that which considers it as a profession to be learned by mastering a series of specific rational knowledge. In view of social changes and the standardization of teaching systems, the representation of the teacher as a professional receiving wages is added to these representations. The stress placed on these components tends to change even today, and the dispute would be over the structuring principle dominating its definition.

Moreover, the epistemology of practice as a teaching education paradigm (Nóvoa 1995; Zeichner; Diniz-Pereira 2005) tends to be affirmed as opposed to the technical-scientific rationality standards that have informed school curricula during the periods of expansion of teaching systems and the courses that prepared their teachers. From this perspective, the school is considered the central axis of teacher education, and the importance of taking into account the life history and experience of the teacher as elements that form his identity and professional work is highlighted.

It is worth remembering that the radical awareness of (1) the precariousness of knowledge and (2) the strategies of domination that underlie it has led not only to the adoption of multireferential investigation approaches, but also to the defense of curricula integrated in the scope of education. This also contemplates multicultural perspectives and the urgent need to contextualize knowledge and work at schools with content that does not fit classical disciplinary approaches.

Various issues that we have pointed out here pervade the pedagogical imagination and influence the creation of curricula and teacher education actions; others not only resist the rules promoted by legislation and the prescriptions of academic production but also populate the universe of representations in teachers' work and enable the creation of new meanings for the teacher formation curriculum.

These are the issues we want to address and go into depth in the research, because we are convinced that the educational reforms have to pay more attention to the subjectivity of the subjects, if they really want to bring about effective changes.

Why undertake this research? Because it creates the possibility of working with many other researchers in an integrated online project—from universities of the capital and the state of São Paulo in Brazil and from other parts of the world—because we have the possibility of expanding the range of approaches converging more and more on our focus of interest as a group, such as the approaches of Tardif and Young, among others; because we are challenged to establish fruitful links between different traditions of thought; because the issue of basic school teaching and curriculum has been my object of study on different occasions, and teacher education is my work as a teacher at a school of education; because it is easier for me to reconcile the intersection of my research activities in the two institutions where I work; because improving the quality of basic education is an issue demanding urgent action in Brazil, and in which teacher education is a contentious subject.

Thus, there is a chance to reconcile the trends of internationalization of research with the national demands to which we have been called upon to respond and with the individual aspirations of the moment as well.

Curriculum Studies in Brazil

When I started the program at the School of Education, the existing bibliography about curriculum in Brazil was poor; both theoretical formulations and empirical studies on the subject were lacking in this country. An article by José Luis Domingues, published in 1986 and based on Habermas, was one of the first works to introduce me to the field of curriculum, situating the main representatives of the paradigms he called technical-linear, circular-consensual, and dynamic-dialogical. At that time, only a few critical texts by Michael Apple and Giroux had been published in Brazil. Abraham Magendzo's *Curriculum e Cultura na América Latina* [Curriculum and Culture in Latin America] was also an important reference for the first courses I taught. I brought it back from Chile after working there for a time.

In 1990, *Currículos e programas no Brasil* [Curricula and School Programs in Brazil], a book by Antonio Flávio Barbosa Moreira, was published. It addressed the complex network of paradigm transfer and the construction/reconstruction of national references in the field, as a result of the country's specific history. During the first half of the 1990s, articles on the approaches of the New Sociology of Education, then a subject little known among us, began to circulate. This dissemination took place through texts published by Brazilian researchers who had obtained their doctoral degrees in the United Kingdom, such as Antônio Flávio and Lucíola Licínio dos Santos. Tomaz Tadeu da Silva also began to become known. The New Sociology of Education and the critical theories on curriculum as a whole shifted the discussions, which had prevailed until then in the psychopedagogy field, to issues of power, ideology, and culture—a shift that has definitely contributed to reflection in the field.

In addition to producing an abundance of work of their own, these and a few other Brazilian researchers have, since then, played a relevant role in the country as disseminators of studies conducted by matrix authors in the field of curriculum, such as Michael Young, Basil Bernstein, André Chervel, Henry Giroux, Stephen Ball, as well as José Gimeno Sacristán, Jean Claude Fourquin, Peter McLaren, John Willinsky, and others such as Stuart Hall and Zygmunt Bauman.

In the 1990s, the post-structuralist and postmodern perspectives also began to be more widely disseminated within academic circles in Brazil. Within the field of education, it is possible to assert that curriculum scholars are those who have most contributed to enhance the debate about the relations between postmodernism and educational theory.

Tomaz Tadeu da Silva has played a decisive role in this sense. At first, he sought to address the central issues of the postmodern thinking and to establish continuities and ruptures with the curriculum critical theories. Next, in 1993, he included eight essays that review contributions from Foucault, Deleuze, Derrida, Rorty, and others in his book *Teoria educacional crítica em tempos pós-modernos* [Critical Educational Theory in Postmodern Times], in search of the production of new meanings for education. Later on, he proceeded with a series of publications within this line.

Studies carried out according to these perspectives have evolved mainly in the University of Rio Grande do Sul, with the contribution of authors such as Tomaz Tadeu himself and Alfredo Veiga-Neto, Rosa Maria Fischer, Guacira Lopes Louro, Sandra Corazza, and Marisa Vohaber. According to the survey conducted by Paraíso (2004) on the literature produced along that same line, the studies have focused on relations of power and subjected identities (inspired by cultural, feminist, postcolonial, and ethnic studies, and the queer theory); on the processes of subjectivation, showing that they are more complex than what assumptions about the "subject" make us believe and which constitute the basis for the critical and traditional theories; as well as on the problematization of the "educational truths," of curriculum knowledge considered as "legitimate," evidencing the artificial nature of knowledge production in education. These studies seek a methodological way out of the totalizations and metanarratives and look out for possibilities of analyzing the singular, the local, and the partial.

But the postmodern provocation goes beyond the post-structuralist perspectives and contaminates the different scientific fields, which reorient themselves toward a multiparadigmatic model in humanities and social sciences. This profusion of models and the hybridism in the theoretical field also characterize the field of education and that of curriculum itself.

From my point of view, one of the most representative lines of curriculum studies is probably centered on school knowledge, and its most important representatives are Antonio Flávio Moreira, Alice Casimiro Lopes, and Elisabeth Macedo from the Federal University of Rio de Janeiro, and Lucíola Licínio Santos from the Federal University of Minas Gerais. More visibly concerned about "discussing" with the different realities of the education systems and with the curriculum policies and practices currently in force in this country, this line of research seeks to understand and shed light upon the theoretical assumptions that have influenced the Brazilian curricular thinking, the hybridizations of the curricular and social discourses, as well as to discuss and sometimes propose perspectives for action (Lopes and Macedo 2002).

This line of research also yields studies on multiculturalism (in schools) that aim to contribute to the destabilization of asymmetrical positions of power that legitimate certain identities and repel others and to discuss how multiculturalism should be treated in educational institutions and in teacher education programs, aiming at a more democratic education. Vera Candau, Ana Canen, and Antonio Flávio B. Moreira himself may also be identified within this line, dialoguing with Michael Apple, John Willinsky, Nicholas Burbules, and others.

At the core of the questioning done from postmodern perspectives, I believe that the emphasis placed on the issue of multiculturalism in curriculum studies conducted in Brazil played a central role in the transition of the paradigm focused on social classes to that which celebrates the differences in the field of education. Nevertheless, the proliferation of essays that started to address the classification of its nuances (resulting in what is "politically correct") seems, at times, to have disguised the fact that there are still very few reliable studies on this subject. Only more recently has empirically based research started to be more widely published.

Moreover, since in the developed countries where this issue was brought about, social discrimination and exclusion predominantly follow the pattern of a more clearly cultural nature, the strong focus on more clearly cultural differences has, in many instances, neglected the difficulties that large numbers of the Brazilian population face in order to gain access to basic social goods, as Brazil has one of the most unequal income distribution in the world. The discourse on differences has frequently contributed to obscure the issue of inequalities or, in some cases, to highlight inequalities only as they affect certain discriminated groups.

In the fertile ground that curriculum studies also helped prepare, the inclusion, in 2003, by a presidential decree, of the Afro-Brazilian History and Culture in the curricula of all Brazilian schools is a tribute that should be paid mainly to the engagement of the Black Movement (*Movimento Negro*). In a country where approximately half of its population consists of mulattoes and blacks, the significant absence of its African roots in the curriculum caused a huge gap in the systematized knowledge about this issue. Cultural entities, ethnic movements, nongovernmental organizations (NGOs), universities and research institutions have advanced toward enrolling, organizing, systematizing and, above all, producing studies and materials that can serve as input to the current proposal, which depends largely on these contributions in order to advance. Aiming at this target, the Ford Foundation sponsored the *Blacks and Education Program* (*Programa Negro e Educação*), coordinated by the National Association of Research and Postgraduation in Education (*Associação Nacional de Pesquisa e Pós-Graduação em Educação*) and by a NGO: the Educative Action (*Ação Educativa*). At the same time, initiatives of teacher education addressing this type of concern start to appear.

Significant changes have also taken place regarding assistance to the indigenous peoples. With the promulgation of the new Constitution in 1988, classes in the first grades of compulsory school started to be taught to these people in their native languages. A movement toward rescuing native languages and cultures, that was formerly ignored, has now emerged, and this movement has grown at the same pace as has the demographic and identity growth of these people. In 2008, the compulsory character of indigenous studies was also extended to all levels of education by the federal government.

Although the increase in the number of affirmative actions concerning populations of African and indigenous origin should be acclaimed, from my point of view, the increasing "racialization" of the discourse of certain identity movements deserves, however, a more profound reflection in the field of curriculum.

Concerning the history of school subjects, there are a few studies developed essentially by researchers in their respective areas of knowledge. However, as pointed out by Lopes and Macedo (2002), there are also those who choose the constructivist approach, outside the hard core of the curriculum field, as well as those from the hard core, who are engaged in deconstructing constructivism as a hegemonic approach in the curriculum guidelines. And there are also studies on school practices and routine, carried out from the perspective of Certeau, Morin, Boaventura Santos, Lefèbvre, such as those conducted by Sonia Penin, and with deviations to the network curriculum, such as those by Nilda Alves.

Even with the large production of quantitative and qualitative curriculum studies, which took place within a very short period—less than two decades, the theorizations yielded as a result of research have little to contribute to curriculum practices and to provide answers to the questions posed by the notorious difficulties the country faces to ensure quality education to everyone.

In addition to losing the curriculum field to other areas, as a result of the detachment from educational approaches on the part of some scholars, and the fragmentation of the studies motivated not only by different views about the objects and disputes in the field, but also by the lack of continuity of some lines of investigation, one certainly has to highlight the lack of research on the historical perspective of the curriculum. The existing research is insufficient, either from the point of view of policies implemented and the ideas supporting them, or the history of subjects, cultural artifacts and school practices.

Teacher Education

For the project "Teaching in Basic Education: Knowledge and Representation of Teachers and Students of Teacher Education Programs" (*A docência na educação básica: saberes e representações dos professores e alunos dos cursos de licenciatura*), developed by the multidisciplinary team with which I am currently involved, perspectives from several fields of study converge and—hopefully—will benefit from the experience accumulated by the researchers. Certainly this is not an easy task, but we have four years ahead of us to arrive at some consensus formulations and to develop complementary analytical perspectives.

Some members of the team have worked with studies that address schools' everyday routine and practices from Lefebvre's perspective, aiming at reviewing the origins of the representation studies by checking aspects of Lefebvre's and Moscovici's theory. Our colleagues who teach Languages and Mathematics have conducted studies on teaching of their respective areas of knowledge and are up to date with the academic production on the subjects. What is still expected from us, pedagogues, is that we contribute toward the discussion of the changes in the social functions of the school and, consequently, in teacher education; analyze the assumptions of the models of education being discussed and the processes of recontextualization which they have been subjected to, either in the context of transposition of models from abroad or in the sphere of the different phases of curricular orientation existing in the Brazilian educational system. Moreover, we are expected to be able to appropriately situate the importance of interaction and reciprocal transformations among the different areas of knowledge. Finally, it is expected that the different views that students of teacher education programs and their respective university professors have about teachers' work can bring a new look to the curriculum established and the one being used, as well as help unravel part of the *imbroglio* that constitutes teacher education in the present.

NOTES

1. In later studies, I would once again reflect on the impact of these approaches over school systems. Although the orientations called constructivist took into

account some cultural determinants of the process of learning the written language and were interested in the school performance of popular classes, they ended up transferring the social and political concerns that motivated the creation of the basic cycle in São Paulo and other states to a domain that was predominantly cognitive and centered on the interaction with individuals. This left behind social factors that affected the life of the entire population (see Barretto's chapter 4 in this volume; Mitrulis 2001).

2. Considering the assertion that Brazil is a country of continental dimensions, with a federal structure that causes school systems to be decentralized, we can conclude that school practices are only superficially affected by the official curriculum.

3. The university programs that educate teachers on higher-level concepts/skills in Brazil are called *licenciaturas*. They include pedagogy programs and programs educating teachers for specific disciplines such as the Portuguese language, mathematics, biology, and others.

REFERENCES

Barretto, Elba Siqueira de Sá. 1998. "Tendências Recentes do Currículo do Ensino Fundamental no Brasil [Recent Trends in the Brazilian Primary School Curriculum]." In *Os Currículos do Ensino Fundamental Para as Escolas Brasileiras* [Primary SchoolCurricula for Brazilian Schools], ed. Elba Siqueira de Sá Barretto. Campinas, SP: Autores Associados.

Barretto, Elba Siqueira de Sá. 1975. "Professores de Periferia: Soluções Simples Para Problemas Complexos" [Urban Schools' Teachers: Simple Solutions for Complex Problems]. *Cadernos de Pesquisa* (14): 97–109.

Barretto, Elba Siqueira de Sá, and E. Mitrulis. 2001. "Trajetória e Desafios dos Ciclos Escolares no País" [Trajectories and Challenges of Learning School Cycles in Brazil]. *Revista de Estudos Avançados* 15 (42): 103–140.

Barretto, Elba Siqueira de Sá., and S. Z. Sousa. 2005. "Reflexões Sobre as Políticas de Ciclos no Brasil" [Reflections on the Learning Cycle Policies in Brazil]. *Cadernos de Pesquisa* 35 (126): 659–688. http://www.scielo.br.

Campos, A. C. de O. 2007. "A Escola Sará: Análise do Currículo nos Ciclos da Rede de Ensino Cuiabana" [Sará School: A Curriculum Analysis of the Learning Cycles in Cuiabá]. Master's Thesis, Faculdade de Educação da Universidade de São Paulo [School of Education, University of São Paulo].

Canen, Ana, and Antoni Flavio Moreira. eds 2001. *Ênfases e Omissões no Currículo* [Emphasis and Omissions in the Curriculum]. Campinas: Papirus.

Cunha, Bilecki Isabel da. 2007. "Postura Docente Diante dos Ciclos de Aprendizagem" [Teacher's Posture on Learning Cycles]. Master's Thesis. Faculdade de Educação da Universidade de São Paulo [School of Education, University of São Paulo].

Domingues, Jose Luiz. 1986. "Interesses Humanos e Paradigmas Curriculares" [Human Interests and Curricular Paradigms]. Revista Brasileira de Estudos Pedagógicos 67, (156): 351–366.

Regina Leite Garcia, and Antoni Flavio Moreira, eds. 2003. Currículo na Contemporaneidade: Incertezas e Desafios [Curricula in the Contemporaneity: Uncertainties and Challenges]. São Paulo: Cortez.

Laville, Christian. 1998. "A Próxima Reforma dos Programas Escolares Será Mais bem Sucedida que a Anterior?" [Will the Next Reform of School Programs Be More Successful than the Previous One?] In Novas Políticas Educacionais: Críticas e Perspectivas [New Educational Policies: Criticism and Perspectives] ed., Mirian. J. Warde. São Paulo: PUC/SP.

Lopes, Alice Casimiro, and Elizabeth Macedo, eds. 2002. Currículo: Debates Contemporâneos [Curriculum: Contemporary Debates]. São Paulo: Cortez.

Magendzo, Abraham. 1986. Curriculum y Cultura en América Latina [Curriculum and Culture in Latin America]. Santiago de Chile: Programa Interdisciplinário de Investigaciones em Educación.

Mendonça, Patrícia Moulin. 2007. "Ler e Escrever nos Ciclos da Escola Plural: Um Estudo de Trajetórias" [Reading and Writing in the Plural School Cycles: a Study on Trajectories]. Master's Thesis, Faculdade de Educação da Universidade de São Paulo [School of Education, the University of São Paulo].

Moreira, Antoni Flavio 1990. Currículos e Programas no Brasil [Curriculum and Programs in Brazil]. Campinas: Papirus.

Paraíso, Marlucy Alves. 2004. "Pesquisas Pós-críticas em Educação no Brasil: Esboço de um Mapa" [Post-Criticism Research in Education in Brazil: Sketch of a Map]. Cadernos de Pesquisa 34 (122). http://www.scielo.br.

Silva, Tomaz Tadeu da. 1993. Teoria Educacional Crítica em Tempos Pós-modernos [Critical Educational Theory in Postmodern Times]. Porto Alegre: Artes Médicas.

Tedesco, Juan Carlos, and Emillo Tenti Fanfani. 2004. "Nuevos Maestros Para Nuevos Estudiantes" [New Teachers for New Students]. In Maestros en America Latina: Nuevas Perspectivas Sobre su Formación y Desempeño [Teachers in Latin America: New Perspectives on their Education and Performance]. Santiago: Cinde, Preal/BID, Editorial San Marino.

Weber, Silke. 2004. "Políticas do ensino fundamental em revista: Um debate pela democracia" [Primary School Policies in Review: A Debate for Democracy]. In Uma história para contar: A pesquisa na Fundação Carlos Chagas [A Story to Tell: Research at Carlos Chagas Foundation] ed. Albertina de Oliveira Costa, Angela Maria Martinez, and Maria Laura Barbosa Franco Puglisi. São Paulo: Fundação Carlos Chagas, Annablume.

Chapter 5

Curriculum as Practiced

Carlos Eduardo Ferraço

Introduction

I have been participating in two directory research groups[1] that have been developing investigations emphasizing analysis of school routines for the comprehension of themes in the educational field, especially in the field of curriculum studies. In general, our objectives are directed toward the *analysis of the established relationships* between practitioners (Certeau 1994, 1996) of the routines of public schools in the first grades of elementary school. These relationships are what I call networked curriculum (Ferraço 2008a).

Thus, the body of my research has included and articulated the following investigation questions: Which narratives and images are produced and shared in the school routines in the processes of negotiation, translation, and mimicry (Bhabha 1998) and which are the uses (Certeau 1994, 1996) that the subjects who practice the schools' routines produce in relation to the declared official curricula? From which implications in the school routines do these processes originate in relation to the methodologies and theories present in the curricular prescriptions proposed by the education offices? How do these processes empower practices of resistance[2] and invention[3] in relation to the homogenizing mechanisms of the official prescriptions? What other discussions about curriculum are being elaborated among these different processes? What clues do the processes give us about other theoretical-epistemological-methodological possibilities of empowering curriculum policies that communicate with the experiences of the multiplicity of the worlds of life?

In general, I am interested in understanding what is going on in the daily lives of educators and students during the processes of production and sharing of curricular knowledge—that is, the relationship established in their knowledge, action, and power networks (Alves 2002) between the content "taught" in the disciplines and the broader contexts of their lives—and what other curricular policies are being produced by them. Thus, I am searching to become epistemologically closer to the networks of knowledge that are woven and shared by the subjects of the schools through their actions and discourses, and how those networks are linked to so many other contexts in their lives.

If it is possible—in analyses of curriculum proposals—to speak about senses and meanings juxtaposed and, sometimes, in contradictory fashion, thereby eliciting the concept of the hybrid,[4] it is even more possible to speak of these—especially the primacy of the hybrid—when investigating those networks characteristic of the daily life of the schools. By focusing only upon proposals and policies, one fails to understand how students and educators integrate them.[5]

Engaging the scholarship and research that have been produced during the last few years,[6] I have analyzed curricula as performed in school routines, assumed as expression of situations and moments lived in the past and the present, and as projections and indications of future situations[7] of production of other discourses in the field of curriculum, and also as a possibility of problematization and enlargement of official curricular policies.

As advocated by Alves (2005), I am interested in developing research focused on understanding the contemporary school routines among the knowledge networks that are being woven by practitioners who involve other environments they live in, presuming, as suggested by Certeau (1994), to elaborate a "theory of practices" or even to try answering Maffesoli's (2007) question from his reading of the *Discorsi* by Machiavelli: *do we still know how to read and interpret the thoughts of the public square?*

Therefore, I do not assume a contraposition between "official curricular policies" and "performed curricula." In fact, I understand that, in the schools' routines, the curricula performed, practiced (Oliveira 2003), or networked (Alves 2001)[8] is expressed as potential possibilities for the problematization and/or broadening of the discursive field of curriculum, including the official proposals from among so many determiners[9] of these networks.

With this research, I try to overcome, as much as possible, the dichotomy between "school knowledge" and "scientific knowledge," keeping in mind that in the weaving of the daily knowledge, action, and power networks, many processes of use, translation, negotiation, and hybridism are performed. These processes imprint themselves with the mark of complexity of everything being weaved together simultaneously.

In my research, I observed that, in the schools' daily life, teachers and students practice different *ways of experimenting-problematizing* the official curriculum. The minor discourse (Deleuze 1992) subjects of education are affirmed as protagonists of the educational scene in those *modes of experimentation-problematization* that are often revealed in extremely *transgressing, powerful, and inventive* ways. These invoke Certeau's (1994) *antidisciplines* that express different ways of thinking and acting and that, at the same time, create, reproduce, negotiate, and thus weave knowledge. As theorized by Oliveira (2008), from Santos (1989, 2004), it is necessary to discuss school routines epistemologically, *considering the indissolubility between the political and the epistemological* and understanding that global justice is not possible without cognitive justice.

> It means that, if we wish to recognize and work for experiences of social emancipation, we need to associate them to the criticism and to the possible formulation of new epistemological premises that incorporate the validity and the legitimacy of different knowledge, practices and ways to be in the world, overcoming the current dominant hierarchization among ones and others and facilitating interactive processes between the different ones that will not make them unequal. (Oliveira 2008, 68)

Thus we problematize curricula performed in schools while elaborating other discourses in the field of curriculum by means of the narratives and images produced, as proposed by Guimarães (2006). We search for ways that will make it possible for us to understand teachers' and students' daily existence without demanding or renouncing what such understanding offers us, returning to existence and to everyday language, in order to revive contact with common life.

Such research also assumes that the school routines follow from the networks of relations that are interwoven and, according to my theoretical references, include concepts of negotiation, translation, and mimicry (Certeau 1994; Bhabha 1998) that are linked to the knowledge-action networks[10] (Alves 1998a). Alves (2005, 3) asserts,

> [I understand] that the human beings, in their actions and to communicate, are loaded with values that reproduce, transmit, but also create.... Thus, in the same process, they go on applying whatever is imposed by the dominant culture, working with those technical products available for consumption and, on the other hand, creating ways to use these technical

inventions, devising new technologies and possibilities of change, not only of the technical artifacts, but of the techniques of instrumentality as well.

Contesting the censorship that science imposes on narrative knowledge (Guimarães 2006), my research is dedicated to listening to the common and everyday, according attention to the daily practices of the subjects in schools, and trying to empathetically understand them in different moments and experienced situations. To this end, together with Guimarães (2006), I have tried to employ a research methodology sufficiently open and flexible to describe the way daily communicative interactions among teachers and students situate them in the world, offering them opportunities for belonging and sociability. As I understand (2006, 14),

> Understanding social life, and not judging it (in the name of what it should be), has been the attitude adopted. Daily life, constituted by implicit knowledge and animated by shared feelings (dedicated to the ordinary events of life, e.g. gestures, habitual speeches, known objects and places, shared affections and passions), in its endless murmuring, its ordinary prose (certainly made of repetition, but also of insistent—and many times unnoticed—invention) has been followed (as a flow, sometimes continuum, sometimes interrupted) in its different significant manifestations.

Therefore, I cite Alves (2005, 2), as she claims that

> the practices that focus our research are not those ones observed by the researcher, but those narrated by the practitioners from the memories they have of varied curricular processes, not only in the past, but also in the present, understanding that possible future practices have to do with the limit situations encountered, consciously or not, in those processes and their overcoming, in the confrontation to many other practices.

What Is Understood by Curriculum in My Research?[11]

The discussion about curricular practices presupposes what is understood as curriculum. In the beginning, I take advantage of the etymology of the word; we find in Goodson (1995, 31) that the word "curriculum" comes from the Latin word *currere*, to run, and it refers to a course or track. The etymological implications are such that the curriculum is defined as a route to be followed or, more specifically, presented.[12]

In this sense, the author helps us to punctuate that it is impossible to separate curriculum form "content to be presented to study." According to Goodson (1995, 31),

> In this view, social context and construction [are] not problems, considering that, etymologically, the power to define reality is firmly in the hands of those who draft and define the course. The link between curriculum and prescription was, thus, forged since very long ago, and, with the passing of time, it survived and got stronger.

In fact, the author leads us to conclude that, when associating curriculum with a racetrack, we are limited to a view of curriculum that takes it as a *path*, a course to be followed, presupposing *stages, sequences, phases, and behaviors* that are to be necessarily guaranteed in the development of the proposed methodologies and contents. As observed by Pacheco (2005, 35), "the term curriculum connotes two main ideas: one of orderly sequence, another of notion of totality of studies."

Even considering that the official prescriptions constitute important elements of the curriculum, I want to problematize that view[13] with the intent to move the focus from the idea of curriculum as an official document to the idea of curriculum as understood in the knowledge, action, and power networks that are woven and shared in the school daily life and whose threads, with its knots and escaping lines (Deleuze 1995), are not limited to daily life but go beyond it, reaching out into different settings inhabited by practitioners.

Alves (2002) advocates that, when participating in the daily curricular experience, even if supposedly following pre-established curricular materials, teachers and students weave practical alternatives with the threads provided by the networks they are part of in and outside school. Thus, it can be said that there is plenty of curricula action in schools, in spite of the different homogenizing mechanisms.

> Unfortunately, many of our curricular proposals have been unable to incorporate those experiences, intending to be above the daily practices of those subjects who constitute the school. Inverting this process means to understand the curricular construction as a process in which alternatives built and performed on a daily basis will appear. (Alves 2002, 34).

Oliveira (2003, 68–69) also helps me in this argumentation in the following statement:

> The school routine appears as a privileged space of curricular production, beyond the official proposals. Specifically, as far as the teaching-learning

processes are concerned, the creative and particular ways teachers aim at their students' learning go far beyond whatever we can capture or understand through the texts that define and explain the current proposals.

Broadening Our View of Curriculum

My research shows that school practitioners produce different ways to experience-problematize the official curricula in multiple processes of use, negotiation, translation, and mimicry, which has made my study of cultural and postcolonial studies more in-depth.

From the point of view of Cultural Studies, one of the ideas that interest me most has to do with the dimension that knowledge assumes. As analyzed by Silva (1999, 136),

> An important fact about the view of curriculum inspired by the Cultural Studies refers to the fact that many ways of knowledge are, to a certain extent, leveled. Thus, there is no strict separation between the knowledge traditionally known as scholastic and the daily knowledge of the people involved in the curriculum.

Alves (2005) also helps me in this argumentation, when she discusses the relationship between curricular and cultural issues. To the author, articulating issues concerning curriculum and culture indicates the need to examine: Are there differences between what is produced as knowledge in schools and outside them, especially in the sciences? What possibilities and interinfluences are there between what is developed by the schools and what is woven in the *space/times* outside schools?

In search of answers, even if partial, to these questions, Alves (2005) refers to Lopes (1999, 222–223) when she claims that

> It is questionable to establish a hierarchy of knowledge and cultures, or to conceive a unity in the cultural plurality. Admitting the plurality of cultures is not only admitting the plurality and the discontinuity of reason, but also admitting the division of work in the society of classes. It is conceiving dominant and dominated cultures as a contradictory and ambiguous blend of repression and liberation, reproduction and resistance.

Thus, when articulating the daily knowledge to the school knowledge, Cultural Studies leads us to think about curriculum beyond the official texts, involving it in the domains of the power, action, and knowledge networks of school routine that are woven in a field of cultural significance. According to Silva (1999, 133–134),

In a way that may be even more important, cultural studies conceive culture as a contested field around struggles for social significance. Culture is a field of production of meanings in which the different social groups, situated in different positions of power, fight for the imposition of their meanings to the broader society. Culture is, in that sense, a contested field of significations.

Because it is constituted in network fields of significance, the curriculum has a dimension of process that cannot be ignored, since it is performed by people *incarnated* (Najmanovich 2001) in determined *social, historical, cultural, political,* and *economic* contexts that are interconnected and that influence each other.

In the articulation and confluence of such contexts, I am going to place the school routines as culture's in-between (Bhabha 1998) in order to problematize the theoretical-epistemological-methodological possibilities that are created in the daily networks of use, negotiation, mimicry, and translation and that express different *cultural engagements.*

According to Bhabha (1998), the terms of cultural engagement, whether antagonistic or affiliative, are produced *performatively*, and the social articulation of the difference in the perspective of the minority is a complex *negotiation* in progress. Negotiation here means movement, in permanent processing, and necessarily without the obligation to get to a consensus, an agreement, or a conciliation point. That makes me a *researcher of daily life* (Ferraço 2003) who is immersed in multiple networks that are characterized by ephemeral negotiations and permeated by ambiguities, and who is experiencing the ambivalence of possibilities that are evident in the interstices but are not fixed or immutable.

In order to complement this idea, I refer to Bhabha (1998, 248) and his proposition of thinking about culture as a *place of enunciation*:

> If culture as epistemology focuses on function and on intention, so culture as enunciation focuses on signification.... The process of enunciation is a more dialogical one that tries to track dislocations and realignments that result from cultural antagonisms and articulations—subverting the reason of the hegemonic moment and replacing it by hybrid, alternative places of cultural negotiation.

To Bhabha (1998), the passage from culture as an epistemological object to the idea of culture as a place of enunciation, promulgation, opens the possibility to other times of cultural significance, establishing a process in which practitioners of daily life routines are assumed to be *protagonists* of their *history and experience.* Thus, the different types of cultural enunciation in the use of the official curricular prescriptions woven in networks produce the *power of invention* in schools and, as a consequence, other uses and discourses of/about curriculum among the multiple *space/times* of translations, mimicry, and enunciations of culture. In fact, in arguments that are in the frontier of cultural differences, many movements of *translation* are performed.

Bhabha (1998) understands translation as a process always alienated from itself, occurring within spaces between cultures, never as a process "in itself" or "by itself," never residing in some core of cultural discourses. Developing that notion, Bhabha (1998) says that translation would be a way to imitate, not as mechanic reproduction, but in a treacherous and dislocating sense: The act of imitating an original is a way that your priority is not reinforced, because it can be simulated, reproduced, transferred, transformed, made a simulacrum, and so on—the original is never concluded or completed in itself.

> The "originary" is always open to translation.... And what this means is that cultures are only constituted in relation to an internal alterity, to its own activity of building symbols that also makes them decentralized structures—and that through this dislocation or transitivity, the possibility to articulate different, and even measureless cultural practices and priorities is open. (Bhabha 1998, 36)

In Bhabha (1998), the idea of mimicry is also emphasized, it is not reduced to mimesis, that is, imitation. On the contrary, mimicry would be a strategy that represents an ironic agreement to the tension between, on the one hand, the panoptical view of domination and demand for identity and, on the other, the back pressure, the change, the difference. In fact, for Bhabha (1998) the discourse of mimicry is produced around ambivalence. To be effective, mimicry must continuously produce its *slippage*, its *excess*, its *difference*.

> Mimicry emerges as representation of difference. It is the signal of a double articulation, a complex strategy of reformation, regulation and discipline that "captures" the Other. It is also the signal of the inappropriate, but a difference or recalcitrance that orders the strategic function of colonial power, intensifies the surveillance but also presents an immanent threat, not only to the normalized knowledge, but also to the disciplinary powers. (Bhabha 1998, 130)

To Bhabha (1998), that immanent threat would be exercised by means of *resisting*[14] *the hegemonic discourses* by using the *inner ambivalence to the colonial power* strategically. Therefore, this ambivalence would make mimicry possible, leading to the constitution of hybrid cultural subjects that would be revealed to be both a similarity and a threat.

The hybrid, for Bhabha, is not a synthesis that solves the conflict between original and essential opposites by blending them. The cultural hybrid is a superposition (and not simply a syncretism), like a bad copy, a dissimulation, a (partial) similarity that is not similitude, but a double inscription, less than one and the double (a metonymy and a metaphor). (Soares 2004, 1–2)

Considering Bhabha (1998), I shall try to deny a vision of school that thinks of itself as an imaginary museum of different cultures, as if it could appreciate and collect them by means of commemorative dates, characters, and habits, or through any other attempt at curricular prescription based on a classic multicultural perspective. Consistent with this view, Silva (1999, 130) claims that in those superficial forms represented as multicultural, the Other is "visited" from a perspective that could be called the "tourist perspective," which stimulates a superficial and voyeuristic brush with foreign cultures. A post-colonial perspective would question those superficially multicultural experiences represented by so-called "commemorative dates." Rather, a post-colonial perspective demands a multicultural curriculum that would not separate knowledge, culture and esthetics issues from power, politics, and interpretation issues. It demands, fundamentally, a decolonized curriculum.

In his discussion about the postcolonial theory for education, particularly, for curriculum, Silva (1999) observes that the postcolonial discourse avoids concepts that conceive the process of domination as a one-way street. To the author, the postcolonial criticism emphasizes, on the contrary, concepts such as hybridism, translation, and miscegenation that allow conceiving cultures as a result of a complex relationship of power in which not only the dominant but also the dominated cultures see themselves deeply modified.

> Concepts, such as those, allow us to focus not only on the processes of cultural resistance, but also on their interaction. Obviously, the final result is favorable to the power, but never clearly, never definitively, as only desirable. The hybrid carries the marks of power, but also the marks of resistance. (Silva 1999, 129–130)

The superficial forms of multiculturalism criticized by Silva (1999) are also underscored by Bhabha (Rutherford 1996), when the latter observes that multiculturalism represented an attempt to simultaneously respond and *control* the dynamic process of articulation of the *cultural difference*, administrating a consensus based on a norm that installs *cultural diversity*.

In that sense, according to Bhabha, although the idea of *cultural diversity* is always welcomed and stimulated, there is also a corresponding argument. In this author's words (Rutherford 1996, 35), "A transparent rule is constituted, a rule given by the host society or dominant culture, that says that these other cultures are good, although we must be able to locate them in our own circuits."

In fact, the schools, teachers, and students, thought as hybrid subjects in that culture's in-between, use[15] the curricula without being imprisoned all the time by *political* or *cultural, original* or *fixed* identities and threaten, in some moments, the official discourse of a unique proposal for the whole system, opening *gaps* that threaten what is imposed. Those gaps also interest me in the performance of this research. To Lefebvre (1991), the insignificant, minor decisions when freedom is experienced are the ones that escape from the state. To him (see Carvalho, Carmo Brant de, and Netto 1994, 17–18),

> If it is true that the State ignores only the insignificant, it is equally true that the political-bureaucratic edifice has cracks and gaps. On the one hand, administrative activity is dedicated to cover those gaps, foreclosing what we may call interstitial freedom. On the other hand, the individual tries to broaden those cracks and cross them.

Therefore, it is necessary to have a political perspective that is based on unequal, negotiated, and translated political identities, neither fixed nor uniform, to produce and act in the gaps. Political identities that are multiple and potentially inventive have been generating other discourses about curriculum in the daily life of the schools. In other words, in the depth of anonymity of the daily networks, the uses and translations of the schools take advantage of the different *logics, ethics,* and a*esthetics.* The knowledge-action of the school subjects is ambivalent. It slides all the time, dislocating institutional reality, thus creating other *possibilities* and simultaneously acknowledging what is given as official reference.

About the Networks Woven by Educators and Learners in the Daily Lives of the Schools[16]

In this section I quote from fragments of narratives by teachers about curriculum, their relation with the students, and some uses that they make of materials and resources in schools. Highlighted among the narrative-images of teachers about curriculum (quoting teachers) are the following:

> "I try to adapt the contents to the students' realities;" "every content is important and I do not ignore anyone, on the contrary, I try to add what

I think it lacks;" "the school curricula must be better explored;" "the curriculum must fulfill the needs of the students, and because of that, it must have clear and direct objectives;" "the curriculum must be varied, a good curriculum is the one adapted to the daily life and to the community where the student lives, it must be always updated, and the teacher taking courses in his or her area;" "the curriculum must be organized, prioritizing the integral formation of the learner to life;" "we must know the disciplines deeply, and be able to identify and conceptualize them, and also form and activate a critical thought, develop social attitudes in the learner, as well as abilities and comprehension of the facts;" "the curriculum must be updated, the teacher must respond to any curiosity of the student, especially about the news in the newspapers or whatever they watch on TV, but cannot understand;" "the curriculum must include civic and moral education and good manners, because nowadays there is no politeness in schools, and the lack of discipline is huge;" "the curriculum must include technological, religious and sexual education, with specialists in those topics, conversations about drugs, especially to pre-adolescent students."

In terms of the *narrative-images* of teachers about their relationship with students, I highlighted the following:

"There are many heterogeneous interests in the classroom;" " with different needs it is much more difficult to do good work;" "the greatest reward is when I teach them some content and they are able to remember another and establish a relationship between them both and apply them, because they show that they have learned;" " there are students who are slower to assimilate the contents and that contribute to the faulty school performance;" "it is difficult to work in a dirty environment, with few didactical resources, students who do not bring their material because they forget it at home, who are not interested and parents who do not help the children and do not even come to school to know what is going on with their children;" " I feel happy to be with the kids, the exchanging of ideas, the discoveries in learning, their tenderness;" "nowadays, there is too much aggressiveness from children, they have no limits, also, there is poor learning and interest from the students because they do not have the basic principles;" "there are excessive absences, the students do not do their work, and play all the time, there is a lot of disorganization;" "I have overcome difficult times in the classroom, nowadays I deal with problems before they form."

Note the use of resources and material—particularly, the blackboard—by teachers:

I think that the best way to teach the contents is through the blackboard. The blackboard is better for explanations. It is better for the student to record. There you can follow more calmly how each one understands the content. On the blackboard, everybody participates. Of course it is dusty. But I read in Nova Escola magazine that there are erasers that aspirate the dust. There are also some teachers who are allergic. I think they still have problems even with anti-allergic chalk, but it is a resource that is there until you erase it, as long as necessary. Then you erase it and it is ready to be used again. However, I do not like the white board, the one that you write with a felt pen. That is a bulletin board, it is not for teaching. Unless you do not write much. In the other school where I was teaching, the board was painted. Then, for the chalk writing to appear, you had to write on the wet board and wait for it to dry, so that the writing would appear. Students like to write on the board. There are many who keep asking for the leftover chalk to write on the board. There are others who make "chalk wars." There are teachers who use the board to punish the students who won't leave the room until they finish taking notes. Teachers draw four columns on the board and write with very small handwriting to be able to give students a lot of content.

Highlighted among the main reports of teachers about the use of the mimeograph are the following:

I use stencil and the mimeograph a lot in school. It is quicker, cheaper and easier to use. The problem is that the image sometimes gets smudged or weak. It is always like that, the first sheets are all smudged and the last ones cannot be read. Once I had the idea to play the game of seven errors and drew two pictures with the errors and printed them in the mimeograph. But alcohol was spilled on the sheet and it resulted in a stain right in the middle of one of the pictures, apart from other stains that happen when you press the stencil very heavily and end up making a hole in the sheet and the ink stains. When the activity was presented, I had them pay a lot of attention and find the differences between the pictures. They immediately started talking about the stain and found a lot of differences. Many more than seven. We got lost in the math. So, we cannot use the stencil for any kind of activity. There are teachers in the school who do not use the stencil when they have their nails done. They prefer to write the tests on the board instead of using stencil because it really stains. Stencil is good to give students some drawings to be colored, to be painted, things like that. My supervisor does not like it very much, because she says it inhibits the students' creativity. But it is the only way to give students the amount of activities that the Bureau demands. It is also a problem when there is no alcohol. There are teachers who have their own bottles of alcohol in their lockers. I've learned that the best way to optimize the stencil is by using the transparent sheet, not the white one. It is much more efficient and it stains less. Another thing is that the students like to smell those sheets printed with stencil because of the alcohol. Especially when we use that kind of perfumed alcohol.

And finally, note the teachers' use of overhead projectors (OHP):

In our school we could buy an overhead projector. The problem is that we must be very careful with the light bulb. We cannot touch the glass or leave it on for a long time. When we set it up for the first time it was a nightmare. The light was projected on the ceiling, to the side, but never forward. After many tries we managed to make it work. Also, there was no instruction manual. We had to take chances. What about the fear of touching the glass or burning out the light bulb before we were able to use it? There are teachers who do not get close to the overhead projector because they are afraid. They say that the light bulb will burn out only by looking at it. I don't know how to use the OHP very well in the classroom. There are times that it is difficult to center the transparency. Then, the students always say: "move it," "the other way around," "move it again," and we get dizzy moving the transparency and it is never good. Another problem is that the transparency sheets are expensive. I use cellophane or even regular plastic, the ones that are very thin. Now, the good thing about the OHP is that it is very light-weight. We can move it from room to room. It is a problem when there is no outlet in the classroom, then it is difficult. I have tried to use an extension cord, but I was worried about a student tripping on the wire and dropping the OHP. Every time a student stood up to go to the bathroom, he/she had to jump over the wire, not to kick it. It was great for the school to purchase the OHP. We project landscapes on the walls of the classrooms as scenery in theater plays. They cannot take long, or the light bulb will burn out. We also use it a lot to make Styrofoam and hard paper panels to decorate the rooms. We draw whatever we want in the transparent sheet and project it on the sheets of Styrofoam or hard paper. Then we draw it with the felt pen, cut it with a knife and paint it.

Fragments of Narrative by Students about Some Content Taught in the Classroom[17]

Why does it rain?

"It rains because God wants it and He feels like watering the plants;" "Because the sun warms the Earth and the water evaporates and makes clouds and the clouds get heavy and drop some water, that is the rain that falls;" "Because when clothes are washed, or something like that, the water is attracted to the sky;" "Because there must be water, so we can go to the beach", "Because the rain drops must water the trees of our Brazil;" "Because it is hot in Brazil and it needs rain;" "Because, if it does not rain, the wells many people get water from, will get dry;" "Because if there is no rain, there is no nature, nor life."

Why does the rain fall in drops?

"Because each drop is a micro piece of the cloud and, when it rains, each micro piece is turned into water, and that is why the drops fall;" "The drops fall because the clouds have little holes;" "When it goes to the sky, it goes like the waterfall, and it goes in drops because it is carried by the wind;" "Because it is a lot of water falling and the wind makes it fall in drops;" "Because if it falls like a waterfall, it defeats the Earth;" "Not to pull down houses and trees;" "Because it is a natural and spontaneous way, and it is the way nature decides;" "Because the clouds are crying;" "To water all the places and crops at the same time;" "Because the angels cry;" " It falls in drops because it cannot fall square-shaped, if it did, it would be weird."

Why do people have different skin colors?

"Because each one has a different hair color;" "Because of the origin and because of racism;" "Because they come from other countries;" "Because God has painted us;" " Because of the relatives of different colors;" "Because they sunbathe a lot;" "Because each one is different and they are of different races;" "Because it depends on the person someone is related to, then the children will have different colors;" "because God has made men of different colors and races;" "Otherwise everyone would be the same;" "Because of the Blacks, they stain the colors;" "Because the mother is different;" "Because, sometimes, there are people who color their skin and put on makeup;" "Because of the kind of blood;" "Because there are the Black and the White people;" "Because the Black people mixture the colors when they marry White ones."

Which questions would you like to know the answer?

"Why doesn't the child come from the man, since he's the one who has the sperm inside?" "Why do we have kids when we don't want to?" "Why are only White girls chosen to be the Queen of Spring?;" "Why do only men get horny when we have sex?;" "What's the minimum size for a penis to cause pregnancy?;" "Is it true that a small penis will not make a woman pregnant? So, why are there so many people in Japan?;" "Why are some people born handicapped?;" "Why are the sexes of males and females separate, and the transvestites are blended together?;" "Why do we lose our vision as we get older?;" "Why doesn't the sun fall?;" "How is the thread made?;" "Where do the colors of the world come from?;" "Why don't the men dry their penises after they pee?;" "Why are men's feelings different from women's feelings?;" "Why doesn't the air have color?;" "Why do we die?;" "Why is there religion?;" "Why are people racist of color or poverty?;" "Why do people say that straight hair is good and curly hair is bad and why does Black people's hair take longer to grow?" "Why are flowers colorful?;" "Why do we have hair in indecent parts of our bodies?;" "Why are there fags, dikes and prostitutes?;" "Why are our parents more liberal with the boys?;" "Why are most of the criminals Black?"

Several Problematics of Curriculum from the Narrative of the Practitioners of the School Routines

When presenting different fragments of knowledge, action, and power networks of teachers and students my intention was to try, at first, to express some of the feelings I have been experiencing in my research from a maze of situations, actions, issues, and decisions that have been lived in the routine of the researched schools.

> Developing research in daily life sounds difficult when we select the school as our field. The school in its realization is a sample of the theory of chaos. Everything happens at the same time, and frequently, not in the time it should happen. The subjects of the research insist on not being translated as research subjects and move according to their own definitions. They will not follow our script, our previsions, not even our agreements: they are absent on the exact day of our visit to the school and talk about everything, but the things we want to know. They act exactly in the way criticized by the theory that supports us. (Esteban 2003, 302)

The daily network sometimes leads us to be suspicious of any conclusion of and/or control over the research data and/or the theoretical/methodological references about curriculum proposed in the elaboration of my research. Interacting with the complexity of school daily life, diving in their networks, and sharing the *action-knowledge* of the subjects have been making me assume the endless dimension of the complexity of curriculum and, as a result, realizing the impossibility of my controlling the diversity of the curricular practice by means of categories and/or closed analysis themes, thought of as limits from where such diversity would be measured, repeated, explained, or framed.

I have increasingly assumed that any intention to frame meanings or to establish tracks of thoughts to be followed in curriculum research is all the time being violated by the movements of the daily networks of the subjects in schools, violations that produce creative meanings impossible to control. According to Bhabha (1998), the everyday conflicts, contra-dictions, antagonisms, and struggles can be as consensual as they are conflicting. They bewilder our definitions and ideas of tradition and modernity and realign our habitual frontiers between the public and the private as they challenge our normative expectations of development and progress.

Therefore, the *action-knowledge* networks of the subjects of my research have helped me infer that, although we can be idealist and utopian and believe in a promising future for education, there is no possibility of an instituted consensual projection of a common ideal prescribed to be reached with the same intensity and willingness by everybody, as it seems to be defended by the official curriculum policies. The strength of the daily life deconstructs any intention in that direction. In other words, the networks woven by the subjects from the prescriptive proposals spread out in multiple directions, weaving different interests, expectations, desires, and needs.

However, *action-knowledge* associated with the school subjects also alerts us to the needs that are set in today's agenda. That is, the utopian ideals of education move from the position of a simple projection, some-thing to be achieved in the future, to become something in the present. Or, as I have advocated, what has interested the subjects of the schools is to think about curriculum from what actually happens in schools, the way it happens, in the context it happens, and with the people who are involved in the events. In my research, I have found out that the points of interest and meaning of school routines to the subjects are, in most cases, issues of daily intensive practice, issues of the present, of today, of the everyday rou-tine. It is as if the future were anticipated everyday, to the present and to the moment of action. There is not, in this sense, any allusion to a certain immediacy, superficiality, or lack of preoccupation in relation to curricu-lum from the teachers' and their students' perspective. On the contrary, the struggle is not only for ideals fantasized in the future to become a daily battle in the school arena, those concrete conditions and contexts where the subjects act.

The fact that the subjects of my research almost always dedicate their attention and effort to the daily issues, situations, and problems of the school has demanded from me, as a researcher committed to the daily practices, a permanent analytical exercise with the intent to contextualize those issues that are locally manifested inside a broader social, political, and economical conjuncture. In that sense, I have been asking the follow-ing question: What are the possibilities of knowledge that are or are not present in schools, that are neither strict nor unique, and that are related to the conditions of material survival, to educators and students?

If we think about each subject as being inserted in different contexts of life, there is no way to ignore that their knowledge possibilities are linked to the relationships between those contexts. The life history of each student and teacher is not just a personal history, detached from the present social, economical, political, and cultural contexts. Thus, there are different possibilities of knowledge that need to be considered and broadened when we are committed to thinking about curriculum in schools.

Therefore, if we assume that each subject has different possibilities of invention and sharing of meanings that are related to different life histories, different backgrounds (Alves 1998a), different social and economical conditions, there is no way to assign the student or, particularly, the teacher responsibility for the lack of correspondence between the meanings proposed by the prescriptive documents and the meanings that are shared by the subjects.

Thus taking into consideration the relationships established between the subjects of the schools and the different contexts of life experienced, expressed, among other aspects, in their beliefs, values, desires, aesthetics, languages, and life projects, I became aware of the fact that, as far as knowledge is concerned, it is not only about defending the search for solutions to the difficulties or for an understanding of local problems, but also, above all, about broadening the possibilities of knowledge, that is, broadening the existent *action-knowledge* networks.

Therefore, fragments of *action-knowledge* networks that are woven and shared by the subjects of the school routines presented here make me think about curriculum beyond the contents and methodologies that are traditionally proposed by prescriptive documents. The diversity and complexity of the answers and argumentations of the teachers and students that I have found in my research oblige me to dive into the daily life of schools searching for clues that point to possibilities of *problematization* of the *action-knowledge* networks weaved and that consider the *individual-collective* subject incarnated as starting and arrival point.

In spite of dominating or not dominating a certain piece of information, the narrative of the teachers and students reveal a maze of logics, ideas, hypotheses, and metaphors, full of arbitrations, hopes, solidarity, religiosity, idiosyncrasies, immediacies, values, absurd ideas, utilitarianisms, and prejudices, that need to be acknowledged as threads and knots present in the weaving of the performed curricula. As subjects immersed in these complex networks that crisscross different *time/spaces* of the curricula, students and teachers invent metaphors of the issues lived in schools. In such processes of invention, there are many ways that challenge, grow distant, or deny the instituted ones that are, most of the time, considered invalid and not deserving attention.

However, despite this depreciation or disregard of the *action-knowledge* networks stipulated by the official policies, they are the existing ones that give the tone and color to what happens in schools. In that sense, we either commit to assume them as possibilities for our analyses, or we will continue, in the way it happens in some studies about curriculum, to talk about schools, students, and teachers that do not exist.

NOTES

1. I refer to the groups "Currículos, cotidianos, culturas e redes de conhecimentos" from PPGE/UFES, coordinated by me and by Professor Janete Magalhães Carvalho, and "Cotidiano escolar e currículo" from PROPEd/UERJ, coordinated by Professors Nilda Alves and Inês Barbosa de Oliveira.
2. I understand that resistance means not only opposition but also deconstruction, transgression, tactics, and tricks produced by the daily networks, in relation to what is imposed as rule, determination, or model.
3. In Kastrup (1999), it is assumed that invention is not a characteristic to be attributed to a subject in an isolated manner. In other words, invention must not be understood from the inventor's perspective, but as part of the process in the daily network relationships
4. From Bhabha (1998), I assume that the idea of hybrid is not synthesis, but juxtaposition.
5. In fact, many "contents" of the curricular proposals are juxtaposed in a segmented way through the school grades, without an effort to establish links between them. For example, in the curricular proposal of mathematics, the concepts of fractions, decimals, and percentages are taught as separate "contents" in different grades, without an attempt at articulation between them, not only in the text of the document, but also in the practices of the teachers.
6. To better understand the production of my research, I suggest the texts Carlos Eduardo Ferraço, Carmen Lúcia Vidal Perez, and Inês Barbosa Oliveira (2008) and Ferraço (2007, 2008a, 2008b, 2008c).
7. As defended by Thomson (1997, 57), "the process of remembering is one of the main ways to identify with a story we narrate. While narrating a story, we identify who we thought we were in the past, who we think we are in the present, and who we would like to be in the future."
8. The expressions used by the daily-life authors to talk about the curricula performed in daily life of schools have many more similarities than divergences.
9. I have been trying to include particularly the projects proposed to different schools by different City of Vitória offices in my analyses, with an emphasis on the education, environment, health and social work bureaus. In this sense, I presented, along with Professor Janete Magalhães Carvalho, the study "Lógicas de currículos em redes e projetos: entre equívocos e possíveis no cotidiano," in

a panel coordinated by Professor Inês Barbosa de Oliveira, in which I could explain the strength of the "projects pedagogy" evident nowadays in the Vitória's Educational System. In fact, we were able to show how the curriculum has been debased by the demand of projects for the schools to perform, emphasizing products over process: what we have been calling "Shop window pedagogy."

10. Using writing aesthetics that I learned from Professor Nilda Alves (2002), I have attempted to link certain words in order to broaden their meanings and invented many others, rupturing the marks of modern science, especially the dichotomized ways to analyze reality.

11. I do not intend to reach a final conclusion about curriculum, because, as observed by Pacheco (2005, 34), "If there is a real and unique definition of curriculum that embrace all the ideas around the structure of the educational ideas, one will admit that curriculum is defined, essentially, *by its complexity and ambiguity*. It is about a concept that *does not have a unique sense*, because it is situated *in the diversity of functions and concepts depended on the perspectives that are adopted*, which can be translated, sometimes, in some imprecision around the nature and the extent of curriculum" (italics ours).

12. According to Pacheco (2005, 29, 35), "The term curriculum was put in the dictionary for the first time in 1663, meaning a course, more specifically, a regular course of studies in a school or in a university, and that is the *meaning adopted by the educational vocabulary....* Although the origin of the term can be found, sometimes, in the classic ancient times, *the point is that school reality has always coexisted with the curricular reality*, especially when the school was institutionalized as a cultural construction with social-economic goals" (italics mine).

13. Even incorporating critiques by different authors into the fact that the sense of vision has been exalted in modern times as a privileged way to relate to "Knowledge" ("see in order to believe," "A certain perspective," "In my point of view," "In my view"...) and, consequently, making it necessary to break up with that mark in our texts and research, especially from the indication of Alves (2001), to exercise "a sense of the world," many times I betray myself and make evident the power that hegemonic discourse of the modern paradigm has had in my education.

14. It is worth recalling the idea of resistance defended previously, that is, resistance as dislocation, subversion, and tactics, and not only as frontal opposition.

15. In Certeau (1994, 39) we find that "many studies, generally remarkable, are dedicated to studying the representations or the behavior of a society. Thanks to the knowledge of those social objects, it seems possible and necessary to mark out the use that the groups or individuals make of them.... *The 'fabrication' that is to be detected is a production, it is poetry*—but hidden, because it spreads in regions that are defined and occupied by the systems of 'production' and because the always more totalitarian extension *does not let the 'consumers' have a place where they can mark what they do with the products.* To a rationalized, expansionist, as well as centralized, noisy and spectacular production, there is another *corresponding production, defined as 'consuming'*:

it is clever, dispersing at the same time it insinuates itself on all sides, silently, almost invisible, because it cannot be addressed, but in *the way they employ the imposed products from a different economic perspective*" (italics mine).

16. At this time, my intention is only to try to present some fragments of the narrative-images that I have had access to in my investigations. Thus, I do not have any intention of generalizing them to all the school routines, but only to show the reader the diversity of situations I have found in those routines.

17. At this point in my research, I spoke with grade 4 students about some of the content taught in the science classes. In that sense, initially, we started from questions that they answered in written form and then spoke with them about their answers. I made it clear that I wanted to hear what they really thought and believed about what was being asked, so that they could, after that, propose any question they would like.

REFERENCES

Alves, Nilda. 1998a. *Trajetórias e Redes na Formação de Professores*. Rio de Janeiro: DP&A.

Alves, Nilda. 1998b. *O Espaço Escolar e Suas Marcas*. Rio de Janeiro: DP&A.

Alves, Nilda. 2001. "Decifrando o Pergaminho: o Cotidiano das Escolas nas Lógicas das Redes Cotidianas." In *Pesquisa no/do Cotidiano das Escolas: Sobre Redes de Saberes*, ed. Inês Barbosa de Oliveira and Nilda Alves (pp. 13–38). Rio de Janeiro: DP&A.

Alves, Nilda. 2002. *Criar currículo no Cotidiano*. São Paulo: Cortez.

Alves, Nilda. 2005. *Artefatos Tecnológicos Relacionados à Imagem e ao som na Expressão da Cultura de Afro-Brasileiros e seu "Uso" em Processos Curriculares de Formação de professoras na Educação Superior: o caso do curso de Pedagogia da UERJ/Campus Maracanã*. Projeto incorporado ao PROCIÊNCIA.

Alves, Nilda, and Regina Leite Garcia, eds. 2002. . "A Necessidade de Orientação Coletiva nos Estudos Sobre o Cotidiano: Duas Experiências." In *A Bússola do Escrever: Desafios e Estratégias na Orientação de Teses e Dissertações*, ed. Lucídio Bianchetti and Ana Maria Netto Machado (pp. 255–296). São Paulo: Cortez.

Bhabha, Homi. 1998. *O Local da Cultura*. Belo Horizonte: UFMG. Meihy, Bom, and José Carlos Sebe. 2002. *Manual de História Oral*. São Paulo: Loyola.

Carvalho, Maria do Carmo Brant de, and José Paulo Netto. 1994. *Cotidiano*: Conhecimento e Crítica. São Paulo: Cortez.

Certeau, Michel de. 1994. *A Invenção do Cotidiano: As Artes de Fazer*. Petrópolis: Vozes.

Certeau, Michel de. 1996. *A Invenção do Cotidiano 2: Morar, Cozinhar*. Petrópolis: Vozes.

Ciavatta, Maria, and Nilda Alves, eds. 2004. *A Leitura de Imagens na Pesquisa Social: História, Comunicação e Educação*. São Paulo: Cortez.

Deleuze, Gilles. 1992. *Conversações*. Rio de Janeiro: Ed 34.

Deleuze, Gilles; Guatarri, Félix. 1995. *Mil Platôs: Capitalismo e Esquizofrenia*. Rio de Janeiro: Ed. 34.

Esteban, Maria Teresa. 2003. "Dilemas de Uma Pesquisadora com o Cotidiano." In *Método: Esquisa com o Cotidiano*, ed. Regina Leite Garcia. Rio de Janeiro: DP&A.

Feldman-Bianco, Bela, and Miriam Lifchitz Moreira Leite, eds. 1998. *Desafios da Imagem: Fotografia, Conografia e Vídeo nas Ciências Sociais*. Campinas: Papirus.

Ferraço, Carlos Eduardo. 2007. "Pesquisa com o Cotidiano. Educação & Sociedade: Revista de Ciência da Educação." *Centro de Estudos Educação e Sociedade, Campinas* 28 (98): 73–95.

Ferraço, Carlos Eduardo. 2003. "Eu, Caçador de Mim." In *Método: Pesquisa com o Cotidiano*, ed. Regina Leite Garcia (pp. 157–175). Rio de Janeiro: DP&A.

Ferraço, Carlos Eduardo. 2008a. *Cotidiano Escolar, Formação de Professores(as) e Currículo*. 2nd ed. São Paulo: Cortez.

Ferraço, Carlos Eduardo. 2008b. "Ensaio de uma Metodologia Efêmera: Ou Sobre as Várias Maneiras de se Sentir e Inventar o Cotidiano Escolar." In *Pesquisa no/ do Cotidiano das Escolas: Sobre Redes de Saberes*, ed. Inês Barbosa de Oliveira and Nilda Alves (pp. 101–117). 2nd ed. Rio de Janeiro: DP et Alii.

Ferraço, Carlos Eduardo. 2008c. "Currículos e Conhecimentos em Rede." In *O sentido da Escola*, ed. Nilda Alves and Regina Leite Garcia (pp. 101–124). 5th ed. Rio de Janeiro: DP et Alii.

Ferraço, Carlos Eduardo, Carmen Lúcia Vidal Perez, and Inês Barbosa de Oliveira, eds. 2008. *Aprendizagens Cotidianas com a Pesquisa: Novas Reflexões em Pesquisa no/do/com os Cotidianos das Escolas*. Rio de Janeiro: DP et Alii.

Ginzburg, Carlo. 1989. *Mitos, Emblemas e Sinais: Morfologia e História*. São Paulo: Companhia das Letras.

Goodson, Ivor. 1995. *Currículo: Teoria e História*. Petrópolis: Vozes.

Guimarães, César. 2006. "O Ordinário e o Extraordinário das Narrativas." In *Na Mídia, na rua: Narrativas do Cotidiano*, ed. César Guimarães and Vera. França (pp. 8–17). Belo Horizonte: Autêntica.

Kastrup, Virgínia. 1999. *A Invenção de si e do Mundo: Uma Introdução do Tempo e do Coletivo no Estudo da Cognição*. Campinas: Papirus.

Lefebvre, Henri. 1983. *Lógica formal, lógica dialética*. Rio de Janeiro: Civilização. Brasileira.

Lefebvre, Henri. 1991. *A Vida Cotidiana no Mundo Moderno*. São Paulo: Ática.

Lopes, Alice Ribeiro Casimiro. 1999. *Conhecimento Escolar: Ciência e Cotidiano*. Rio de Janeiro: Eduerj.

Maffesoli, Michel. 2007. *O Conhecimento Comum: Introdução à Sociologia Compreensiva*. Porto Alegre: Sulina.

Morin, Edgar. 1996. *Ciência com Consciência*. Rio de Janeiro: Bertrand Brasil.

Najmanovich, Denise. 2001. *O Sujeito Encarnado: Questões Para Pesquisa no/do Cotidiano*. Rio de Janeiro: DP&A.

Oliveira, Inês Barbosa de. 2008. "Estudos do Cotidiano, Educação e Emancipação Social." In *Estudos do Cotidiano & Educação*, ed. Inês Barbosa de Oliveira and Paulo Sgarbi (pp. 67–106). Belo Horizonte: Autêntica.

Oliveira, Inês Barbosa de. 2003. *Currículos Praticados: Entre a Regulação e a Emancipação*. Rio de Janeiro: DP&A.

Pacheco, José Augusto. 2005. *Escritos Curriculares*. São Paulo: Cortez.

Rutherford, Jonathan. 1996. "O Terceiro Espaço: Uma Entrevista com Homi Bhabha." *Revista do Patrimônio Histórico e Artístico Nacional* 1 (24): 34–41.

Santos, Boaventura de Sousa. 1989. *Um Discurso Sobre as Ciências*. Porto: Edições Afrontamento.

Santos, Boaventura de Sousa. 2000. *A Crítica da Razão Indolente: Contra o Desperdício da Experiência*. São Paulo: Cortez.

Santos, Boaventura de Sousa. 2004. *Conhecimento Prudente Para uma Vida Decente: Um Discurso Sobre as Ciências Revisitado*. São Paulo: Cortez.

Sgarbi, Paulo. 1999. "Era uma vez um Cotidiano que se Queria Epistemologia ou Modernos e Pós-modernos e Seus Conhecimentos." In *Documentos de Identidade: Uma Introdução às Teorias do Currículo*, ed. Inês Barbosa de Oliveira and Tomaz Tadeu da Silva. Belo Horizonte: Autêntica.

Soares, Maria da Conceição Silva. 2004. *O Local da Cultura: Considerações Acerca das Idéias de Homi Bhabha*. Mimeograph.

Chapter 6

Libraries and Identities

Alice Casimiro Lopes

(…) tracer nettement une frontière, c'est déjà la dépasser.

Gaston Bachelard (2002, 71)

Curriculum and Subjects

Brazilian curricular studies, according to a Marxist perspective, has as one of its primary themes investigations into curricular organization. According to this narrative, once the initial approaches were surpassed—which depicted that organization as a set of psychological or epistemological principles referring to the order of the contents, adapted to students' age and grade level, as means of conceiving curricular integration—politically committed (or "critical") investigations were conducted in order to understand how the organization of knowledge constituted curricular conceptions. Such organizations of knowledge, comprising the dominant forms of the school curriculum, were then problematized according to Marxist categories.

The work of Nilda Alves, Regina Leite Garcia, and Inês Barbosa Oliveira (Alves 1999; Alves and Garcia 1999; Alves and Oliveira 2005), questioning linear forms of organization of knowledge and proposing the possibility of our thinking about the curriculum as in a network, has been powerful in establishing a critical debate on the disciplinary curriculum. This debate has occurred in association with the revalorization of everyday life in schools. For these scholars, whose publications are strongly based on

Boaventura de Souza Santos, Michel de Certeau, and Humberto Maturana, knowledge is produced in everyday life in a network of subjectivities. This way of understanding is consistent with those critiques of modern science that argue that its methods of legitimation devalue everyday narrative knowledge. The focus of these curriculum studies is not, however, the specific problematization of the school subjects, as these are understood only in their relationship with the broader disciplinarity of academic knowledge based on empirical positivism and Cartesian rationality that anchor the scientific development of modern science.

Alfredo Veiga-Neto, similarly, problematizes the subject, in view of its action as a mechanism-regulating knowledge. He is developing a Foucault-based research program through criticism of a line of thinking prevailing in Brazil related to interdisciplinary studies centered on a humanist-essentialist perspective.[1] In this perspective, disciplinarity is a kind of pathology of knowledge (Japiassu 1976) resulting from the association of that knowledge with instrumentalism and correlating to the interests of capitalist development. Veiga-Neto (1994, 1995, 1996) questions that conception because it is based on a unitary vision of reason incorporating all disciplines and because it disregards those knowledge-power relations that engender disciplinary knowledge, which are not dismantled due to the will or action of a supposed conscious single subject. For him, the school has its rituals of space and time marked by the disciplinarization of knowledge. It is those rituals that maintain relationships with the processes of governmentality.

For Veiga-Neto (2008), the curriculum is an artifact of school culture centered on order, representation, and transcendence. That makes the school subject exhibit specificities with regard to scientific knowledge, insofar as the knowledge-power relations that form it are not part of a *continuum* of the knowledge. These relations depend on power strategy games that are specific to that modern institution called school. A more specific approach to the school subjects does not dwell on understanding the institutional specificities of the subjects, nor does it aim to consider the trajectories of different disciplinary communities. These approaches are developed by those who research the history of school subjects.

Studies on the history of school subjects, based on the sociohistorical understanding of the school subject, sustain the research done under the coordination of Antonio Flavio Moreira, in which Elizabeth Macedo and I have participated. Based specifically on the studies of Ivor Goodson, Thomas Popkewitz, and Stephen Ball, our research investigated how the logic of the school subject is evident in private educational institutions. In this line of research, although there is the view that disciplinarity is a regulating mechanism that operates through both schools and institutions producing scientific knowledge, the specificity of curricular organization in pedagogic work in general is the focus of these investigations.

In my investigations (Lopes 1999), I argue that disciplinary organization acts in the transformation of scientific knowledge into school knowledge. Didactic transposition, as interpreted by Chevallard (2002), is the mediation between different social practices, between scientific and everyday practices. Also in that work, based on a vigorous dialogue with epistemology, I try to understand the school subjects as specific levels of knowledge that form a school epistemology.

While developing this research program, I questioned the axiological perspectives of an analysis of school knowledge whose standard is based on definitions of scientific knowledge. To do so, I went beyond an understanding of culture still marked by epistemological categorizations of scientific and everyday knowledge, going on to point out the contextual practices of legitimizing this knowledge. Socially, the operation continues with the hierarchies and divisions of culture—erudite culture, popular culture, systematized knowledge, and commonsense knowledge. All the same, understanding through a sociohistoric viewpoint how those hierarchies are maintained becomes more fruitful. And also how interrelationships are constructed between those knowledges—how cultural hybrids are produced in multiple contexts, among them the schools.

If in an epistemological focus there is more importance given to understanding why and in what way the school subject differs from the scientific subject, in a sociohistorical approach the issues are modified[2]. It is important, for example, to understand the stability of the subject-centered curriculum as organization technology and specific school control. It is with this understanding that, in partnership with Elizabeth Macedo (2006), I maintain that the subject-centered organization does not prevent curricular integration movements but submits them to its logic.

In research on curricular organization policies (Lopes 2008), I seek to demonstrate how much the specific policy changes in disciplinary curricular organization depend on the understanding of the school subjects. To understand how school subjects prepare us—to investigate how the interrelationships between knowledges are developed in schools and what meanings the different disciplinary communities give to the curriculum—seems to me to be a more productive research program than to compare binarily one or more modalities of curriculum aligned with the subject-centered curriculum. To then question the social goals associated with curriculum (whether disciplinary, integrated, or even simultaneously disciplinary and integrated) becomes even more promising, as does any actual criticism of the subject-centered curriculum and, above all, any critique of the power relations embedded in the curricular organizations.

Bearing in mind that the trajectory of the curriculum field in Brazil, only briefly mentioned here, and my own research trajectory, I shall try to place the debate on disciplines that I am proposing in this chapter. A field in which the discussion on relationships among school subjects and modalities of integration of contents is strong can contribute to the wider debate about relationships between knowledges in the educational field. I am, therefore, engaging in a movement contrary to the trajectory described: I am separating myself from the specific discussion of the school subjects to concentrate on the interpretation of the disciplinarization of knowledge, focusing on the field of the curriculum. It is not a case of a return to epistemology. Based on discussion in the field of curriculum regarding school curricular organization itself, my investigation reflects on the disciplinarization of knowledge that constitutes us as researchers. Why are we still so disciplined in the actual organization of our research? Even in a field where critical debate on the subjects is so strong, why do we still organize our journals, congresses, development agency evaluation processes, and classes in such a disciplinary way? In my view, the answer even to these questions is not found in a general dynamic of organizing scientific knowledge, nor can it be reduced to a dichotomy between being for or against the disciplines, as the actual trajectory in the field of curriculum teaches us. I shall analyze how the discussion on disciplines reminds us of debates on politics and identities.

Subjects and Libraries

Thinking about disciplinarity, a metaphor that comes to my mind is the relationship we make between disciplines and libraries. We tend to define disciplines as groups of knowledges, as methods, and as common thinking devices capable of producing and reproducing knowledge. Accordingly, very often we consider that we can put together in our minds, and on our bookshelves, the library we form on a given discipline. It is not the library of Babel described by Borges,[3] because the intention is not to put together the universe of all possible books but to exercise the power of selection of what is considered, due to the time or to enlightened judgments, to be the best. Even if we affirm continually that the knowledges are socially constructed, many times we refer to the disciplines as if they constituted a stable repertory resulting from that selection.

It is possible to perceive a harmony among the more usual conceptions of curriculum as a selection of culture and the conception of disciplines as libraries, even among practitioners of Marxist theory. Michael Apple's

(1989) idea, for example, that what is important is to discuss *who* makes the selection of culture for the curriculum is associated with the idea of the formation of that legitimated repertory and of the existence of a certain reification of what is chosen for the school curriculum. If it is possible to discuss the subject of selection, it is also possible to stabilize the selection for which the subject—dominant class, more powerful social groups—is responsible. Both the subject that chooses and the chosen object are materialized in certain interests and have their identities fixed, in this case, according to an essence associated with social class parameters.

Even the most sophisticated construction of selective tradition in Raymond Williams (1961)—the basis of a large part of the theorizations on the topic in the field of curriculum studies in Brazil and the United States—points to the idea of a repertory of cultural assets. Williams (1961) develops that concept from his research into the history of culture. According to Williams, the culture of selective tradition is the connective tissue of culture as experienced (the culture of a certain time and place, accessible to those who experience this time and place) and culture as displayed (the recorded culture of all kinds, from art to the most varying events of everyday life). Theoretically, the culture of a certain period is always recorded, but in practice all that recording is absorbed by a selective tradition that makes us learn certain aspects of a period and not others. Both are different from the culture experienced. As Williams says, this selection generally reflects the organization of a given period as a whole, although this does not mean that the values and emphases are confirmed later on. Selective tradition then creates a general human culture, the historical recording of a given society and a rejection of considerable areas of the culture experienced. The selection process involves continual reinterpretations, because the selections are constantly made and remade. It is a process that is not carried out solely by education, although education has a preponderant role.

Williams stresses that education tends to be treated as if it were an abstraction and the curriculum as if it were an established body of knowledge to be taught and learned, whose only problematic refers to its distribution: in what quantity, in which period of time, and to what group. On the contrary, Williams maintains, the contents of education is subject to major historical variations; it expresses, consciously or unconsciously, certain basic elements of culture: it is a determined selection, a particular set of emphases and omissions. Furthermore, if this selection of contents is examined more thoroughly, decisive factors are noted that affect its distribution; the cultural choices involved in selecting contents have a core relationship with the social choices involved in its practical organization.

The certainty that omissions in the constitution of what is understood by tradition may not always be positive, that what stays, contrary to what is often thought, may not always be considered as the *best*, in any interpretation of the word, drives the desire to recuperate the loss. There is the desire to assemble a cemetery of forgotten books, as Daniel Sempere's father does in *A Sombra do Vento* [The Shadow of Wind], by Carlos Ruiz Zafón.[4] In that cemetery, a library that society abandoned is kept in the hope that it will live forever, that its books may be brought back in the future by new readers. At the same time, as the cemetery's maintenance is passed on to new generations, keeping the secrecy of the place of accumulation of that repertory of stories and abandoned knowledges is required. As in life, it is a repertory to be perpetuated by and for initiates as members of a brotherhood.

Later on, Williams again discusses the process of selective tradition, associating it with the discussions of hegemony and broadening its definition. Common sense composes hegemonic knowledge: an entire body of conceptions, meanings, and values that form everyday practices and our understanding of humanity and the world. That dominant culture, exercising its hegemony, is transmitted as the fruit of a tradition, as systematized universal knowledge. Such knowledge is understood as the dominant culture, simultaneously economic and cultural. Through processes of domination, tradition (which is always selective) is presented as a tradition without adjectives. Moreover, there is a continual remaking of the dominant culture to make it hegemonic, disguising its selective nature.

Williams' analysis is capable of deconstructing the idealized concepts of systematized knowledge and universal wisdom, as well as stressing that every systematization is, above all else, a selection marked by the most varied interests, whether of class, gender, or ethnic group. It also contributes to the understanding that hegemonic culture is not imposed on us authoritatively by easily identifiable practices and meanings of the dominant class but is incorporated ideologically as something of value, whose conflicts throughout time have been purged; hence, they are not easily deconstructed. He fails to point out, however, that culture is an ongoing production in different spaces and times. As may be concluded from Macedo (2006), a tradition that is not fixed by distinctions between culture, economics, and politics and that incorporates discussions of cultural difference has no relevance for categories such as selection of knowledges, cultural repertory, and fixed dualities of identities in the school's cultural policy. Affirmations such as "dominant knowledges and popular knowledges" presuppose fixed positions in the political struggle, as if those antagonisms might not be modified during the course of the actual struggle for the signification of culture in the curriculum.

Trained in that interpretation of culture as selection, we are avid consumers and readers and are constructing the library of our dreams, more or less successfully. That library is one that we want not only to have and read, but also to master the disciplinary body, and for which we care with the diligence of Peter Kien, in the *Auto-de-fé* [Act of Faith] by Elias Canetti.[5] But it is a library we want to transmit to those who come after us. In academia, in the process of scientific production, we want our students and collaborators to have access to that library. In schools, we hope that our children and pupils know what we believe to be basic or fundamental, and we will guarantee access to those libraries that form the collection of human knowledge.

In the different sciences, libraries specialize in different ways. The recognition of that particular library that serves us is one of the attributes by which we are valorized in academia. In the so-called physical and biological sciences,[6] that library will be composed of more periodicals than books; in the field of human and social sciences, more frequently the opposite occurs. The actual choice of the means of socialization of those texts—journal or book—is related to the way in which each disciplinary community relates to the knowledge it produces, criteria that control the legitimation of what can/should or should/not be published, and the target public. Journals are defended by physical and biological sciences because they ensure peer review of subject specialty, and because they guarantee rapid communication, particularly over the Internet. The human and social sciences tend to favor the book, assuming that, even without the usual referee mechanisms, they acquire greater public assessment, specifically because they circulate beyond the specialty, also reaching a non-academic public. But another possibility is that the book encloses what is considered *essential*.

Understanding the formation of a library, including the significance of collections, enables us to understand the formation, indeed, the self-identification, of the disciplinary subject. The essence of the library is the actual essence of the subject that is considered capable of being fixed. Even if the idea of a social construction is formulated, that construction is very often located in the past, not in the everyday practice of social relations in the present. I am what I am because I was made like that and because those are the books that I read. At the extreme limit, the existence of an order of learning these knowledges, an order of reading the texts of that library, is sequenced in the curriculum.

The ideas of minimum curriculum, curricular standards, a national curriculum, and science for all meet that expectation: to select what is supposed to guarantee access to legitimate and fundamental libraries and to project the supposed identities of disciplinary subjects. Many times criticisms are not about the process of forming collections according to centralized guidance, but about the specific collections formed and the political interests that act in their selection. Other groups seek to insert their *books* and their knowledge, projected as authoritative for everyone. They propose logical principles in an attempt to organize the knowledge into a certain order considered as best for everyone.

Lima Barreto, an early twentieth-century Brazilian writer,[7] in his tale *A Biblioteca* (The Library), describes the efforts of a father, Fausto Carregal, to maintain a library of classical books capable of teaching his son chemistry. He also describes his deep suffering when he knows that the same son will not learn to read and, therefore, will not gain the knowledge that was so carefully collected during the life of the boy's grandfather, characterizing the passing from one generation to the next a subject-specific training. In a way, we do not want to lose our forefathers because we do not want to lose ourselves.

This library is the expression of the mechanism of collecting that which, as Canclini (1998) discusses, not only organizes and ranks our symbolic assets but also differentiates among those who are capable of understanding the logic of the collection. Those who gather it are identified with that collection; they are disciplinarized. With changes in scenarios taking place even as we try to learn about our time that we call postmodern, the old libraries, like that which Fausto Carregal kept for his son, do not seem to make sense any more. Often that troubles us and makes us feel as if the ground has given way under us, a ground that we felt prevented us from falling into relativism like someone who falls from Paradise. Instead of diving into that abyss, I think it is more productive to understand why libraries are vanishing.

Decollections and Reconfigurations

Nowadays we perceive more quickly how much libraries are reconfigured by principles that constitute collections and perhaps even the actual idea of collecting. First, due to the displacement of knowledge as facts and the shifting of focus to performance, with the application of modern scientific ways of proving, science has entered into a new relationship with technology (Lyotard 1986). This is marked by the insistence on producing an increase in value and, in that way, on reintroducing resources into the scientific process for its continual development. The close connection established between performances that are prerequisite to economic development and those that are produced by introducing technological advances in scientific development provides, as Lyotard (1986) observes, the interpenetration of the organizational rules of entrepreneurial work with the dynamics of scientific research. To guarantee what is understood as scientific-technological development, the appropriation of scientific content is no longer controversial. These are understood as susceptible to being accessed in various databases, rendered easily accessible through the transformation of knowledge into information, of books from our libraries into *bytes*. The focus, then, of teaching-learning is displaced by the performances necessary for processing and accessing such databases. With the acceptance of the logic of close relationships between education, work, and scientific production, efficiency in teaching and in the other fields is seen as equivalent, measured in terms of competencies and skills for producing certain performances (López and Lopes 2010).

Second, due to hypertext links on the Internet, as well as the constant and ultrafast deterritorializations, the decollection of libraries is accelerated. Canclini (1998) considers the imminent death of collections to be symptomatic of the vanishing of classifications between high and popular culture, as well as of the fading away of the actual subject. The more fluid and more complex circulation of knowledge makes for new identities and hierarchies and thus new disciplines are formed.

In an attempt to cope with the fading away of the disciplines, we hold on to the memory as if it were itself a tangible tool and not the constant reconstruction of the past in the dynamics of remembering, forgetting, and recreating. What we remember from the past—frequently interpreted as if it were better than the present, because we remove from it the marks of oppression, limits, and difficulties that we feel in the present—becomes an expression of our desires for the future. That relationship with memory ends up influencing the theories with which we work. On occasion we escape from facing up to the present by taking refuge in the past and in its supposedly stabilized libraries.

The past, however, seems to be more capable of stabilizing our identities. As Appadurai (2001, 5) notes, the past is no longer a territory that is lived in only through memory. It is also a set of cultural scenarios that can be traversed by spatial changes—the past of one place is the present of another—so that our own past can be manipulated in such a way as to become "a normalized modality" of the present. The American cinema has been especially efficient in that regard. Films such as *Down with Love*[8] and *Far from Heaven*[9] are period recreations whose makers are proud that many of their viewers believe that they may actually have been made at the time they portray. They are presented as nostalgia films, recalls Jameson (1997), in which historic times are frozen and presented as beyond the actual historical time. Simultaneously, they project a past with experiences and issues exported from the present, thus reinventing it. To be faithful to the past, their "presentification" is produced. Those processes attribute even greater importance to imagination as a form of action and a social fact in the globalized world. How we imagine the world and how we put ourselves into action as a result of what we imagine are also modified.

This accelerated process of decollecting, deterritorializing, and reconfiguring, a characteristic of what we call global times, is then seen as a threat to our libraries and identities. The new forms of work engendered in late capitalism (Jameson 1997) are held responsible for the creation of a knowledge ever more disconnected from people and more associated with the products they generate. Education is questioned because it does not guarantee that young people are cognitively and behaviorally disciplined, as much by those who defend adaptation to the new forms of work as by those who repudiate them. If what is sought is the formation of a stable repertory, the question is whether the criteria that are formed to differentiate between the emphases and omissions are adequate. An anguish is produced due to the perception that there is much less reading of books that are increasingly being published in greater numbers. What is feared is the loss of the notion of whole, when it is perceived that, given the diversity of texts written on paper, filmed, put into circulation on the Internet, photographed, put on television screens, on palmtops and cell phones, each one has his/her own choice of what to read or not to read in the most varied tribes.

However, I endorse Appadurai's (2000) treatment of globalization as a phenomenon that is not new. Globalization, in his view, is a producer of disjunctive flows that have existed for a long time. The flows characterize the constant movements of ideas, ideologies, persons, images, and technologies that are provisionally seen as stable structures or organizations only due to the incapacity of our mechanisms for identifying and dealing with the movement. These flows, he continues, are not convergent—they do not have the same direction, speed, and origin—and maintain among them only disjunctive relationships. These flows today are only accelerated by the new technologies.

Even in the past, collections were assembled as if to produce a certain order in the chaos—perhaps before considering that the chaos was apparent and that the effort to gain knowledge was in the service of discovering the order that was concealed in that appearance. Today it is easier to accept the order as apparent. It is easier for us to see the untiring collectors, including those who organized libraries of records, such as the personage José of Saramago[10] in *Todos os nomes* [*All the Names*]—someone who is suffering from metaphysical anguish because he cannot bear that chaos rules the universe and who seeks unceasingly to overcome that anguish by defending his very well arranged collections; even to penetrate that order, they need an Ariadne's thread tied to the ankle. It is due to that interpretation that I think it is possible to understand Fausto Carregal's library as not so solidly disciplinary. Also, in it, flows of knowledge emerge, perhaps at a lower speed that does not make them so notable. Lavoisier, Camões, and Euclides are also in his library.

With the acceleration of the decollecting processes, however, even stronger is the certainty that basic books do not exist, that founding libraries are capable of identifying us once and for all, or at least for a long period of stability. That enables us to look to the past and also to question the actual interpretation of what it did or does through such well-consolidated libraries. It seems to me that the concept of hybridism can help us to understand the decollections, the deterritorializations, and the impure genres (Canclini 1998) that characterize our subjects and libraries, if we view these cultural hybrids not only as a postmodern scenario but also as a category for us to rethink the very well-grounded stability with which we construct history.

I am returning then to the topic that I proposed at the beginning of this chapter: why are we still so disciplinary? Why do we still discuss disciplines, in light of so many transdisciplinary networks of knowledge? Why do I still position myself disciplinarily, even in the preparation of this chapter? I maintain that this happens because the discipline is not in focus in its epistemological sense, as I mentioned earlier: for example, categories of knowledge, methods and common thinking mechanisms capable of producing and reproducing knowledge. Disciplines are social constructions that achieve certain ends. They gather together subjects on certain territories; they sustain and are sustained by power relationships.

It is possible to think, for example, of the specificities of Education. Perhaps from the epistemological point of view, at least from a certain epistemology, such specificities may be classifiable as disciplinary and non-disciplinary. There are defenders for each one of the two hypotheses of formation. There are also those who defend as well the distinction between what is seen as the founding disciplinary basis of education (philosophy, sociology, psychology, and anthropology) and what is seen as an applied field of that same area (curriculum, didactics, teacher training, and genre studies). There are those who presuppose that we can surmount the difficulties of organizing specificities, a presupposition based on research and its articulation with social movements.

In the perspective that I propose, however, that distinction vanishes, loses meaning. All those fields of knowledge are equally disciplinary, with their own social and historical constitutions, struggles, conflicts, and agreements. In that perspective, there is no one a priori knowledge that, once mastered, allows us to belong to a discipline. We construct this knowledge in the process of becoming disciplinary. In that process, I feel that equally interrelationships between knowledges and cultural hybrids are included. Through different political struggles we hegemonize disciplinary fields and form our identities in those struggles. Disputes in the construction of our libraries and identities are, above all, political struggles for hegemony.

Politics and Identity

A social demand is characterized by Laclau (2005) as the expectations of social groups that, if not fulfilled, can turn into demands, in defense of which varied groups unite in political struggle. Once these demands that are at stake in the political situation are defined, the groups organized around those demands are defined. For such articulation to be developed in a given concrete political struggle, such as the struggles that take place regarding the legitimation of knowledge in disciplines, identities cannot be closed in the difference. Rather, they are weakened—indeed differential demands are sacrificed—in order to guarantee articulation.

No political identities are established a priori, whether they result from positions of subjects in relation to class, gender, race, or even disciplines. There are no political identities constituted before the articulatory process, because, as Mouffe (2001) discusses, political practice in a democratic society forms political identities on precarious and always vulnerable terrain. These hybrid processes correspond to those alterations in which the differential identities "waive" their particularities on behalf of a common project.[11] However, through articulation on behalf of that project, hybridism is, simultaneously, the negation and affirmation of a particularity. In that process, a given identity (particularity) is emptied of its meaning becoming the empty signifier into which meanings of the multiple differential identities slide. In the production of articulatory practices, an equivalence is necessary—never an equality—among different elements. That equivalence is ensured by the antagonism that acts as a constitutive exterior of a chain of signification, and also by empty signifiers that are filled in differently by differential identities. Simultaneously, antagonism empties the signifiers because it opposes the logic of the difference that gives it meaning.

The process whereby a particular identity is emptied of significance, becoming an empty signifier, into which multiple meanings will slide capable of forming a discursive nodal point, is called hegemony by Laclau. To hegemonize is, therefore, to fill in the emptiness of a signifier making a nodal point in the chain of signification. As Burity (1997) discusses, hegemony is a type of political relationship and a social logic, not a place in social topography. For that reason, hegemony is always unstable, ambiguous, and plural—and hegemonic processes can be multiple. In the constitution of hegemonies we are formed as collective wills capable of defending certain demands (Laclau 2005).

A subject, therefore, cannot fix identities. Who and how the subjects are positioned as members of a disciplinary community depend on political struggle, and not on knowledge. The collective wills of those communities are formed from a hegemonic articulation in which traditions constitute the subjects of that struggle. I am referring to the sense of tradition theorized by Chantal Mouffe (1996): a historical insertion in certain discourses, including the practices and language games that constitute us as subjects. Groups of people recognize certain political forms of organizing themselves into communities according to traditions they have in common. Those traditions also condition their lifestyles and their ways of interpreting. Traditions do not fix the political struggle, as they are submitted to different interpretations during that same struggle. In that sense, tradition is not selective, as Williams insists, but becomes produced in the political struggle for the meaning of the event, for the meaning of culture itself.

Curricular traditions—ways of conceiving, for example, curricular choice and organization—provide outlines for the communities of specialists that organize themselves around certain educational demands. How different subjects fill, for example, the empty signifier "teaching quality" depends on their curricular traditions that have been constructed historically in specific communities. These disciplinary communities, whose constitution depends on disciplinary curricular organization and on an entire series of social actions associated with school subjects as sociohistorical constructions, struggle politically for certain demands and are articulated with other communities due to the possibility of fulfilling those same demands. In the articulation process, both their identities and their demands are hybridized and have their meanings reconfigured. For that reason I consider that acknowledging hybrid identities does not mean disregarding the history of those traditions, as they are themselves comprised by the negotiations that we make with traditions, the negotiations we make with our multiple libraries—of books, theories, films, theater plays, images, and memories—of everyday life, and their decollections.

That hybridism characteristic of theoretical tendencies, identified in the trajectory of curricular thinking in Brazil (Lopes and Macedo 2003) and in the United States (Pinar et al. 1996) is a good example of that process. It contributes, and greatly so, to the complexification of the understanding of curriculum, as well as to the expansion and diversification of the research topics. The maturity and fertility of the field are easily perceived in the production of articles and books as well as in theses and dissertations. Administrative-scientific studies that characterized the field until approximately the end of the 1970s are today almost nonexistent as academic production (Lopes, Macedo, and Paiva 2006). Marxist perspectives predominate, but the contributions of post-structuralist and postmodern perspectives, above all those from the 1990s, have increased. However, if in the 1990s the field was very often interpreted as a clash between Marxist and post-Marxist perspectives, today we tend to surmount that dichotomy in order to understand what research object (e.g., topic) we constructed and how we formulated our research questions.

New incoming theories—from philosophy, politics, sociology, and cultural studies—are incorporated, in order to try to articulate problems for specific research investigations. That movement, at times, makes the curriculum so ambiguous and multifaceted that it loses a certain harmony with the history of curricular thinking. Even so, I feel that this hybridism is important for opening up new perspectives. The way for the field to advance, in my view, does not go through an attempt to treat its characteristic hybridism as a loss. As Laclau (1996, 65) says, "only a conservative identity, closed on itself, could experience hybridization as a loss."

However, hybridism does not always lead to overcoming the somewhat prescriptive nature that marks curriculum research in the instrumentalist tradition. To think of curriculum research as constructing proposals for schools or as making conclusions about the guiding theoretical principles of practice is still considered a productive political-academic attitude. It is common for relationships between proposals and practices, between political guidelines and political practices, to be treated in a verticalized manner, resuming on a new basis the conception that it is up to the theory, even if a theory of post-structuralist inspiration, to illuminate the paths of practice.

It is possible that this tendency will continue, at least partly, due to the actual hybridity characteristic of the curriculum field in Brazil. The hybridism of theoretical tendencies contributes toward making the field multifaceted and productive, but it also makes for more fluid frontiers, subjecting the field to mobility among different inflows of theories. Such mobility, which I would in no way call negative or mistaken, favors the incorporation of new theories into the traditions already known, those in which we feel more comfortable. Hence, the contemporary valorization of *culture* and *discourse* becomes blended with the effort to construct an alternative emancipatory practice, often treated in the singular, or with investigations into school practices and cultures (treated as examples of what is desired for all and any practice), reintroducing the claim of homogeneity or totality.

Even so, I feel that the identification and analysis of the theoretical mobility (characterized by porous borders among theories) in which we are involved can be productive for understanding the cultural hybrids we produce. We might rethink what "libraries" can contribute to the understanding of our historical traditions, when these concepts are juxtaposed—in negotiation—with contemporary processes of signification. I think that understanding this negotiation can be powerful for what is being constructed as curriculum.

I share the analysis of Pinar (2007) regarding the importance of a disciplinary field that is willing to understand which older ideas influence the thinking of people now in the field and how that influence develops. When he refers to the complicated conversation that characterizes the debate that constitutes the field of curriculum, he stresses its both vertical and horizontal dimensions, the history of curricular thinking and national history, cultural and political events, and the institutional processes that prepare us as thinkers in a certain field, because we respond to them in a specific way, and we form the field through our discourses, including those we direct or intend to direct to the schools. In the words of Pinar (2007, xv), "without knowledge of the intellectual history of curriculum studies, without understanding of its past and present circumstances (both internal and external to the field), one cannot contribute to the field. One cannot advance its conversation and thereby complicate its understanding. Nor without such knowledge can one claim expertise."

Through the valorization of "canon" we thus return to the libraries, although without essentialisms or the effort to fix identities. The definition of what we understand by canon in a disciplinary field depends on the negotiation of meanings that our own field establishes. To conceive that there are multiple libraries capable of training us and that, politically, we reconstruct their meanings as we construct our disciplinary field seems to me a way of our conceiving our subjects in a less fixed way, and simultaneously, of our perceiving why we continue disciplinarity. But these are disciplines without certainties. However, as much as we long for it, there is no Ariadne's thread to guide us, a cemetery of forgotten books (as "truth") waiting for us somewhere, a library from the past to applaud or guarantee the universe of knowledge. We know that our children will not necessarily read the library we leave to them. There is no certainty that they will even remember us. Collections are made and remade every day, new readings and new meanings are articulated, cultural hybrids are constructed, political actions on a terrain of uncertainties are undertaken. Living with the uncertainty of the political game seems to be what remains for us. It is a game that is always played on uncertain terrain—there is no rational basis that defines a priori the political options to be chosen—and it requires us to rethink what we now understand as standard slogans such as social justice, equal rights, teaching quality, and democracy. In part, that depends on our understanding, not only in curriculum studies but across the field of education, that the construction of a library is itself political, whether it is established on the bookshelves, in files, on a computer hard drive, or just in our own imagination.

NOTES

1. I am referring to the works of Hilton Japiassu and Ivany Fazenda, developed on the basis of Gusdorf's theory. Those studies were widely disseminated in Brazil both in the criticism of university disciplines and in the school subjects. As examples, see Japiassu (1976) and Fazenda (1995).

2. Disciplinary organization in the school is expressed, for example, in a timetable that controls which teacher will teach what, to which group of students, in which physical space, and at what times. In that perspective, there is a relationship between school knowledges and scientific knowledges. Even so, knowledges as teaching civic pride or citizenship, or sex education, are submitted to the timetable and to disciplinary control. Even when there is a strong relationship with the academic and scientific knowledges, they are not the same knowledges that circulate in research centers, in universities, and in schools. In each of those institutions different communities are formed that produce knowledges to attend distinct social purposes. Those social and historical differences also produce differences in the epistemological level. Physics, for example, has its forms of organization in the scientific field sustained by the mathematical discourse. Teaching physics in a school means constructing a language that expresses many of those physical, mathematically constructed concepts. But that construction needs to be developed in a non-mathematical language or at least in other mathematics (usually, at least in Brazil, we do not work with differential and integral calculus in school mathematics, for example). In that epistemological difference, I am theorizing beyond the didactic transposition discussed by Ives Chevallard. While Chevallard limits himself to the epistemological level, I try to interpret how that *episteme* is constituted socially and historically as a discourse legitimating different knowledges.

3. Jorge Luís Borges, Argentine writer who was born in 1899 and who died in 1986. The tale *A Biblioteca de Babel* [The Library of Babel] is in his book *Ficções* (Fictions).

4. Catalan writer, born in 1964 and currently living in Los Angeles, California.

5. Elias Canetti was born in 1905, in Bulgaria, and died in 1994. He wrote in German and won the Nobel Prize for Literature in 1981.

6. It is always hard to choose the adjective to be used for classifying sciences usually considered non-social and non-human. Not all are physical and biological, not all are mathematical or technological, not even all of them are hard and

certainly much transcends the natural. To call them non-social and non-human, by exclusion, also seems to me the most incorrect denomination, insofar as we can have some consensus, it occurs because we consider that they are human beings in specific social relations that produce them. Perhaps they should be treated, as Perelman (1997) does, as sciences that are usually not used for argumentation and prioritize demonstration, but there would be much to explain in that context. In the midst of that controversy, until I choose a better option, I am opting for the denomination of physical and biological sciences, in the expectation that the different areas of knowledge that are not understood as human and social sciences may be understood as represented in that sphere.

7. Afonso Henriques de Lima Barreto, was born in 1881, in Rio de Janeiro, Brazil, and died at the age of 41 in 1922. He worked as a journalist and is considered one of the great Brazilian writers of the so-called pre-Modernist phase.

8. North-American production, 2003, directed by Peyton Reed, starring Renée Zellweger and Ewan McGregor.

9. North-American production, 2002, directed by Todd Haynes, starring Julianne Moore, Dennis Quaid, and Dennis Haysbert.

10. José Saramago, Portuguese writer and winner of the Nobel Prize for Literature in 1998, was born in 1922 in the province of Ribatejo and died at the age of 87 in 2010, in Canary Islands.

11. One of Laclau's most significant contributions lies in the relations between the particular and the universal. The universal for Laclau is an empty signifier, therefore, it does not have its own content. The horizon of the universal is always beyond, it is never the result of a chain of equivalences between distinct demands. In that sense, the universal is incommensurate with the particular, and at the same time does not exist without it, because everything universal is a particular that has universalized. For further development of this point, see Laclau (1996).

REFERENCES

Alves, Nilda. 1999. "Tecer conhecimento em rede." In *O sentido da escola*, ed. Nilda Alves and Regina Leite Garcia. Rio de Janeiro: DP&A.

Alves, Nilda, and Regina Leite Garcia. 1999. "Atravessando fronteiras e descobrindo (mais uma vez) a complexidade do mundo." In Alves, Nilda and Garcia, Regina Leite (Ed). *O sentido da escola*, ed. Rio de Janeiro: DP&A.

Alves, Nilda, and Inês Oliveira,. 2005. "Uma história da contribuição dos estudos do cotidiano escolar ao campo do currículo." In *Currículo: debates contemporâneos,* ed. Alice Casimiro Lopes and Elizabeth. Macedo (pp. 78–102). São Paulo: Cortez.

Appadurai, Arjun. 2000. "Grassroots Globalization and the Research Imagination." *Public Culture* 12 (1): 1–19.

Appadurai, Arjun. 2001. "Dislocación y diferencia en la economía Cultural Global." In *La modernidad desbordada—Dimensiones culturales de la globalización*, ed. Arjun Appadurai (pp. 41–61). Buenos Aires: FCE.

Apple, Michael W. 1989. "Currículo e poder." *Educação e Realidade* 14 (2): 47.

Bachelard, Gaston. 2002. *Études*. Paris: Vrin.

Borges, Jorge Luís. 1975. *Ficções*. São Paulo: Círculo do Livro.

Burity, Joanildo A. 1997. "Desconstrução, Hegemonia e Democracia: o Pós-Marxismo de Ernesto Laclau.". In *Política e contemporaneidade no Brasil*, Org. Marcos Aurélio Guedes de Oliveira. Recife: Edições Bagaço Ltda, p. 29–74.

Canclini, Nestor García. 1998. *Culturas híbridas—estratégias para entrar e sair da modernidade*. São Paulo: Edusp.

Canetti, Elias. 2004. *Auto-de-fé*. São Paulo: Cosac-Naify.

Chevallard, Yves. 2002. *La transposición didáctica—del saber sabio ao saber enseñado*. Buenos Aires: Aique.

Fazenda, Ivani. 1995. *Interdisciplinaridade: história, teoria e pesquisa*. Campinas: Papirus.

Jameson, Fredric. 1997. *Pós-modernismo—a lógica cultural do capitalismo tardio*. São Paulo: Ática.

Japiassu, Hilton. 1976. *Interdisciplinaridade e patologia do saber*. Rio de Janeiro: Imago.

Laclau, Ernesto. 1996. *Emancipation(s)*. London: Verso.

Laclau, Ernesto. 2005. *La razón populista*. Buenos Aires: Fondo de Cultura Económica.

Lima Barreto. 1956. "A Biblioteca." In *Histórias e sonhos* (pp. 139–150). São Paulo: Brasiliense.

Lopes, Alice Casimiro. 1999. *Conhecimento escolar: ciência e cotidiano*. Rio de Janeiro: EdUERJ.

Lopes, Alice Casimiro. 2008. *Disciplinas e integração nas políticas de currículo*. Rio de Janeiro: EdUERJ/Faperj, in press.

Lopes, Alice Casimiro and Elizabeth Macedo. 2003. "The Curriculum Field in Brazil in the 1990s." In *International Handbook of Curriculum Research*, ed. William F. Pinar (pp. 185–204). New Jersey: Lawrence Erlbaum Associates.

Lopes, Alice and Elizabeth Macedo. 2006. "An Analysis of Disciplinarity on the Organization of School Knowledge." Paper presented at the *Second World Curriculum Conference of the International Association for the Advancement of Curriculum Studies* . Tampere: Finlândia1.

Lopes, Alice Casimiro, Elizabeth Macedo, and Edil Paiva. 2006. "Mapping Researches on Curriculum in Brazil." *Journal of the American Association for the Advancement of the Curriculum* 2 (1): 1–30.

López, Silvia Braña, and Alice Casimiro Lopes. 2010. "A performatividade na política de currículo: o caso do ENEM". *Educação em Revista* 26 (1): 89–110. Available at www.scielo.br

Lyotard, Jean-Francois. 1986. *O pós-moderno*. Rio de Janeiro: José Olympio.

Macedo, Elizabeth. 2006. "Currículo como espaço-tempo de fronteira cultural." *Revista Brasileira de Educação* 11 (32): 285–296. Available at http://www.scielo.br.

Mouffe, Chantal. 2001. "Identidade democrática e política pluralista." In *Pluralismo cultural, identidade e globalização*, ed. Cândido Mendes and Luiz Eduardo Soares (pp. 410–430). Rio de Janeiro: Record.

Mouffe, Chantal. 1996. *O regresso do político*. Lisboa: Gradiva.

Perelman, Chaim. 1997. *Os âmbitos sociais da argumentação. Retóricas*. São Paulo: Martins Fontes.

Pinar, William F. 2007. *Intellectual Advancement through Disciplinarity: Verticality and Horizontality in Curriculum Studies*. Rotterdam and Taipei: Sense Publishers.

Pinar, William F., William Reynolds, Patrick Slaterry, and Peter Taubman. 1996. *Understanding Curriculum*. New York: Peter Lang.

Saramago, José. 1997. *Todos os nomes*. São Paulo: Companhia das Letras.

Veiga Neto, Alfredo. 1996. *A ordem das disciplinas*. PhD Diss., Porto Alegre, Tese de Doutorado, Universidade Federal do Rio Grande do Sul.

Veiga Neto, Alfredo. 2008. "Currículo e cotidiano escolar: novos desafios." Paper presented at the *II Congresso Internacional Diálogos sobre Diálogos*.

Veiga Neto, Alfredo José da. 1995. "Interdisciplinaridade: uma moda que está de volta?" In *Paixão de aprender II*, ed. Luiz Heron da Silva and José Clóvis de Azevedo. Petrópolis: Vozes.

Veiga Neto, Alfredo. 1994. "Disciplinaridade versus interdisciplinaridade: uma tensão produtiva." Paper presented at the *VII Encontro Nacional de Didática e Prática de Ensino*, Goiânia, UFGo.

Williams, Raymond. 1961. *The Long Revolution*. London: Harmondsworth/ Penguin Books.

Zafón, Carlos Ruiz. 2007. *A sombra do vento*. Rio de Janeiro: Objetiva.

Chapter 7

Curriculum as Enunciation

Elizabeth Macedo

The Tagus is more beautiful than the river that flows through my village
But the Tagus is not more beautiful than the river that flows through my
*   village*
Because the Tagus is not the river that flows through my village

(Pessoa 1998, 50)

The task of producing an autobiographical vision of a field of studies might lead one to compose a chronology involving a supposition of progress, whether linear or not, and an urge to narrate one's own history and that of the field. In this text, however, I intend to introduce another movement, starting with theoretical questions that I am asking myself today and thereby initiating a dialogue between these and the curriculum field inside which they were being asked. I do not feel that this movement will produce a vision of the field itself that differs entirely from what would be possible in a chronological approach—as this also would carry the mark of my present worries—although I consider that it is capable of better explaining the non-exhaustive nature of any attempt to give meaning to a field of knowledge that is formed through supposedly rational political decisions, albeit also through projections of our many fantasies.

The concept I intend to use as the guideline of my history is that of curriculum as enunciation, with which I have been working in recent years.[1] This is a formulation I began to develop due to approximation with postcolonial scholars, especially Homi Bhabha (2003), Stuart Hall (2003), and

Arjun Appadurai (2001), in order to discuss the thematics of difference. Although I may have always considered dialogue and negotiation to be fundamental both to the curriculum and to democratic practice, my first formulations had consensus as a fundamental category and rested on communicative action as expressed by Jurgen Habermas (1982): a consensus based on rational principles and guided by a discourse ethic that had the status of foundation.

Both my approximation with and my withdrawal from communicative action were decisions made in the space of a curriculum field that was being organized in Brazil after almost three decades of predominance of Tylerian rationality. In the 1980s, when Brazil was redemocratized, both this field and education in general came under the strong influence of Marxist theorists, a tendency that began to be diluted in the mid-1990s. About that time, the field shifted in the direction of post-structuralism, and culture emerged as one of the major topics, a change that, according to Pinar (2002, 114), also happened in the United States with the "explosive growth of cultural studies." It is that moment of transition between a political concept of curriculum and the centrality of culture that I want to emphasize in my situated history, because it involves sliding between knowledge and culture that is at the root of my discussions about curriculum as cultural enunciation.

The majority of curriculum theorists in Brazil who began to dedicate themselves to the thematics of culture had their roots in critical theory and, therefore, focused on the selection and distribution of school knowledge as fundamental aspects of the field. A dialogue with the English New Sociology of Education, which presented itself as a sociology of knowledge, became visible in the definition of the theory of curriculum as an attempt "to understand relationships between the processes of selection, distribution and organization and teaching of school content and the strategies of power inside the inclusive social context" (Moreira and Silva 1994, 20).[2] The centrality of knowledge in critical theory was not specific to Brazil. Reference to earlier works (Wexler 1982; Apple 1993; Giroux 1983) by influential U.S. scholars reveals the importance they had already given to the discussion about knowledge.

The fact that knowledge has been a fundamental category of critical theorization in curriculum created a zone of ambiguity when that theory began to incorporate culture. In the same text in which Antonio Flavio Moreira and Tomaz Tadeu da Silva (1994) defined curriculum in strict association with school contents, they described—as the main themes of curriculum theory—ideology, power, and culture, defining the latter sometimes as a repertory of knowledge and at other times as a practice of signification. In more recent texts (Moreira 2004, 2005, 2007) that focus on culture, Moreira emphasizes the relationship between curriculum and knowledge, very often referring more explicitly to content. Returning to the New Sociology of Education (specifically to Raymond Williams), his definition of curriculum as a selection of culture has a horizon of questions posed by the political theory of the curriculum and, although he references culture, he treats it as a group of knowledge or source of content.[3] That tension has been common in discussions of different theorists of the field. The question that Pinar (2002, 123) puts to curricularists shows that it is a tension not limited either to Brazil or to the critical theory: "when moving to cultural studies, we specialists in curriculum are asking, as we once did, which knowledge is of most worth." Although this conception of knowledge involves the act of knowing and, therefore, he does not see knowledge as a thing to be learned, it does not seem to me to be irrelevant to the use of the term and to the even more insistent return of Spencer's question "what knowledge is the most worth?" What I am maintaining is that the importance the category of knowledge seems to have in the theory of curriculum leads to culture being accepted as an epistemological object, as a repertory of meanings, and as a tradition to be passed on. In that sense, culture and knowledge become almost synonyms.

I feel there is a clear tension between knowledge and culture that perhaps could be described as a tension between culture as repertory and culture as meaning production. This is a debate that was not introduced by cultural studies. In the 1980s, the discussion about school as a space for cultural production and reproduction questioned the idea of culture as only curriculum content. In Brazil, although most of the works in that line might be more clearly associated to the field of didactics[4] or even to something that could diffusely be called ethnography of the school, the intersection between those areas and the curriculum makes it necessary to mention them. Studies centered on the idea that the school is a space for cultural production intensified in Brazil as a reaction to positivistic quantitative research methodologies and are today still much in evidence (Macedo et al. 2006a, 2006b). As in the anthropology of the time (Appadurai 2001), cultural production and reproduction were viewed in an additive perspective. In education, that binomial was presented by terms such as school culture and scholastic culture (Forquin 1993).[5] Scholastic culture, as a kind of didacticized culture that was up to the school to transmit, defined socially accumulated knowledge that would have to be socialized via curriculum. School culture, as a complementary dimension, involved the symbolic and material production that takes place in the heart of the school. With similar structures, many studies of that time created ways of dealing with the growing importance of culture without disregarding the school as a place that would have to deal essentially with the accumulated knowledge.

The same discussions about reproduction and production taking place
in the field of anthropology and appropriated by the ethnographies of
the school were also present in a more specifically curricular literature,
with concepts such as formal and experienced curriculum. Luciola Santos
(1992),[6] in a widely referenced didactic text, introduced English debate in
Brazil that extended preoccupations of the curriculum to go beyond the
socially prescribed knowledge to be mastered. Although the seminal work
of Maxine Greene (1977), in which she urges the curriculum to open up to
the experience of the subjects, has not been translated, texts influenced by
her work have circulated widely in Brazil. Long before that (in the 1930s),
the work of John Dewey, in which the philosopher maintained that curricular experiences transcended the activities planned and projected in
the written documents, had been widely disclosed in a movement called
"New School." Although they contained local specificities, all those discussions pointed to the fact that culture as production—as a practice of
meaning—was being neglected in the curriculum and its theorization. At
the end of the 1980s, it was the turn of Marxist theory to underscore the
importance of what was happening in the schools and classrooms. In the
remainder of this chapter, as a way of simplifying the discussion, I will
approach that debate on the bifuraction of the curriculum as formal and
experienced, considering them as references to the double dimension of
culture as reproduction and production. In the first, the reproduction of
culture is emphasized and the selection and distribution of knowledge gain
prominence, while, in the second, the main concern is with the production of meanings in the school. While my description of the field can be
criticized as simplistic, curriculum researchers in Brazil define their work
as curricular documents or curricular practice,[7] justifying their research by
the importance of one or the other.[8]

There is no clearer example of the importance that distinction took
on in Brazil than the debates accompanying research on everyday life.
Initially referred to in Henri Lefebvre (2008)[9] and later in Michel de
Certeau (1988, 1998), the Brazilian works (Alves 1998, 2002, 2004; Alves
and Garcia 2001; Oliveira 2005) conceived the curriculum as articulated
as social practice in order to invert the hierarchical relationship between
theory and practice. Throughout the last two decades, practice has been
seen as a web of curricular alternatives that articulate knowledge networks
(and later knowledge, wisdom, and power). The curriculum that matters
is that practiced in schools, in clear contrast to the formal documents and
policies. In that sense, even if it grants centrality to culture as production,
the reproduction dimension continues to be its opposite and gives rise to
a series of other binaries associated with that dualistic conception of culture. Initially, those binaries opposed the science that was at the base of

school knowledge (reproduction) and endorsed common sense understood as knowledge produced in everyday life, not solely but also in schools. The dialogue with postmodernity, especially with Gilles Deleuze, in the 1990s, brought the metaphors "tree" and "rhizome," and the networked curriculum was marked by a conception of rhizomatic knowledge. Knowledge continues to be a central category in the discussion of the networked curriculum, although the focus on everyday life tactics might broaden the concept itself, incorporating the impromptu (Alves 1998b) and the powerful (Alves 1996; Alves and Oliveira 1998). The polarization between modern knowledge that defines the official knowledge, on one hand, and the everyday production of the practitioners of the curriculum, on the other, emphasized the separation between reproduction and production of culture, while valorizing the experienced curricula over the formal curriculum.

I have been concerned about this additive solution that has been enabling the curriculum theory to deal with culture as the production of meanings without abandoning the idea of a shared repertory of meanings. From the point of view of a theory of the curriculum, it concerns me that the curriculum might be seen as a transnational cultural museum in which cultural assets are selected and distributed, even in extensively contested processes. However, before going on to question that solution, I think it is advisable to mention contributions more specifically derived from cultural studies for the field in Brazil, even if it is possible to perceive in them a sliding between culture and knowledge.[10] They are works in a more clearly post-structural perspective, the great majority of them depositories of Foucault's discussions. Without wanting to pinpoint a moment of origin, I am stressing the above-mentioned important article by Moreira and Silva (1994). In it, going beyond the connections with the New Sociology of the Curriculum and with the critical theory of the curriculum I mentioned, comments were made about the emergence of a linguistic turnaround—considered postmodern—and the realism of the critical theories was criticized.

While Antonio Flavio Moreira began to advocate an association between modernity and postmodernity, the work of Tomaz Tadeu da Silva underwent a strong change in the direction of post-structuralism,[11] following a tendency that had been observed in U.S. curriculum theory (Pinar et al. 1995). That decision gave centrality to the practice of meaning (Silva 1999a), altering the prevailing conception of culture as a source of content to be taught as it questioned the transparency of the language that marked the discussion of critical theory. In another more recent text that also had an impact in Brazil,[12] Silva (1999b, 136) slipped between culture and knowledge maintaining, for example, that the cultural studies "would equate, in some way, specifically school knowledge with knowledge explicitly or implicitly transmitted through a publicity advertisement." Even if the curriculum were to be defined as productive and significatory practice, as a social and power relationship, and as a practice that produces identities, school knowledge as an object of transmission would continue to dominate the horizon of curriculum studies in Brazil.

My intention with this situated but non-chronological history is to understand how the ongoing discussion on knowledge and culture came to operate in the actual definition of curriculum. Although cultural studies and the linguistic turn have been important milestones of the field in Brazil since the 1990s, the idea of prevalent culture in the field remains that of a shared repertory of meanings, which blurs the borders between knowledge and culture. I hope I have shown, however, that the reproductive dimension of culture has been distended by the idea of cultural production and, after the linguistic turn, by the notion of practices of meaning. I maintain, however, that the distension in the field of curriculum in Brazil did not dissolve the dichotomy between reproduction and production but, rather, contributed to its strengthening in binary pairs, such as formal and experienced curriculum, scholastic culture and culture of the school, scientific and everyday knowledge. I feel it is necessary to overcome these binaries. My argument is that it is not possible to escape from the dichotomies by pluralizing the possible positions. What is necessary is to deconstruct the logic in which they can be thought, which in the case of curriculum can be accomplished by characterizing it as cultural enunciation.

The Other and the Same

> (...) I'd have
> nightmares of other islands
> stretching away from mine, infinities
> of islands, islands spawning islands,
> like frogs' eggs turning into polliwogs
> of islands (...)[13]

> (Bishop 1984)

In order to consider the curriculum as a *space/time* of cultural enunciation, I shall begin by analyzing the dichotomies within which the field of curriculum has been operating. These are dichotomies also visible in U.S. and English literature, such as the concepts of formal curriculum and the experienced curriculum, and culture as reproduction and production.[14]

Dichotomies are regulated by the valorization of the latter terms (to the detriment of the former, at the same time as the former are considered powerful, as the power against which one should struggle). Studies of curriculum policies, for example, make that distinction very clear both in critiques of the top/down models and in the proposition of down/top strategies. In Brazil, these studies have been an important part of the field (especially during the 1990s when the state's intervention expanded) and clearly illustrate the binary distinctions to which I refer. Although more recently the theoretical foci of the studies on curriculum policy have been increasing, the great majority of them (Macedo et al. 2006a, 2006b) are still governed by a conception of curricular policy as something imposed by the state on a school that resists or compromises (top/down model). The formal curriculum and the notion of culture as reproduction are the focus of attention, which is mostly critical. There are also in that area studies of policy, although fewer in number, centered on curricular alternatives woven into the everyday life of schools (down/top model), emphasizing the creative dimension of everyday life but minimizing its reproduction dimension and the importance of formal curricula (Alves and Garcia 2001; Oliveira 2005). In both approaches, the distinction can be seen between production and implementation of the curriculum—pointed out by Stephen Ball (1997); Ivor Goodson (1995); Taylor et al. (1997)—that broadens the dichotomist perspectives I have been mentioning and, I maintain, needs to be surmounted.

I consider that the valorization of the experienced curriculum over the formal curriculum expresses the fantasy of perfect representation and the prevalence, in Western thought, of a realist epistemology. The written nature of the formal curriculum makes the mediation of language obvious and displaces the authorship to the point that it appears anonymous, while the experienced curriculum pretends to maintain a direct and natural relationship with the lived meaning of the written documents. Presumably this appears as a perfect representation of what occurs, while the former embeds (presumably) an oblique and artificial representation of the reality. It is as if the formal curriculum disassociates itself from the thinking that produced it, as if it were a distortion of the lived experience in relation to what was written. Something so bastardized would not produce any type of resonance, because it is the illegitimate expression of the reality, a stance assumed by some works in the down/top model used in analyses of curricular policies in Brazil. The majority of the studies, however, insist on the power of curricular documents, frequently attributing it to the imposition of the instituted state authority. Although it may be acknowledged that vertical power strategies are evident in some cases, I feel that, in most of them, the formal curriculum is not implemented as purely imposed action. Also, the hypothesis that there is no resonance from the curricular documents—that curriculum exists only in the sphere of lived experience—seems to me to be fanciful.

For the advancement of curriculum theory, I consider that it is necessary to deconstruct the binary distinctions between the formal/experienced curriculum and the reproduction/production of curriculum. Derrida's notion of supplement appears to me to be useful for overcoming such binaries in understanding curriculum. The supplement functions like a non-essential increase to something that is already complete but paradoxically lacks a certain something. For Derrida (1973), presence is always deferred; there is never anything beyond supplements and substitute meanings. Hence, what is supplemented communicates the incompleteness that it identifies in the supplement. The experienced curriculum is supplemented by the formal curriculum, but it does not incarnate the presence that supposedly would differentiate it from its opposite in a binary scheme. *Both* are marked by the absence attributed to the formal curriculum, making the distinction between them opaque. We could say the same of terms such as cultural production, which depends on the supplement reproduction. How would it be possible to think of experienced curricula or cultural production inside schools without the historical sharing of some meanings, without the iterability that characterizes the signs and that allows signification? Consequently, the experienced curriculum must share with the written curriculum a past understood as instituted outlines, as would cultural production communicate processes of reproduction. None of them is the immediate representation of an accessible or isolated reality; none is a text comprised of only outlines that preexist any lived structure of which they might be the outline. Experienced curricula, to which the fantasy of the perfect representation attributes the possibility of referring to something concrete, of invoking presence, are, like written curricula, only infinite deferrals, without origins.

If there is no immediate representation, but only deferrals, distinctions such as those we have been discussing—formal/experienced and reproduction/production—become unsustainable. From the theoretical point of view, they catch us in the trap of continuous-time—that knowledge and cultural artifacts already existing are selected and distributed by the curriculum, or that the formal curricula are produced and later implemented—in a scheme in which creation exists only as a possibility of resistance to or subversion of a past imposition. In a situation of infinite deferments, the relationships between past, present, and future meanings are complicated in a scheme whose keynote is movement, articulation, and the antagonistic negotiation of meanings.

I have referenced Jackson Pollock's *Full Fathom Five* painting as emblematic of the curriculum, because it manages, like no other painting, to express the paradox between the fluidity of the act of painting and its fixing onto the canvas as a condition of its own existence. Similarly, the curricular text interrupts the flow of meanings created by the infinite deferral, fixing them momentarily in documents. Without that fixing there would be no text or meaning, but at the same time the formal curriculum interrupts the actual fluidity of the creation. In a certain sense this is an impossible fixing and, in the same movement, also a necessity.[15] At the same time as Pollock's painting is fixed on the physical canvas, it shows a decentered image. We cannot perceive what is underneath or above, what emerges and what recedes; there are no formats. The layers interpenetrate each other with outlines that seem to go in one direction and right away get lost and open in other multiple possibilities. While our eye follows one of the paths that the outlines show, we construct a different work for each observer and at each moment. We are the ones who are centering the image, in a perception always partial to that presented to us. When we center it, we lose the fluidity of meanings, but without doing so it would not be possible for us to see it. Not all can be seen because the decentered image has no limits; it always opens over the closings that are being constructed.

For me, it is the image of the text as successive deferrals that opens like "islands spawning islands," but whose meanings are stanched for the construction of a specific text. The textual structure, like Pollock's painting, is decentered, without limits, but is momentarily fixed around a provisional center every time that we produce a text and, then, open it to new possibilities of meanings. I think that Derrida's concept of *brisure* (1973) enables us to grasp what I am saying. Curricular texts, like open structures, are overdetermined and, thus, are closed, constructing modes of address that in themselves have a provisional quality.

Besides the concept of *brisure*, the notion of hybridism has enabled me to treat curricular texts—always permeated by the *différance* of the writing—like ambivalent enunciations because they are marked by the separation between the enunciated "I" and the "I" of the enunciation. That separation creates what Bhabha (2003, 68) calls a third space, "which although in itself is not representable, constitutes the discursive conditions of the enunciation which guarantee that the meaning and the symbols of the culture do not have unity or primordial fixity and that even the same signs may be appropriated, translated, rehistoricized and read in another way." Accordingly, every enunciation articulates, for Bhabha, a pedagogic dimension—associated with the tradition and outlines of shared meanings—and another performative that becomes a project by virtue of negating what has been already said. The iterability of the pedagogic dimension works as a return to the past and as a "strategy of representation of the authority," while the *différance* of the language ensures that curricular meaning is not transparent or mimetic (Bhabha 2003, 65).

That ambivalence of the enunciation is, for Bhabha (2003), what opens up the possibility of multiple significations and explains the impossibility of total control of what Ball (1997, 23) calls, following Foucault, a discursive dimension of the curriculum: "a moving picture that articulates and constrains the possibilities and probabilities of interpretation and enunciation." In the postcolonial literature of Bhabha (2003) and Hall (2003), control creates hybridity, because absolute saturation of the senses is impossible. Domination is always partial because it requires recognition of the other that it wants to dominate and is, thereby, checking the completeness that would accomplish it (Bhabha 2003). In that sense, every enunciation is hybrid because it is obliged to negotiate, antagonistically and incompletely, its meanings with the other.

In the perspective of the enunciation, dichotomies such as those that have marked the field of curriculum in Brazil no longer make sense, because creation dialogues with tradition, spawning a zone of ambivalence, an in-between space that is neither past nor future, but both and neither of them. The curricular texts produced in that frontier zone, whether they are written or experienced, are constructions of meanings that hybridize the impossible objects we create through a would-be differentiation. Accumulated knowledge (what is worth teaching), experienced cultures, future expectations—all of them also hybrid in their own constitution—are named as controllable entities that can or cannot cohabit. Meanwhile, in that frontier zone, all that exists are cultural flows we are stanching in a process that creates pitfalls that make it hard for the theoretical work to grasp the complexity of the social and the human (Appadurai 2001).

In Brazil there have been severe criticisms of perspectives that point to the formation of networks of meanings and to the recreation of meanings, accusing them of neglecting the power involved in the negotiations. On the contrary, I feel that those perspectives have enabled us to work in a more consistent way with the prevalence of power and, more specifically, with the agency of the subjects. They enable us to glimpse a way out of the cruel struggle against an absolute power that Marxist theories associated with the new sociology of the curriculum have pressed upon us. That way out involves the politicization of the processes of meaning that are at the root of concepts such as *brisure* and hybridity and point to a theory of hegemony on a post-Marxist basis such as that defended by E. Laclau and C. Mouffe (Laclau 1998, 2000; Laclau and Mouffe 2001; Mouffe 2003). Concluding on the basis of dialogue with those authors, I feel it is possible to bring to curriculum policy studies the dimension of agency in the enunciation that escapes from the easy relativism that some readings by authors such as Derrida (1973, 1998) and Bhabha (2003) at times imply. That is, the discursive theory of hegemony has been my tool for understanding the overdeterminations of the curricular texts and the discursive closings they allow, so as to respond to the criticisms of relativism.

About Relativism

> ora se nos mostra o agora:
> este agora.
> a g o r a.
> mas ele já deixou de o ser
> quando nos é posto à mostra:
> e vemos que o agora
> está exatamente nisto:
> enquanto ele é
> de já não mais ser.
>
> (Campos 1997, 68–69)[16]

Every cultural enunciation, as an act of signification, depends on difference but cannot be formed only by that difference. The excess of meanings that a differential and displaced structure produces constitutes the discursive as a condition and the impossibility of particular enunciations. These are possible only when the logic of the difference, of infinite deferral, is permeated by a logic of equivalence that allows the provisional closing of the structure and sharing of meanings. For Laclau and Mouffe (2001), that closing is always produced by hegemonic articulations capable of contingently positioning certain *significants* as nodal points along a chain of equivalences that passes through the differential logic of the system maintaining with it a relationship of undecidability. That equivalence is possible only when a radical difference is present, a constitutive exterior that makes the differential elements of the system begin to share something in common, which is the radical difference in relation to that exterior. With that, the structure is provisionally centered and closed and a determined text may be produced.

The challenge, therefore, is to understand how hegemonic articulations occur that enable certain *significants* to act as nodal points and thereby close the system provisionally. In an attempt to reach that objective Laclau (1998) deviates from Derrida (1998) and repositions the subject as locus of decisions that occur in the undecidable space of the displaced structure. The discussion about hegemony is, therefore, also a discussion about the constitution of the subject and of its agency. It is agreed that in a displaced structure there are no previous subject positions (identities), but only contingent identifications invented by the decision that closes the system. The subject does not exist before the decision is made but is constituted by its own incorporation into the symbolic order when deciding how to constitute itself as subjectivity. As the decision occurs in a concrete context, in a partially destructured structure, there are limits within which the decision will occur, which does away with totally relativist perspectives. For Derrida (1998, 164), however, the decision makes it impossible beforehand to constitute a subject, seeing that the identification process is also "a disidentification process, because if the decision is identification, it destroys itself."

In spite of Derrida's provocations to Laclau's notion of subject and agency, I feel that formulation is useful for discussing the curriculum as text. It allows the articulation of a discursive perspective, which introduces contingency and temporariness to the old social preoccupations with agency and the subject. In this, I think that I am admitting to my Enlightenment heritage—which enables me to think of education as the symbolic self-construction of the subject—but aware of Laclau's critique of a free and conscious subject. That impossibility does not eliminate the necessity of either. In his words (Laclau 1998, 118), it "puts back the agent of the decision in the aporetic situation of having to act as if it were a subject, without being equipped with the means of a totally constituted subjectivity." Along the same lines, Slavoj Zizek (2004) considers that every subject looks for a *significant* that might express subjectivity within the symbolic order, but in an act of signification that will never be entirely possible.[17] Acts of signification are thereby attempts to fill in a constitutive deficiency, so as to establish the plenitude of identity already denied to it.

The political struggle for signification may be viewed as an attempt by certain groups to set themselves up as subjects when presenting their demands to the hegemonic order. If it were not for an antagonistic rupture, those demands would proliferate infinitely, resulting in a relativism that would make negotiation impossible. It is, therefore, that rupture that approximates the different demands, articulating them around a nodal point that closes the text temporarily and permits the sharing of meanings. Some positions are more effective than others in compensating for the displacement of the structure, in that they manage to inscribe the different demands. However, that effectiveness occurs at the expense of its literal content in favor of a metaphorical dimension that condenses meanings and significations. By and large, the more emptied of meaning, the more effective a significant is as a nodal point, temporarily closing the signification system.

Although there is nothing essential that transforms a *significant* into a nodal point of the structure, that process can occur only through articulations (hegemonic) that transform these into a provisional center of the structure and fill it partially with certain *significants*. In that sense, an emerging hegemonic discourse articulates a group of subject positions and appears as a universal object, which incarnates the absent completeness. It appears as the political alternative for the representational system, functioning as a myth that wants to fill in the displaced structure and stanch the deferral of meanings. That process is, however, partial and contingent, as the system goes on being confronted by non-symbolizable events. For Laclau (2000, 192), hegemonic relations "are not [,therefore,] self-regulated totalities, but precarious articulations that are always threatened by a constitutive exterior."

I consider that this approach allows us to perceive the hegemonic articulations that occur in curricula to the effect of fixing their meaning and addressing the subjects. Fixing meaning through modes of address can never be completed because, as cultural enunciations, curricula are always already ambivalent texts that articulate past meanings and recreate them constantly through potentially infinite deferrals of meaning. To illustrate how I have worked with that insight, I reference a discussion that has recently arisen in the field of curriculum studies in Brazil and is related to those preoccupations that led me to define the curriculum as enunciation.

The shift in the field of curriculum studies toward culture was not an isolated fact related only to Brazil's social panorama. It coincided with the greater consolidation of democracy in Brazil and with the political gains won by cultural minorities, especially the Black movement. The racial equality law, the recognition of Zumbi dos Palmares as a national hero, the implementation of affirmative action in the universities and in the public sector, and the inclusion of History of Africa in school curricula are among the examples of those gains. Although headlined by the Black movement, political demands for recognition of cultural difference expanded, in effect guaranteeing more space in the national scenario for many, in clear contrast to a constitutive exterior that was antagonistic to each. In the field of curriculum, these demands resulted in conferring the position of prominence that cultural difference (for some, the concept of diversity) has assumed in recent decades. That is, at the same time as the theory of curriculum began to consider culture among its main preoccupations, an articulation of minority demands could be perceived as gaining representation in curricular texts. Earlier universalist conceptions of curricular knowledge ceded textbook space and the demands of the difference entered into the interstitial spaces of curriculum.

Obviously, the movement for representing the demands of minority groups is much more complex than this, as it involved contradictory articulation processes. I will not explore this complexity here. My point here is that the connection between curricular theory and knowledge—based on the conception of culture as a repository of meanings that approximates culture and knowledge—constructs curricular texts whose principal modes of address imply the formation of universal subjects. In Brazil, where economic and social inequalities are flagrant, the idea that public policies should be a tool of social equality has irresistible appeal and, for decades, has been animating discourses of a universalist nature. More recently, with the expansion of demands in the name of difference, provoking moments of antagonistic rupture in the social fabric, discourses emphasizing difference have coalesced into an idea of quality of education. This idea hybridizes different discourses into a defense of accumulated knowledges as the objective of the school curriculum. That articulation involves discourses based on critical and post-critical presuppositions, as well as on conservative discourses associated with the market, which is made possible by the pressure of the minority groups' demands for inclusion.

Understanding the antagonism between claims for difference and for universality—it also acts as an element that constitutes both—is a prerequisite for understanding the sliding between culture and knowledge that I referenced in my situated history. In recent curricular proposals, questions of cultural difference, although present, are inserted in a text whose principal mode of address is a universal subject (Macedo 2008a; 2008b) who requires socially accumulated knowledge. In the Brazilian field of curriculum studies that I have been discussing throughout this chapter, the defense of "formal contents of the scientific subjects" (Moreira 2005, 40) surfaced again at a moment when cultural studies and post-critical theories seemed to accord centrality to culture. The sliding I mentioned in the first part of this chapter becomes more problematical, in that it can express a contraposition to the space that has been won by viewpoints affirming difference. Deconstructing this sliding, therefore, has become an urgent task for curriculum studies in Brazil. That is why I have proposed understanding curriculum as cultural enunciation, a conception that challenges the authority of culture as referential knowledge and allows it to emerge as a heuristic resource for discussing difference (Appadurai 2001, 28).

NOTES

1. This concept has been used in my research and in theses of students I have supervised (Destro 2004; Frangella 2006; Oliveira 2006; Agostinho 2007).

2. This is one of the texts most used when defining curriculum in Brazil. Consulting Google Scholar (on November 25, 2007), for example, shows 110 quotations when the great majority of texts on curriculum in Brazil are only 10–20 quotations. A study of theses and dissertations defended in Brazil between 1996 and 2002 (Macedo et al. 2006a, 2006b) also indicates that this work is one of the most quoted. In addition to being the writers of that important text, its authors are two of the most distinguished scholars of curriculum in Brazil; their work has great influence in configuring the field.

3. In a 2004 text, entitled "Por que ter medo dos conteúdos?" [Why Be Afraid of Contents?], Moreira maintains that it is necessary "to go back to considering more strictly the processes of selecting, organizing and systematizing the knowledges to be taught and learned in the school" (Moreira 2005, 38).

4. In Brazil, the fields of curriculum and didactics coexist in universities as a product of the dual influence of the French and American models of training. Although no epistemological difference between the fields is clear, I feel they are clearly delimited as symbolic fields in the words of Bourdieu (Lopes and Macedo 2003).

5. Forquin's book was translated in 1993 and had great influence in the ensuing years. It is not a work that was focused on the field of curriculum, but it impacted studies about the school. Especially relevant was the use of the concepts of culture of the school and scholastic culture, disseminated, among others, by Candau (2001), one of the leading names in didactics in Brazil with a scholarly production that could be easily understood as belonging to the field of curriculum. This researcher has had an extensive career in training researchers in the area, meaning that her influence has been extended by the works of her former students.

6. It is interesting to note that the author is a researcher who works in the field of didactics of the curriculum.

7. In a recent study of theses and dissertations on the curriculum of elementary education (Macedo et al. 2006a, 2006b), that distinction is clearly explained in a large number of studies.

8. That is also not a particularity of persons studying in Brazil. Goodson (1995), Young and Whitty (1977), and Young (2000) have defended an integrated approach to the written and experienced dimensions of the curriculum. That defense, however, is much more focused on pointing out the importance of the study of the formal dimension, or of the conflicts involved in its definition, as a reply to what they have defined as "an absolute belief in the properties of transformation of the world that the curriculum as practice might have" (Goodson 1995, 21).

9. Especially relevant in this work was the pioneer work of Nilda Alves, very often in partnership with Regina Leite Garcia, both regarding the theoretical formulation as in the preparation of curriculum for training teachers focusing on the idea of everyday life. Because it is a group that is very closely knit and active in postgraduate-level training, the penetration of that concept in the field of curriculum in Brazil has been very extensive in recent decades.

10. The field of curriculum in Brazil has attracted a relatively small number of scholars, which facilitates the circulation of the concepts I am mentioning. Often Brazilian scholars fail to cite their local written production at international meetings and seminars. Moreover, Brazilian scholarly publication is controlled by very few groups. Somehow these conditions create an atmosphere in which hybrid perspectives circulate.

11. The influence of T. T. Silva on Brazilian curricular theory was very great in the 1990s due to his strong presence in the publishing market, translating many American texts and producing others based on post-structural literature. He worked also as a supervisor of many researchers in the field. A study of the dissertations defended between 1996 and 2002, however, showed that few studies took that theoretical path. Although Silva as well as Moreira and Alves were the principal Brazilian references in those studies, seldom were his studies or post-structural passages quoted (Macedo et al. 2006b).

12. This book, called *Documentos de Identidade* (Identity Documents), is a didactic work summarizing in a few pages the most common curriculum discourses. There is no doubt that it is one of the most quoted texts in the field in Brazil (in Google Scholar, on November 25, 2007, there were 210 quotations) and it is part of an enormous set of bibliographies of graduate and graduate courses on curriculum. In some way it seems to be inspired by the work of Pinar et al. (1995) without, however, being exhaustive or containing the level of detailing of this book. In that sense, it offers simplified, even hazardous, reading of the field because it leads the reader to understand that the theorizations that it calls post-critical are better or more up-to-date than the critical perspectives and these are more than the traditional viewpoints.

13. Although the poem begins with a foundational event ("A new volcano has erupted"), this serves as a contraposition to the author's island, which is "still un-discovered, un-renamable," used as an allusion to the nightmare, because she knows "that I had to live on each and every one, eventually, for ages." Movement and fixation create an ambiguous zone.

14. When establishing these two sides, I do not maintain that knowledge, formal curriculum and culture as reproduction or culture, experienced curriculum and culture as production are the same thing. I just feel that they are related as binaries.

15. The impossibility and the necessity I mention are not separable, so that we could suppose that in spite of the impossibility, something might be necessary and an attempt should be made to surmount the impossibility on account of the necessity.

16. So, the now shows itself, this now, now; but it no longer is what it was when it appears to us and we see that the now is exactly in this, while it is no longer being.

17. The symbolic order is upset by the Lacanian reality that introduces a disturbance that resists totalization and, thus, displaces structure. That radical negativity will prevent the subject from finding a *significant* through which it can express itself. That makes symbolic action fail and produces the deficiency that is, precisely, the subject. In that sense, the significant and the

subject will be the deficiency, retroactive effects of the impossibility of its own representation (Torfing 1999).

REFERENCES

Agostinho, Patrícia. 2007. "Produção Curricular e Formação Docente no Cotidiano Escolar: Práticas de Enunciação e Atividade Política." Dissertação de Mestrado, Faculdade de Educação. Rio de Janeiro: UERJ.

Alves, Nilda, and Regina Leite Garcia. 2001. O Sentido da Escola. Rio de Janeiro: DP & A.

Alves, Nilda. 2004. "Imagens de Professoras e Redes Cotidianas de Conhecimento." Educar em Revista 1 (24): 19–36.

Alves, Nilda. 2002. "Sobre Redes de Conhecimentos e Currículos em Redes." Revista de Educação AEC 1 (122): 94–107.

Appadurai, Arjun. 2001. La Modernidad Desbordada: Dimensiones Culturales de la Globalizacion. Buenos Aires: Fondo de Cultura Econômica.

Apple, Michael. 1993. Official Knowledge. New York: Routledge.

Ball, Stephen. 1997. Educational Reform: A Critical and Post-Structural Approach. Buckingham: Open University Press.

Bhabha, Homi. 2003. O Local de Cultura. Belo Horizonte: UFMG.

Bishop, Elizabeth. 1984. The Complete Poems: 1927–1979. New York: Farrar, Strauss & Giroux.

Campos, Humberto de. 1997. O Arco-Iris Branco. Rio de Janeiro: Imago.

Candau, Vera Maria. 2001. "Cotidiano Escolar e Cultura(s): Encontros e Desencontros". In Reinventar a Escola, ed. V.M. Candau. Petrópolis: Vozes.

Certeau, Michel de. 1988. Practice of Everyday Life. Berkeley: University of California Press.

Certeau, Michel de. 1998. Practice of Everyday Life II. Minneapolis: University of Minnesota Press.

Derrida, Jacques. 1973. Gramatologia. São Paulo: Perspectiva.

Derrida, Jacques. 1998. "Notas Sobre Desconstrucción y Pragmatismo." In Desconstrucción y Pragmatismo, ed. Chantal Mouffe. Buenos Aires: Paidós.

Destro, Denise. 2004. A Política Curricular em Educação Física do Município de Juiz de Fora-MG: Hibridismo Entre o Contexto da Produção do Texto Político e o Contexto da Prática. Master's Dissertation, Faculdade de Educação. Rio de Janeiro: UERJ.

Forquin, Jean Claude. 1993. Escola e Cultura. Porto Alegre: Artes Médicas.

Frangella, Rita de Cássia. 2006. Na Procura de um Curso: Currículo- Formação de Professores- Educação Infantil Identidades em (Des)construção. PhD Dissertation, Faculdade de Educação. Rio de Janeiro: UERJ.

Giroux, Henry. 1983. Theory and Resistance in Education: A Pedagogy for the Opposition. South Hadley: Bergin & Garvey.

Goodson, Ivor. 1995. Currículo: Teoria e História. Petrópolis: Vozes.

Greene, Maxine. 1977. "Curriculum and Consciousness." In *Curriculum and Evaluation,* ed. A. Bellack and H. Kliebard Bekerley: McCutchan Publishing Corporation.

Habermas, Jurgen. 1982. *The Theory of Communicative Action.* London: Beacon Press.

Hall, Stuart. 2003. *Da Diáspora: Identidades e Mediações Culturais.* Belo Horizonte: UFMG.

Laclau, Ernesto, and Chantal Mouffe. 2001. *Hegemony and Socialist Strategy.* London: Verso.

Laclau, Ernesto. 1998. "Desconstrucción, Pragmatismo, Hegemonía." In *Desconstrucción y Pragmatismo,* ed. C. Mouffe. Buenos Aires: Paidós.

Laclau, Ernesto. 2000. *Nuevas Reflexiones Sobre la Revolución de Nuestro Tiempo.* Buenos Aires: Nueva Visión.

Lefebvre, Henri. 2008. *Critique of Everyday Life.* London, New York: Verso.

Lopes, Alice Casimiro, and Elizabeth Macedo. 2003. "The Field of Curriculum in Brazil in the 1990's." In *International Handbook of Curriculum Research,* ed. William F. Pinar. Mahwah, NJ: Lawrence Erlbaum.

Lopes, Alice Casimiro, Elizabeth Macedo, and Edil Paiva. 2006. "Mapping Researches on Curriculum in Brazil." *Journal of the American Association for the Advancement of the Curriculum* 2 (1): 1–30.

Macedo, Elizabeth, Alice Casimiro Lopes, Edil Paiva, Inês Oliveira, and Rita de Cássia Frangellaet Rosanne Dias. 2006b. *Currículo da Educação Básica.* Brasília: MEC/ INEP.

Macedo, Elizabeth. 2008. *"Hegemonic Struggles around the Notion of Quality: The Case of Multi Education (Brazil)."* Paper presented at the American Educational Research Association Annual Conference, New York,

Macedo, Elizabeth. (In Press). "Como a Diferença Passa do Centro à Margem nos Currículos: O Exemplo dos PCN." *Educação e Sociedade* 28.

Moreira, Antonio Flavio. 2004. "Articulando Desenvolvimento, Conhecimento Escolar e Cultura: Um Desafio Para o Currículo." *Cadernos de Educação* 13 (22): 55–74.

Moreira, Antonio Flavio. 2005. "Por que Ter Medo Dos Conteúdos?" In *Políticas e Práticas Curriculares: Impasses, Tendências e Perspectivas,* ed. M. Z. da C. Pereira and A. P. Moura (pp. 11–42). João Pessoa: Idéia.

Moreira, Antonio Flavio. 2007. "A Importância do Conhecimento Escolar em Propostas Curriculares Alternativas." *Educação em Revista* 45: 265–290.

Moreira, Antonio Flávio B and Tomaz Tadeu Silva. 1994. "Sociologia e Teoria Crítica do Currículo: Uma Introdução." In *Currículo, Cultura e Sociedade,* ed. A. F. B. Moreira and T. T. da Silva. São Paulo: Cortez.

Mouffe, Chantal. 2003. *La Paradoxa Democrática.* Barcelona: Gedisa.

Oliveira, Inês Barbosa. 2005. *Currículos Praticados: Entre a Regulação e a Emancipação.* Rio de Janeiro: DP&A

Oliveira, Ozerina Victor. 2006. *O Processo de Produção da Poítica de Currículo em Ribeirão Cascalheira-MT (1969–2000): Diferentes Atores, Contextos e Arenas de Uma Luta Cultural.* Tese de Doutorado. Faculdade de Educação. Rio de Janeiro: UERJ.

Pessoa, Fernando. 1998. *Fernando Pessoa & Co.: Selected Poems* ed. and trans. (from Portuguese) Richard Zenith. New York: Grove Press.

Pinar, William. 2002. "'I Am a Man': The Queer Politics of Race." *Cultural Studies—Critical Methodologies* 2(1):113–130.

Pinar, William, William Reynolds., Patrick Slattery, and Peter Taubman. 1995. *Understanding Curriculum*. New York: Peter Lang.

Santos, Luciola. 1992. "O Discurso Pedagógico: Relação Conteúdo-Forma." *Teoria e Educação* 5: 81–90.

Silva, Tomaz Tadeu. 1999a. *O Currículo Como Fetiche*. Belo Horizonte: Autêntica.

Silva, Tomaz Tadeu. 1999b. *Documentos de identidade: Uma Introdução às Teorias do Currículo*. Belo Horizonte: Autêntica.

Taylor, Sandra, Fazal Rizvi, Bob Lingard, and Miriam Henry. 1997. *Educational Policy and the Politics of Change*. London/New York: Routledge.

Torfing, Jacob. 1999. *New Theories of Discourse: Laclau, Mouffe and Zizek*. Oxford: Blackwell.

Wexler, Peter. 1982. "Structure, Text and Subject: A Critical Sociology of a School Knowledge." In *Cultural and Economic Reproduction in Education*, ed. M. Apple. London: Routledge & Hegan Paul.

Young, Michael, and Geoffrey, Whitty. 1977. *Society, State and Schooling*. Lewes: Falmer Press.

Young, Michael. 2000 *O Currículo do Futuro*. Campinas: Papirus.

Zizek, Slavoj. 2004. *Conversations with Zizek*. Malden, MA: Blackwell.

Chapter 8

The Primacy of the Quotidian
Inês Barbosa de Oliveira

Since 1999, I have been working on research projects focused on the quotidian, those various practices that the different school subjects develop through interaction with each other, as well as the emancipating sense that these practices can assume in different circumstances. I have observed and tried to understand events in the schools' quotidian life that are invisible to quantitative traditional methods of research and its search for models and explanations of particular practices through generalizations of plural *makings/knowings*, movements, or mobilities and differences found in schools. In this sense, we consider the various different elements entangled in the production of the curriculum practiced by the schools' subjects.

In the current project, centered on the possibilities of understanding these dimensions that were until now invisible, we work to unveil those possibilities registered in school reality that are as yet not realized as the school's contribution to the democratization of the society. Keeping in constant dialogue with other studies in the curriculum field, in which subjects are related to the contemporary social context and its influence over policies and curricular practices (Apple 1995; Goodson 1995; Macedo and Moreira 2002; Macedo and Lopes 2002; Macedo 2006), we labor to understand the specificities of the school quotidian in the weaving of the various practiced curricula, which are always subject to multiple influences (Ball 2001, 2006).

So, while writing this chapter, I gave a little attention to matters such as globalization and the political, social, and economic issues that are linked to it (however they influence politics and curricular practices). In my research I am mainly trying to deepen the theoretical reflection on the quotidian and the methodological development of the research in/of/ with the quotidian. My other aspiration is to increase understanding of the schools' daily dynamics, woven by the ways of action, interaction, and thinking about the subjects involved in this quotidian, leveraging what we identify as emancipating *doing/knowing* from researchers, teachers, and students in the schools. Through Boaventura de Sousa Santos' *Sociology of Absence* (2004), we intend, in the current research, to think concretely about the emancipating potential registered in quotidian curricular practices. In addition, after *Sociology of Emergence*, we think of the possibilities to diffuse these practices on a larger scale, as an inspiration for others to develop their own. That we want because we understand each reality as a product of the singularities and specificities of subjects and circumstances that define them, constituting potential for social emancipation not only separately, but also as a set that respects a logic different from the structures in which they are inscribed but possibly follows another logic, one of the practices (Certeau 1994). I perceive the pedagogic practices as a way to social emancipation, even knowing that they are specific and singular as woven into different contexts and circumstances by different subjects, stakeholders in possible formal education contributions to society's democratization. The quotidian's common aspects and shapes, once properly understood, can lead to the recognition of concrete elements that favor the school's democratization, thereby contributing to actual processes of social emancipation.

This idea draws from *Sociology of Emergence*, which discerns in reality what it might be but is not yet, a concept that Santos (2000) borrows from Ernst Bloch. By working with this idea, I believe, we are contributing to the recognition of practices that enact the emancipating educative project and, subsequently, of its possible contribution to the establishment of social democracy (Oliveira 1999, 2002, 2005).

Drawing on what we have already learned from working *in/of/with* quotidian research regarding the impossibility of framing the reality in fixed and constant cages, under penalty of loss of its complexity and wealth, the idea of the current project is to formulate possible reading contexts,[1] starting with premises of the sociology of absence. We will search for everything that was not crushed by the hegemonic logic of the Western modernity and its reductionistic means of conceiving and investigating social reality. We conduct that search by studying those dynamic and constant processes of dialogue among knowing, doing, values, and cultures (Ginzburg 1989).

Practiced Curricula in Times of Globalization

Thinking about curricular subjects today demands bringing to the scene the idea that globalization has real effects on the local curriculum. Moreover, we must appreciate that globalization's influence surpasses questions limited to the production of inequalities and exclusions. Therefore, it is necessary to think about them as practices that are not only political but also curricular, as we understand from Macedo (2006) that these instances cannot be separated but are rendered complementary through reciprocal influences.

Also after Santos (1999), we appreciate that the processes of globalization in their contemporaneousness must be treated in the plural and not in the singular. Santos considers that referring to the complex processes of "globalization" in the singular can lead to misunderstanding the multiple economical-political processes underlying the term. Distinguishing among societal movements of opposition to "hegemonic globalization," Santos points out that we should focus on different concrete realities as well as on "in-progress" political and social struggles, which oppose dominant ways of understanding that function to support further globalization. Santos argues that mere opposition to globalization, in the name of human rights or the importance of the "local," does not help in either understanding globalization or ameliorating the problems caused by it. Processes and struggles for other forms of globalization are in progress and need to be studied, understood, and evaluated.

We can, then, think in terms of hegemonic globalization as well as initiatives against it. Santos points to two processes: globalized localism and located globalism. Their analysis helps us to understand why these two processes contribute to structural inequalities. Through globalized localisms—which make us believe in the universality of particular products, values, and habits of a specific people, country, or culture—non-hegemonic cultures are kept subordinated. Parallel to these processes of globalized localisms, there are located globalisms, which designate the different ways established society's practices and logics penetrate different localities and impact local populations. Inequalities tend to increase when an established logic tends to become hegemonic. Many local cultures have origins, habits, and traditions dissonant to what is imposed on them by capitalism and its forms of work organization, as is the case, for example, with some tribes and rural populations.

Defended by educators from all over the world, compulsory education is problematic for rural populations, nomadic people, and oral cultures.

Without attacking the idea of making schooling universal, I consider it fundamental to raise the question of cultural imposition that underlies this idea. In particular, I question universal schooling's aggression against certain cultures as it maintains the predominance of Christian-Jewish traditions. What seems fundamental to contemporary curriculum studies, derived from notions of globalized localisms and located globalisms, is the creation of inequalities and exclusions that the hegemonic Western capitalist world is producing by the ways it manages cultural differences. Understanding globalization demands a deeper understanding about not only the question of equality but also of difference (Santos 1999).

The universal human right to dignity, to the minimum standards of consumption that are prerequisite to a fulfilled life, cannot coincide with dominant social models or with the values and cultural habits produced by capitalism with its emphasis on individualism and competitiveness. Different modes of existence must remain legitimate in the daily life of threatened populations. This requires us to abandon any opposition between equality and difference and regard them instead as complementary (Oliveira 1999). Equality is opposed to inequality but not to difference. Difference requires *sameness*,[2] they are complementary but not identical, as Santos (1999, 65) explains:

> We have the right to be the same whenever difference discriminates against us; we have a right to be different whenever equality takes away our distinctive characteristics.

Santos (1999, 72–73) also identifies anti-hegemonic concepts of globalization—the cosmopolitism and the common heritage of the humanity.

> [Cosmopolitanism] treats the transnational organization of the resistance of states-nations, regions, classes or social groups victimized by unequal exchanges....This resistance consists in turning unequal exchanges into exchanges for shared authority, and is translated into struggles against exclusion, subordinate inclusion, dependence, disintegration, downgrade.

Regarding humanity's common heritage, Santos describes it as a set of transnational struggles for the protection (thereby removing from the market) of those resources, entities, products, and environments considered essential for the life and dignity of the human species and whose sustainability can be guaranteed over the scale of the planet (75). Such struggles refer to resources that, by nature, will be managed by a logic other than exchange (76). In other words,

> Humanity's common inheritance constitutes anti-hegemonic globalization as we fight for the transformation of unequal exchanges through exchanges

of shared authority. This transformation will take place in all constellations of practices, but it will assume different profiles in each one of them.

The idea of humanity's common inheritance may sound somehow naive. Surely we do not live on the same planet as George W. Bush.[3] Nor is physical reality sufficient to think about the social. Physically we all live on the same planet, but the effects of the damages caused by modern capitalism will be felt in a differentiated way, the dominated ones will suffer the worst effects.

Can cosmopolitanism be the only option for thinking globally? Let's fight cosmopolitanism! We need to discover where our struggle is located: is it in the home of the Colombian Indian, with the May Square grandmothers, or the Palestinian refugee? The struggle is against processes of subordinated inclusion, of exclusion, against the dominant. It is inevitably unique. The struggle seems different because sites are differentiated. In other words, each circumstance enables possible particular action on behalf of the excluded, the subordinated, and the dependent. How do I twist unequal exchanges into shared authority relations in each localized circumstance? This is the challenge of daily political action, and it is this challenge that we face in the creation of the curriculum, its limits and its possibilities of contributing to emancipation. Even in different circumstances, through differentiated actions and reflections, we are always immersed in struggles for the transformation of unequal exchange into shared authority, including internal struggles against our prejudices, authoritarianism, and other anti-democratic tendencies. In each quotidian reality, the struggle occurs in different forms, and the better we understand our reality, the better are the chances of entering in this struggle effectively. That explains the need for plunging into the quotidian. It is not possible to fight in the abstract field! To transform unequal exchange relations into shared authority relations requires knowing the particularities of circumstance. Not because one is going to fight against that circumstance, as the object is the social, after José Machado Pais (2003). The idea of humanity's common heritage makes sense only if thought of as a battle for recognition of a truly common heritage. At present, however, there is no such thing as a common heritage!

The School's Social Function

In times of globalization, the common curriculum is reduced to schooling success, measured by global systems of evaluation, national and international. These assessment systems assure greater control over daily curricular practices while allowing workers to adapt to new circumstances, for example, these new exigencies occurring with dizzying speed in advanced capitalism. Presumably, it is necessary to establish rigid mechanisms of control over production in a way that guarantees the productivity necessary to the competitiveness of the products in the globalized market. The market assumes the central role; it becomes the primary regulatory principle, as it co-opts state-owned policies, social relations, groups, and political controversies.

In developing a common curriculum—in fashion especially in the 1990s and nowadays less discussed—national and international systems of evaluation play key roles. They define what and when to teach and reduce the freedom of schools and local systems so that it amounts to adaptation to evaluated realities, thereby defining their programs and teaching methodologies. Therefore, through control of the legitimating mechanisms of differentiated learning processes, educational policies accommodate international capitalism. Michael W. Apple (1995) points out that control over the teacher's decision making is one of the main objectives of politicians' proposals for a national curriculum in the United States. Miguel Arroyo (in Oliveira 2000) affirms that while defining what enters the curriculum (for example, which knowledge is necessary for students), the system defines what cannot enter, making obvious the arbitrariness of the political process of choice: the curriculum entering the school comes from the dominant power; staying outside is knowledge associated with subordinated cultures.[4]

But hegemonic speech, which defends, formulates, and legitimizes these policies, is not only about "choice." Controversies occur, referenced in curriculum scholarship, in various governmental spheres, as well as in everyday practices in schools, in the sometimes silent translation of official curriculum according to local interests, values, and means. This translation of the ways different social, individual, and collective subjects dialogically encounter rules that are apparently imposed on them (Certeau 1994) is not only political but also, and especially, epistemological.

The *Enlightenment* served as a portal to modernity, enabling many to assume that formal/scientific knowledge is always superior to that of the quotidian. Michel de Certeau (1994) believes that this formalist/scientific view is illusory. As I affirmed before, I think that quotidian practices, besides their organizing, quantifying, and classifying aspects, enacted through repetition, scheme, and structure, are developed in circumstances, opportunities that define directions for using whatever is provided by others. The tools, the discursive forms, and the general rules of being in the society are, in the quotidian, marked by the operations they undergo.

Our studies are devoted to discovering, finding out, and unveiling the educative policies/practices that are not included in the official models and point to different directions, starting from practices not incorporated in the rules of the hegemonic globalization. Let us perceive those anti-hegemonic educative politics and practices developed by the *apprentices of the quotidian*, their knowledge and epistemological sources, ways of doing, and needs and possibilities. We labor to perceive in these practices conceptions of knowledge and ways of creation that question modern *epistemicides* (Santos 1995) and the ethnocentrism associated with them. In the quotidian we find conceptions of apprenticeship not characterized by hierarchies. These findings provide the conceptual foundations of the work I am developing now and to which I dedicate myself from this point onward.

Theoretic-Epistemological-Methodological Foundations

The theoretical-epistemological-methodological foundations of my research derive from a long and deepened reflection about the thought of Boaventura de Sousa Santos.[5] I have articulated these in previous texts (Oliveira 2003, 2005, 2006). My epistemological research that is reflected in this chapter is related specifically to the appropriation of Santos' sociologies of *absence* and *emergence*, not only as theoretical-epistemological references, but also as methodological possibilities. Santos presents these concepts as *proceedings*, for example, reflection and action in the world. Therefore, while recognizing the political and epistemological validity of these sociologies, I incorporate his epistemological analyses into methodological principles of concrete thought so they become integral to my research's methodology. While studying *Sociology of Absence*, I immediately recognized myself as a presence in the research I had been conducting regarding those emancipative practices undertaken by teachers[6] in schools. Santos (2004, 778) affirms,

> Firstly, social experience is much wider and varied than what the western science or philosophy knows and considers important. Secondly, this social wealth is being wasted.... Thirdly,... to fight the waste of social experience, it is not enough to propose another type of social science. It is even more necessary to propose a different model of rationality.

This new model would be a cosmopolitan rationality based on three "proceedings": the two sociologies of *absence* and *emergence*, and the work of *translation that enables the former to become the latter.* The study of these proceedings contributes to education reflection and to the development of emancipating pedagogic alternatives; it is my privileged theoretical and methodological reference. Santos (2004, 779) says,

> Understanding of the world exceeds Western understandings of the world..., the form as it creates and legitimizes social power has very much to do with conceptions of temporality..., the most fundamental characteristic of the western rationality is in fact, on one side, to contract the present and, on the other, to expand the future.

Subverting this logic, and in line with the research in/of/with the quotidian, it is necessary to expand the present by creating conditions for such *inexhaustible social experience* in our schools. The *sociology of absence* becomes a method that enables the discovery of modes of existence rendered invisible by modern scientism, which tries to exclude everything that does not fit its model of rationality. Once the immensity of current experience of contemporaneousness becomes known, understanding them in their diversity requires the constitution of an intelligibility marked by mutuality, a rationality that, for example, neither diminishes specific identities nor makes them irreconcilable. In other words, it is imperative, when studying everyday experience, to do so with ways of approaching it that enable us to understand its convergence, differences, and specificities.

The relationship between present and future shifts Santos calls "a sociology of the emergence." The notion that we can transform practice from abstract objectives is naive: the future resides within the present. In other words, only what is registered in contemporary reality will be able to give rise to what will be the future. It is necessary to amplify the present, not only in the recognition of the already existent potentialities but also in the weaving of new ones.

The primacy of the whole over its constituents, inferred in the idea of totality with which Boaventura says *metonymic reason* is obsessed, leads to the conviction that there is only one logic that governs behaviors, not only for the whole but also for every one of its parts, resulting in the homogenization of the whole and its parts. The existence of each part is understood only in respect to the whole in which it is included; every variation is understood as a peculiarity. Metonymic reason finds, in the dichotomy, the most finished form of totality because it combines symmetry with hierarchy. Opposed to what metonymic reason considers, Boaventura understands that the whole is less and not more than the sum of its parts given that one of them is turned into a reference. Due to that move, all the dichotomies approved by metonymic reason contain a hierarchy. The importance of underlining this fact has two main consequences.

> Firstly, since nothing exists out of the totality that is or deserves to be intelligible, metonymic reason affirms itself an exhaustive, exclusive and complete reason.... Metonymic reason is not able to accept that understanding the world is much more than Western understanding of the world. Secondly, for metonymic reason none of the parts can be thought outside its relationship with the totality.... Therefore, it is not admissible for any of the parts to have its own life beyond what is given by the dichotomous relation and much less could it be another totality. (Santos 2004, 782–783)

In other words, *metonymic reason* suffers a limited understanding not only of the world but also of itself.[7] The absence of arguments, imposed coercively through non-recognition and silence, renders experience invisible. Moreover, the dizziness of rapid change becomes a sensation of stagnation. This paradox would be associated with the reduction of the present time as a "fleeting instant between what already is not anymore and what still is not. With this, what is considered contemporary is an extremely reduced part of what is simultaneous" (Santos 2004, 785). Much of what exists as experience, in its contemporaneousness, stops being considered as existent and is thought of as past or, simply, irrelevant.

To recover this lost experience, to amplify the world through the amplification of the present requires criticism of metonymic reason. Only through a new space/time will it be possible to identify and to valorize the inexhaustible wealth of the world. In other words, to identify and to valorize non-hegemonic ways of thinking and being in the world—besides what *metonymic reason* realizes and accepts as existent—requires new, methodologically revised inquiries. To understand what, in fact, happens in the quotidian educative processes—*that which escapes from pedagogic models and official curricular proposals*—it is necessary to consider ignored forms of knowing/doing/thinking/feeling/being in the world. It means studying everything that the school has neglected in the name of "scientific" knowledge and Western white bourgeois culture. In order to understand everything that is present (if ignored) in school and in student life, we study what otherwise gets discarded as diversion or mistakes—for example, events that do not fit in what metonymic reason requires—thereby recovering real life. To do so, it is necessary to make visible practices and events through methodological procedures in/of/with quotidian research. By identifying those associated with the *sociology of absence* and, next, recognizing the emancipating potential in them, we employ these to multiply emancipating experiences in a sociology of emergence.

To transform absences into presences, thereby recognizing emancipating innovations in daily curricular practices, has been the point of our studies in/of/with quotidian. We aspire to achieve a more systematized understanding of these various modes of existence, aiming to formulate the means of their multiplication, thereby amplifying social and epistemo-logical diversity in the present world, with an eye toward social emancipation and democratization in the future. In this sense, the different logics of nonexistence identified by Santos and the different ecologies that become visible from its overcoming enable us to restructure what would otherwise be raw data.

Santos distinguishes five different logics—or ways to produce nonex-istence—linked to rational monoculture. He understands that "there is production of non-existence whenever a given entity is disqualified and made invisible, unintelligible or disposable in an irreversible way" (Santos 2004, 787). Nonexistence is produced as social forms, disqualified seg-ments of homogeneous totalities, for example, excluding totalities. Each of these logics has to be disproved in order to overcome them. In other words, for each production of nonexistence, the *sociology of absence* reveals the diversity and multiplicity of social practices. This idea of multiplicity and of non-destructive relationships between agents who compose them is underlined by the concept of ecology that constitutes, in Santos' view, the overcoming of the monocultural logic of *metonymic reason* and allows the constitution of horizontal relationships between the different possibilities of each cultural field and, in so doing, discloses the absentees.

> Common to all these ecologies is the idea that the reality cannot be reduced to what exists. It is an amplified version of realism, which includes the absent realities that have been silenced. (Santos 2004, 793)

The "sociologist of absence," through an "archaeology of the invisible exis-tences," tries to surpass, with the establishment of different ecologies, each form of nonexistence and monoculture associated with it. In order to do so, he needs to adopt proceedings that, being specific to each nonexistence, have in common the possibility of making viable what metonymic reason murdered. Such proceedings point to two major associations with edu-cation. The first one is methodological: bringing to presence everything metonymic reason made invisible, especially everything that comprises the schools' quotidian existence. Our intention is to legitimate the *knowing-making* that characterizes educative spaces, highlighting its contribution to social emancipation. Not only in the sense of the educative process itself, but also in the widest sense of possibly contributing to democratizing social transformation, the methodological adoption of the proceedings of the *sociology of absence* seems to be not only relevant but also fundamental.

Second, the epistemological aspects of this sociology focus our atten-tion on the school content itself, including the structures of the school and the hierarchies they follow and define, the demands associated with them, as well as the values disseminated through its supposed scientificality. The multiplication of practices is made visible through the practice of this "archaeology of the invisible existences" in different school universes and takes us to the criticism of *proleptic reason*. The conception of future based on linear time emanating from monoculture—its presupposition that the history has one unique sense and that progress is without limits—underscores the indolence of this reason, of supposing that the future is already known, enabling us not to think of it. Santos points out,

> The sociology of emergence consists in substituting the emptiness of future according to linear time (an emptiness that is everything as much as it is nothing at all) for a future that is plural and concrete, simultaneously utopian and with realistic possibilities, which are built in the present through activities of care. (Santos 2004, 794)

I believe that the great contribution of Santos' *Sociology of Emergence* is in the idea that the future can be built from the plural and concrete possibilities discernible in the present, through individual and/or collective action. Contrary to determinism, we appreciate that the future of social subjects resides in their own actions; we have to conceive *education as action of social subjects who are able and interested in "taking care" so that the future can be better than the present.* When the future stops being an automatic, predictable continuation of the present and starts to be a product of real social actions, the future shrinks in the same proportion as it risks being thought of as the product of only those actions that built it. In other words, to use an old metaphor, what was not planted will not be harvested. Instead of thinking of a dichotomy and a static pair—the present that is and the future that is not yet—we start to think processually in the creation of the possibilities to come.

The possibilities and capabilities characterizing the quotidian are going to reconstruct everything they touch, questioning and modifying the preceding determinations. However, this reconstruction does not mean the introduction of any certainty of something that does not yet exist. The uncertainty of possibility rests on the fact that the conditions that can make it concrete are only partially known and, moreover, exist only partially. In other words, potential is recognizable but not its result. Therefore, the contraction of the future gives us the responsibility to not waste these ever-changing and concrete opportunities.

> In each moment, there is a limited horizon of possibilities and therefore it is important not to waste the unique opportunity of a specific transformation offered by the present: *carpe diem*. (Santos 2004, 794)

The future to be built, then, can come into being only from the enactment of possibilities inscribed in the present and, therefore, cannot and should not be understood as infinity. Because the present contains more than one possibility, it includes a multiplicity of invisible but existent realities that can potentially be made concrete, but that have not materialized as yet.

Therefore, the complementarity between these two proceedings— the *sociologies of absence* and *emergence*—becomes discernible. "The more experiences are made available in the world today," Santos (2004, 799) tells us, "the more experiences are possible in the future." In other words, while the first set of proceedings devotes itself to unveiling already exis-tent experiences of what is already in existence, the second is dedicated to studying possible experiences, *what is yet to come.* Both allow us to rethink the future, relating it to the concrete elements of its many realities, radical-izing expectations suited to real possibilities, surpassing the idealism of the falsely infinite and those universalizing expectations postulated by moder-nity. Let us abandon fantasies of a great future that will never come as we search for a more nuanced relation between experience and expectation. Santos reminds us that "the Not Yet, far from being an empty and infinite future, is a concrete future, always uncertain and in danger.... The *sociol-ogy of emergence* is the investigation of the alternatives that fit the horizon of the concrete possibilities" (Santos 2004, 796).

The sociology of emergence enables us to analyze the possibilities of future that are already inscribed in actual practices, experiences, or forms of school knowledge, identifying *signs, tracks, and traces of future possi-bilities in everything that exists.* Our research is, yes, an investigation of absences, but not only about what is not viable as in the *sociology of absence,* but also the absence of "a future possibility still to be identified and [of] a capacity still not fully formed" (2004, 796). In the *sociology of absence,* the multiplication and diversification of the available experiences are achieved by the different ecologies—of knowledge, of the moment, of differences, of scales, and of productions. In the *sociology of emergence,* the symbolic amplification of the traces and signs of possible futures achieves the multi-plication and diversification of the possible experiences.

Conclusion

Working on our "data" with the premise of Ginzburg's indices para-digm (1989), we can affirm that the first results of this inquiry disclose emancipating possibilities, demonstrating transgressing static charac-teristics (de Certeau 1994), for example, rupturing those monocultures that dominate capitalist Western society, referenced in the *Sociology of Absence*. I acknowledge the influence of associated studies, especially those of Ball, Lopes, and Macedo, on our work, as well as on associated studies of subordinated social groups (Blacks, natives, homosexuals, women; see Gomes 2008; Santomé 2008). As dialogue enhances understanding and thereby the field of curriculum studies, it is crucial, even when not done in an explicit way, to weave ideas and perceptions into the fabric of one's own scholarly production.

Finally, I have to say that although this analysis is focused on the school quotidian, no social analysis of a particular context can ever be considered to be finished. Understanding the school quotidian does not produce final truths but functions to open doors to multiple approaches that acknowledge a differentiated school reality. I seek no consensus, a concept that reflects the monolithic conformity of social life against which I am fighting, but, instead, provisional, circumstantial agreements. While not professing to any religion and without any pretension to be resolving the problems of the world, I offer this conclusion because I believe that participating in the processes that may contribute to a better life for more people, and in more *space/times*, is worthwhile. To fight for further happiness makes me happier, without engendering frustration for not having succeeded.

In abdicating the impossible dream of accomplishing everything, we learn to be happy with the success of what we can do, always motivated by strong desires that I see as sources of possible pleasure and happiness. The ambiguity, precariousness, and limitations of our research results are part of quotidian existence, and of all existences, never the ideal, always merely the best possible.

NOTES

1. This expression is inspired by the notion of knowledge net weaving and its provisional and dynamic characteristics.
2. Sameness in this instance refers to a complete equality between all the people, in spite of individual differences.
3. The name is symbolic and represents the most politically and economically powerful people in the world.
4. It is important to acknowledge current educational politics in Brazil, which recently made the teaching of African and Indian cultures in every school in the country mandatory.
5. In 2002, I spent the year in an internship with Professor Boaventura.
6. I develop the idea that one of the specificities *in/of/with* the quotidian is the intimacy between epistemologic reflection and political intentionality. I insist

upon a tripartite relationship among the political, the epistemological, and the methodological (Oliveira 2005).

7. Edgar Morin already announced a similar idea in his *Ciência com consciência* [Science with Conscience] (1995) when he referred to modern science's incapacity to think about itself.

REFERENCES

Apple, Michael W. 1995. "A Política do Conhecimento Oficial: Faz Sentido a Idéia de um Currículo Nacional?" In Moreira *Currículo, Cultura e Sociedade*, ed. A. F. Barbosa and T. T. da Silva. São Paulo: Cortez.

Ball, Stephen J. 2001. "Diretrizes Políticas Globais e Relações Políticas Locais em Educação." Currículo sem *Fronteiras* 1 (2): 99–116. Available online at: http://www.curriculosemfronteiras.org

Ball, Stephen J. 2006. "Sociologia das Políticas Educacionais e Pesquisa Crítico-Social: Uma Revisão Pessoal das Políticas Educacionais e da Pesquisa em Política Educacional." *Currículo sem Fronteiras* 6 (2): 10–32. Available online at: http://www.curriculosemfronteiras.org.

Certeau, Michel de. 1994. *A Invenção do Cotidiano: As Artes de Fazer*. Petrópolis/RJ: Vozes.

Ginzburg, Carlo. 1989. *Mitos, Emblemas e Sinais: Morfologia e História*. São Paulo: Cia das Letras.

Gomes, Nilma Lino. 2008. "Descolonizar os Currículos:um Desafio Para as Pesquisas que Articulem a Diversidade Etnico-Racial e Formação de Professores." In *XIV ENDIPE—Encontro Nacional de Didática e Prática de Ensino*, EdiPUCRS 3: 516–529. Trajetórias e Processos de Ensinar e Aprender: Sujeitos, Currículos e Cultura. Porto Alegre.

Goodson, Ivor. 1995. *Currículo: Teoria e História*. Petrópolis/RJ: Vozes.

Macedo, Elizabeth. 2006. "Currículo: Política, Cultura e Poder." *Currículo sem Fronteiras* 6 (2): 98–113. Available online at:. http://www.curriculosemfronteiras.org.

Macedo, Elizabeth, and A. Lopes. 2002. *Currículo: Debates Contemporâneos*. São Paulo: Cortez.

Macedo, Elizabeth, and A. F. Moreira. 2002. *Currículo, Práticas Pedagógicas e Identidades*. Porto: Porto Editora.

Morin, Edgar. 1995. *Ciência com Consciência*. Rio de Janeiro: Bertrand Brasil.

Oliveira, Inês Barbosa de. 2006. *Boaventura e a Educação*. Belo Horizonte: Autêntica.

Oliveira, Inês B. 2005. Aprendendo a ler/ver/ouvir as Práticas das Professoras no Cotidiano Escolar. CD_Rom do *III Seminário Internacional "Redes de Conhecimentos e a Tecnologia: Textos, Imagens e Sons."* Rio de Janeiro: Realizado na UERJ.

Oliveira, Inês B. 2003. *Currículos Praticados: Entre a Regulação e a Emancipação.* Rio de Janeiro: DP&A.

Oliveira, Inês B. 2002. "Aprendizagens Culturais Cotidianas, Cidadania e Educação." In *Redes Culturais, Diversidade e Educação,* ed. B. I. Oliveira and P. Sgarbi.Rio de Janeiro: DP&A.

Oliveira, Inês B. 2000. "Alternativas Curriculares e Cotidiano Escolar." In *Cultura, Linguagem e Subjetividade no Ensinar e Aprender,* ed. V. M. Candau (pp. 21–37). Rio de Janeiro: DP&A.

Oliveira, Inês B. 1999. "Sobre a Democracia." In *A Democracia no Cotidiano da Escola,* Inês B. Oliveira. Rio de Janeiro: DP&A.

Pais, José Machado. 2003. *Vida Cotidiana: Enigmas e Revelações.* São Paulo: Cortez.

Santomé, Jujo Torres. 2008. *Multiculturalismo Anti-racista.* Porto: Profedições.

Santos, Boaventura de Sousa. 1995. *Pela Mão de Alice. O Social e o Político na Pós-modernidade.* São Paulo: Cortez.

Santos, Boaventura de Sousa. 1999. "A Construção Multicultural da Igualdade e da Diferença." *Cadernos do CES:* (1–63).

Santos, Boaventura de Sousa. 2000. *A Crítica da Razão Indolente. Contra o Desperdício da Experiência.* São Paulo: Cortez.

Santos, Boaventura de Sousa. 2004. "Por Uma Sociologia das Ausências e Uma Sociologia das Emergências." In *Conhecimento Prudente para Uma Vida Decente,* Boaventura de Sousa Santos (pp. 777–823). São Paulo: Cortez.

Chapter 9

The Exchanges

William F. Pinar

What we remember from the past…becomes the expression of our desires for the future.

(*see Lopes' chapter 6 in this volume*)

In this chapter I summarize the exchanges[1] between the participating Brazilian scholars and the international panel members. The summary is organized according to the Brazilian scholar to whom questions were posed and the order in which his or her chapter appears in the collection. My commentary concludes this chapter and comprises the next.

The Exchanges

Antonio Carlos Amorim

Addressing his Brazilian colleagues as well as the members of the international panel, Amorim suggests that "instead of forgetting the categories of experience and the subjectivities, the field of curriculum in Brazil works with them and seeks other possibilities." He invokes the concept of "pellicles" to denote those "membranes" of "experience" and "subjectivity" that enable visibility. He links these to the "plurality of boundaries" between cultures in Brazil, accentuating the visibility of "hybridization" in Brazil, reflected in distinctively postmodern (in Amorim's words "not taught to us by modernity") "inventions" of curriculum. He trades the concepts of "context, belonging and cultural identity" for the ideas of "plane, differing and singularizations without a subject." From the "intellectual decolonization" of globalization comes the distinctiveness—including the "neologisms"—of Brazilian scholarship. No longer split-off as representational, these new concepts construct an "immanent relationship with the event." As an example, Amorim references those Brazilian film studies that point to the "figuration" of the Brazilian people as a "deformity" of utopic expectations, "ending our longing for revolution and fantasies of social equity." This end becomes an "entry point" for thinking about what is a "disfigured social[2] layer," a "plane" from which curriculum is theorized. From these concepts "experience" and "the event" achieve, he suggests, a "deepening."

After thanking Autio, Baker, and Hoadley for their "attentive, generous and provocative reading" of his chapter, Amorim announces that the final version will incorporate their questions and his replies to these. His "main dialogue" is, however, with Deleuze rather than with concepts associated with curriculum studies. Curricular concepts are the result of "verbal actions," casting curriculum "onto the plane of thought wherein French poststructuralism is juxtaposed with the Brazilian curriculum theorists Croazza, Tadeu, and Veiga-Neto," thereby proposing a "plane of sensation and composition to curriculum." The constitution of such a plane is the challenge of "thinking without representing," for example, engaging the "power of words, images and objects" as "political commitment." Why, replying to Baker, does he "continue to [focus] on the centrality of the look?" As a language, the image preserves the "possibility of difference without identity," in which "disfiguration" is not equivalent to stylistics (with concomitant claims for transformation), but "lines of force in which violence is fundamental." That is Amorim's definition of learning: "a violent act of thought." He is not proposing any substitution of the word (or image) for "the silence that screams," rather to think (through images as well as words) an escape from representation, freeing the "subject" from "man." Amorim aspires to free thinking from its subsumption in critique and politics, to enact the eventfulness of thinking through difference in the world.

Baker points to Amorim's "post-humanist" move past critical theory, to a "sense of innovation" that is "overdue" in the field. She wonders whether there is a "broader and deeper" point in Amorim's use of film juxtaposed to his critique of ocularcentrism. If film itself—with its "moving pictures"—provides no "source" of "disfiguration/transformation, nor the properties of the viewer," where, Baker asks, is the source for "disfiguration/transformation"? Is there an "unnamed reservoir" from which Amorim composes "planes of sensation"? What roles do his central concepts—image, word, visual—play? Are they in service of the withdrawal of "power" and the "eventualization of the subject"?

To think without a subject, Amorim asserts, renders education a "sign in the middle" of a "field of forces." To think in the "intensity of encounters and sensation"—not "who" or "what" or "when" but in the differences between these—provokes "experience" and "subjectivation." In this plane of composition, "reality" compels our presence in the present, not suspended in a future split off by "how it could be." The eventfulness of sensation intensifies desire, not as instrumental action but as "vertigo," accentuating "dream" as "substance." Amorim emphasizes "shapes" and "colors" and "sensations" as "objects" of curriculum research. Art enacts such assemblages of sensations; duration—not substance—is "what matters." In duration, figuration disfigures itself in its becoming "affect...incarnated in bodies." These are not "objectives"—the implementation of which can be measured through evaluation (we are in Amorim light years away from Tyler)—but unpredictable and perhaps indiscernible forms in a zone in which cliché is cleansed from the screen. There is no "totalitarian" wish to fill up the screen with an "alternative" to Tyler, but to provide sketches that tend to disappear after drawing them, allowing something else to come after, out of them—no diagrams of action, no codes of conduct then, but connectivity formed through difference. The "production of the new" provokes "forces unknown before, forces which surpass imagination and experience." Amorim summarizes, "The curriculum *disfiguration* bears this potency; affiguration is a series of events released by/in this potency of curriculum creation." Through images in his text Amorim "teaches" these concepts; through images is the "lucidity" of "learning" made clear.

After acknowledging Amorim's "fascinating...experimentations," Autio starts with his "Finnish association" of his "rhizomorphic thinking" with—it is for Autio an experience of *déjà vu*—"shamanist remnants in Finnish culture that may have rendered the strong traditional role of imagination" in Finnish life, poised, as Finland was (and is), between West and East. Autio cites the Finnish philosophers of education Johan Wilhelm Snellman (1806–1881) and Juho August Hollo (1885–1967) who endorsed the potential of imagination at all educational levels, especially during the elementary or primary years, when, they recommended, children should start with fairy tales and activities and only later move to abstract concepts. One is reminded of developmental schemes (moving from the concrete to the abstract) typical of Western curriculum rationales (Pinar et al. 1995, 707), including Egan's theorization of romantic understanding (1990). Associating these two Finnish "pioneers" with Amorim, Autio wonders whether there is not "some universal but not authoritatively defined desire of learning and education." For all three, it seems to Autio, "the core of this desire and blissful joy of learning through the imagination is its perpetual movement, expanding beyond any core subjectivity or self, without fixed identifications or Kantian antagonism between individuality and society." Autio also associates this "deep human desire for unconditional and all-encompassing freedom" with "Buddhism." "Our being can always be otherwise," Autio writes, "[it] does not belong entirely and finally to anything but it can be everything, everywhere." Autio asks Amorim four questions: (1) How can we "intertwine the unavoidable celebratory and consumerist use of art with its vital role...in our theories"? (2) Will pressures for a new orthodoxy appear as the "contingency and intertextuality of art meet institutional power"?[3] (3) What curricular forms—"interdisciplinary spaces"— might we devise to enable "new forms of intellectual engagement"?[4] (4) Can conceptions of "text" and "inscription" not only function self-referentially but also point us to the world, specifically to "social processes"?

Amorim registers the withdrawal of "imagination" in cinema studies in Brazil. The focus is instead on articulating "image" with "thought." Amorim prefers the concept of "fabulation...a radical displacement of reality that could be represented as true." Referencing the visual artist Tom Lisboa and Amorim's 2008 "School and Culture" class in the University of Campinas undergraduate teacher education program, Amorim describes his "professional practice of curricular disfiguration" in which "image visualities" evoke pedagogical representations of cultures, wherein reality "can be told, understood, but not located." Fabulation is, then, "an image-less visuality, a photograph transferred by writing, an eyeless image." There is no coincidence between representation and reality, except, Amorim suggests, on the Internet, where "constant intervention ensure that the relationships between the virtual and the real are always updated." He adds, "In education, as well?"

Baker asks about Amorim's reference to violence. Does it denote "displacement, brute force, substitution"? Baker notes that "violence has very specific and buried meaning in people's daily lives" as well as in "popular media and philosophical texts," referencing both Bourdieu's notion of symbolic violence and feminist theory's forefronting of "psychological and emotional violence." Does Amorim's definitional use of it—"learning as a violent act of thought"—function to "deflect the seriousness of the effects raised by postcolonial, feminist, and disability studies scholarship"? Amorim replies by specifying his use of the concept, for example, "the violence [is] the force that transforms figuration...into figure." Responding to Baker's question regarding his emphasis upon "duration...while 'simultaneously' questioning...linear time," Amorim (referencing Deleuze and Bergson) invokes the "immanent force of movement-duration, a source from which creating potencies emerge," in contrast to "movements...structured by habit...or automatized perceptions." From "in-between images" comes (Amorim here references Maurizio Lazzarato) "a power of affection, creation, thought." It seems to me that Amorim is emphasizing the non-coincidence of representation that duration produces, a non-coincidence that is associated in North American scholarship with Bhabha and the concept of "third space" (see Wang 2004). Amorim is emphasizing imagery that is not only spatial but also visual and temporal to depict (my terms here) the relations among representation, duration, experience, and "the there" of "empirical" reality.

Can the "there" of reality be associated with the "nation"? Indirectly Baker challenges the very conception of this project when she asks Amorim, "how does one recognize Brazilian curricular discussion? Does one have to be born and raised in Brazil? Or received their PhD in Brazil? Or use particular springboards? Are there strategic essentialisms?" Amorim replies by disavowing any "essentialism." He is making no comparison with other countries; indeed, he notes, many of his references derive from work conducted outside Brazil. Amorim works, he explains, with "encounters with situations...which I do not believe are universal or generalizable." Referencing "the site that is Brazil," Amorim asserts, "What stands out, for instance, in the invention of language in our research, as well as the experimentation [is our] neologisms. [These] are examples of resistance to colonization, for example, the creation of a non-submissive linguistics." Not persuaded, Baker counters by pointing out that "non-submissive linguistics" are not unique to one "location." She continues: "This is not to disparage the inventiveness and creativity which the chapters in this volume embody but to question the analytical explanation for them that you seem to be developing through implicitly privileging the coding of the nation, no matter how tethered or temporary the shifting coagulations and constitution of Brazilian-ness is presented as."

Baker also questions Amorim's depiction of "internationalization" as "global," as contrasted to the "local," to the nation, challenging "the [very] impulse to code at all, to have classificatory practices that sort differences between international and Brazilian," suggesting that this seems "a particularly (and circularly) Modern and Euro-Americas enterprise—the instantiation, vehicle, and effect of logocentrism." Baker contrasts Amorim's dialogic invocation of "Brazilian" with his chapter: "if the absence of the subject is one of your concerns, can there still be a Brazilian (or American or French or whatever) *anything*, whether it's cinema, curriculum studies, or food? I would be fascinated to discuss with you in person such nation-speak." Baker concludes, "Reference to other countries of the world is acceptance of modern geographical discourse and its version/s of the subject and of the world." Finding Baker's remarks "very pertinent," Amorim replies, "I propose we objectively think of meeting soon." He disclaims research-as-resistance to "colonizing movements" or "a humanistic substance for the curriculum field." He is, he insists, "working with lines, rather than with polarization points."

Elba Siqueira de Sá Barretto

Replying to Hoadley's question regarding "curriculum integration," de Sá Barretto replies by providing a historical account of the concept in Latin America, specifically in Brazil, linking curricular integration with national integration, a "homogenizing process" guided by "European standards...even though miscegenation [was] intense." She emphasizes that the "crushing" of indigenous Indian and African cultures occurred during the early colonial period *before* public schooling. During the last century, while states were given the responsibility of formulating curriculum guidelines, in the "most developed" municipalities additional guidance was provided. Devised during the 1990s, the National Curricular Parameters (PCN) supplemented but hardly eliminated state and municipal guidelines. They left undisturbed the disciplinary structure of the curriculum while introducing "transversal themes" such as "preservation of the environment, respect for differences, and education for health." Recently, studies in African history as well as in Afro-Brazilian and indigenous cultures have also been incorporated into the curriculum.

As confirmed by UNESCO, the PCN provided greater curricular continuity from early childhood through secondary school education, as had national curriculum reform in other Latin American countries. While curricular integration was non-controversial during its development, after its implementation scholars worried that the large-scale assessment accompanying it would function to "impose the competitive logic of the private sector onto the public sector." Indeed, "performance indicators" allowed states and municipalities to increase their power over the curriculum, restricting content to what can be measured. Postmodern curriculum theorists expressed skepticism that a "common curriculum [could represent] the wide diversity of [Brazilian] society." A "large number" of scholars remained supportive of a national curriculum, however, while asking for a "broader and more democratic consultation process" during its preparation. Among those consulted were University of Barcelona professors César Coll and Anna Teberosky, as well as other major players in Spanish curriculum reform, whom de Sá Barretto characterizes as "psychologists with a cognitive orientation." Despite an excessive "psychologization" of the Spanish curriculum, Brazilian scholars took comfort in the fact that state-directed assessment had not dominated curriculum reform. Even so, scholars such as da Silva questioned the uncritical acceptance of constructivism, particularly its reduction of social, political, and cultural issues to questions of "learning."

In reply to Hoadley's question concerning Freire's influence, de Sá Barretto acknowledges his centrality to "popular education movements" in Brazil. After the dictatorship ended, these movements coalesced into "informal education," the leaders of which considered formal education as serving the interests of the dominant classes. By the end of the 1980s, Freire was head of the educational system of the municipality of São Paulo, managing an "integrated, interdisciplinary curriculum" inspired by his proposals for adult education, structured around "generative themes" formulated by schools in dialogue with their communities. Rejecting curricular prescription by the state, this curriculum relied on students' cultural experience; it was adopted by other municipalities. Nationally, Freire's influence was "more diffuse." Today he provides an indispensable "reference point," but he is associated with "generic principles" concerning the "incorporation of popular culture" in the curriculum and the contribution education can make in the creation of a more just social order.

Regarding Hoadley's questions concerning Lefebvre's contribution to Brazilian curriculum research, de Sá Barretto points to the adoption of his formulation of representation as in-between the social and personal, enabling researchers to emphasize the moment between the "lived" and the "conceived" (or established concepts and theories). In this "in-between" moment are opportunities for "action" and "creations of new meaning." In this space of mediation are blockages and breakthroughs as well. Barretto seeks to identify both as they inhere in daily practice, thereby underlining teacher agency and creativity. Hoadley asks whether there is class-differentiated research of this space of mediation; de Sá Barretto replies that such research has waned in recent years. What has appeared is public concern over the class origins of new teachers: are the low levels of student achievement attributable to their limited cultural capital or/and to the courses comprising teacher education?

Alice Casimiro Lopes

Regarding Hoadley's question concerning the role of "disciplinary organization" in the transformation of scientific knowledge into school knowledge, Lopes replies by emphasizing the multiple meanings of "disciplinarity." Among these are the various divisions of knowledge and communities of social actors engaged in struggles for knowledge legitimation. In this sense, disciplinarity becomes a technology for controlling actors and knowledge in institutions. There are multiple disciplinary sites, including those within the academic disciplines and within the locality of the school, where not necessarily disciplinary concerns, such as "citizenship," may predominate. Even those school subjects that are closest to their parent disciplines—chemistry, for instance—assume different forms as the social actors who articulate them are different, as are their localities. After Goodson and Ball, Lopes acknowledges the importance of struggles for resources and status; after Chevallard, Lopes studies how the *episteme* is constituted socially and historically. Hoadley finds "fascinating" this question of "translation," not only its internal features (i.e., structures) but also the conditions of its production, including ideological conditions.

Lopes references the distinction between publication in the natural versus social sciences (periodicals versus books, demonstration versus argumentation), suggesting that the readership of the social sciences may exercise more influence in the constitution of knowledge than that of the natural sciences. In postmodernity, rationalization (including empiricism and logic) becomes questioned, leaving us (after Lyotard, Lopes notes, but in her own words) with "legitimation through performance," rendering the political and the epistemological intertwined. "Disciplinary identity," then, "shapes the ways in which we ask questions," rendering research always already "contingent and provisional," implicated in "our processes of signification of the world."

Hoadley wonders what roles agency and identity play in this view. How, she asks, do we understand the generational gift of providing knowledge (and making choices about which knowledge) to the young? Invoking Gramsci, Hoadley points to knowledge of the "highest achievements of human endeavor"—what Michael F. D. Young terms "powerful knowledge"—as prerequisite for historical transformation: are not these lost in an exclusive preoccupation with hegemonic processes of signification? "What is depressing to me about the postmodern position," Hoadley confides, "is its complete denial of possibilities for striving to define the best that we have accomplished, establishing what knowledge is worthwhile and good. Maybe I am stating it too strongly, but I would argue that nihilism is inimical to the project of education." Within South African curriculum studies, Hoadley worries, the predominance of the political over the epistemological means that it sometimes seems that "almost anything passes as curriculum studies," and "what results is a weakening of the field."

"First of all," Lopes begins, "I would like to say that your comments are very important to me....Before all else, my thanks." "Secondly," Lopes emphasizes, "the way for the field to advance...does not go through an attempt to treat its characteristic hybridism as a loss." After Laclau, Lopes suggests that only a self-enclosed identity can experience hybridization as "loss." That is not to say that hybridism does not produce problems of its own, but in her view the "vagueness of [disciplinary] frontiers" is not necessarily "a weakening of the field." Indeed, Lopes asserts that the contrary is true. Incorporating theory from other fields renders curriculum studies "more dense and mature...contributing to strengthening the reasoning" of the field. Moreover, Lopes does not dissociate epistemology from politics, as each informs the other. Epistemologies always encode political preferences; they become "hegemonized" within the curricula we develop. Within this perspective it becomes important to study the history of the field, as the constitution of the field involves renegotiating its traditions. Hoadley concurs on this point, but she worries that hybridization means "the loss of a common language...[and] thereby cumulative understandings." Hoadley thanks Lopes: "this has been a very thought-provoking and productive exchange for me."

Lopes concurs with Baker's characterization of the collection as "exciting, dynamic, and energizing" exhibiting a "synergy" informed by the chapters' "incommensurability," a synergy characteristic of the field of "curriculum." Lopes disassociates political struggle from any conception of "totality," or (quoting Baker) "as an implicit kind of activism/morality." For Lopes, "knowledge is not a thing." The disappearances of libraries, Lopes suggests, signals the disappearance of any "reified" conceptions of knowledge and curriculum. Nor, for Lopes, can "culture" be rendered "substantial" in the sense of fixing identities; for Lopes "culture" is "signification of the world," always involving politics. Lopes shares Baker's linking of political struggle with "Darwinian evolutionary theory and masculinist historiography that privileges war and violence." Such struggle is over signification. For Lopes (as for Laclau) "discourse is the primary terrain for constituting objectivity," those "articulatory practices" that structure "totality" through "relations of difference." Always relational, discourse is never static or complete but also "susceptible to subversion." Lopes thus emphasizes the point: "There is always a polysemy, a multiplicity of meanings."

All is not flux always; there are moments of constitution, including of identity formation (nodal points in Laclau's phrase). Such moments establish relations among elements of difference. These relations are never static but, rather, "antagonistic...always tensioned." Excluded elements remain as the "constitutive exterior," thereby rendering totality simultaneously "necessary and impossible." Political solidarity (my phrase, not Lopes's) would seem to follow from "differential identities" suspending their "particularities on behalf of a common project." Hybridism (or synergy) is both the "denial and affirmation of particularity." In such nodal moments of configuration hegemony occurs, but it is itself "always unstable, ambiguous and plural." Political action, then, is enacted through decisions taken on "an undecidable terrain: we constitute ourselves as subjects [even though] there is no *a priori* that sustains our decision as rational or obligatory." Strategic essentialisms are never more than that; there are no "political identities prior to the articulatory process." It is the political process of signification, then, not the static "social demands" of essentialized "social groups," that characterizes democratization. Lopes signifies curriculum policy as articulatory practice, inviting resignification by teachers and students.

Regarding Autio's question concerning "cross-cultural borrowing and grafts" in Brazilian curriculum studies, Lopes acknowledges the "hybridism" of the Brazilian field due, in part, to these global flows, especially from France and the United States. She characterizes these as "relations of dependence," as knowledge from these two countries have been, on occasion, uncritically incorporated. Thanks to the emphasis upon hybridism in postcolonial studies, scholars have become clearer about their own reinterpretation of knowledge, as well as the interrelations among disciplines as these are reconstituted in curriculum studies. Given these conditions, Autio questions as to what happens to canonical knowledge, as in the "Great Books" or *Bildung* traditions. Relatedly, Autio references the contributions of information technologies to a "globalized Encyclopedia" asking whether such "a global archive of knowledge" decenters European, indeed, Western, knowledge, thereby implying not only a hybridized curriculum theory but also new roles for the field.

Lopes replies by reiterating the primacy of articulatory processes in the constitution of new knowledge, processes that are not always apart from its disciplinary but self-conscious of its political meaning. Referencing her reply to Hoadley, Lopes affirms her sense that the "new technologies and the acceleration of cultural exchanges" function to "blur" the disciplines "without eliminating them." Epistemological issues are at stake in disciplinarity, and so are political ones, as "communities are constituted that control who has the right to talk about what, when, and where and with what legitimacy." These communities are not only local and national, but also global, and how these "communities act globally as epistemic communities, in knowledge-power relations" enable us to understand the "hegemonizing of certain meanings for curriculum policy."

Elizabeth Macedo

In her reply to Baker, Macedo acknowledges the "difficulty of translation" in both "internationalization" and "interdisciplinarization." By these concepts Macedo is referencing issues of "translation" between "academic cultures...marked by national bias." Although Macedo is "familiar" with curriculum studies in the United States, she is located outside the "space-time" in which U.S. curriculum debates occur. Her intellectual self-formation in Brazil was influenced more by European (specifically French and German) philosophical traditions than by those associated with the United States. By that phrase—"space-time" (about which Baker asks "does it relate to History?")—Macedo is drawing upon a post-Einsteinian notion of time and a non-Euclidian geometry to theorize a "non-structured" or "non-centered structure." In aesthetic terms, Macedo invokes Cubism to specify a "multidimensional space" represented in "different moments of perception." Such a view has "profound implications" for concepts such as history (and "authority" and "influence," about which Baker also asks) as a "decentered structure" that is, as such, not determinative of "any position of the subject." History, Baker continues, is produced through processes of decontextualization, not as a series of a priori, not as foundational, essential, or self-same, or as repressive of difference.

Baker invokes Foucault's analysis of the modern episteme (in which dividing practices become pivotal in the very notion of knowledge) when asking Macedo about the epistemic genesis of her concepts of "knowledge" and "culture." Are both "discursive practices" regardless of their relation to "production, reproduction, or enunciation"? If so, what is the "a priori...out of which these formations becomes recognizable"? Or would the a priori be "different in each modality" (e.g., production, reproduction, enunciation)? Without an "a priori," how does recognition—including of hybridity—occur?

Macedo replies by wondering whether "we are facing a new temporality" in which a "new" episteme—"an episteme of contemporaneousness"—is emerging "independently of the time lived"? If there is such an emergence, such a *dispositif* (a less "homogenizing" concept than "episteme," Macedo adds), it is marked not be any a priori but by the very answer the question produces. For Macedo, "culture" as "production" or "reproduction"— indeed, as an "epistemological object"—is a construction of the modern episteme, enabling "culture" to have "content" and "presence." In such an episteme "culture" is "marked" by "history" and the "materiality of everyday life." Such "positivity" renders "culture ... an imagined museum," in which "multicultural" perspectives focus on "diversity." The articulation of difference is thereby theorized into silence. In Macedo's reformulation, "culture" becomes "signification," an "enunciation," a "production, irregular and incomplete, with meaning and value." Referencing Bhabha, Macedo notes that enunciation becomes institutionalized as "the political reinvention" of the complex contemporaneousness of "signification." In "culture as epistemological object," hybridity is "a blend of preexisting cultures" or it becomes a "third term that eases the tension between cultures." For Macedo, hybridity becomes the "condition" in which enunciation occurs. The "cultural" is the flux that precedes the fixing of "culture." Without hybridity, there would be only "culture" as endless repetition.

Macedo extends this point in her reply to Baker's question regarding her juxtaposition of Laclau, Mouffe, Derrida, and Zizek, theorists situated in very different, even dissonant, traditions. This "option for bricolage" does not, she allows, dissolve the obligation to acknowledge their differences (as she does in regard to the notion of the "subject" in Laclau/Mouffe and Derrida, and "discursive practices" as employed by Zizek). Macedo's reference to Zizek, she notes, is specific to the notion of the "constitutive exterior." In their analysis of binary logic, Macedo finds that differences between Derrida and Laclau/Mouffe recede when relocated into a "destructured structure." Although acknowledgment of differences in traditions is important, Macedo agrees, "bricolage" becomes warranted when specific theorists themselves bridge differences and/or when those differences, now relocated, function in specific ways to make specific points. To illustrate the former, Macedo references the Derridean conception of *différance* as "demanded" in efforts to understand hegemony, mixing, in a sense, "deconstruction" with "late structuralism." Macedo's conception of "curriculum as enunciation" requires both traditions. That conception implies a notion of the subject—replying here to Baker's questions regarding silence, fixity, and violence—whose constitution (after Laclau) implies a "constitutive lack" in structure, and not only in those intrasubjective processes (after Derrida) of identification/disidentification, as when the "violence" of "fixity" is accepted as a "necessary and impossible operation for constructing meaning." Macedo reiterates, "A subject inside displaced structure...[implies] contingent identifications." Replying still to Baker's question, Macedo reserves the right to assert "meaning" despite its hermeneutical antecedents, separating the concept from hermeneutics' tendency toward "totality" by emphasizing enunciation's embeddedness in "negotiation, displacement, and realignment."

These theoretical issues become concrete when Hoadley asks Macedo to specify their significance in understanding the empirical realities of schools. Macedo replies by linking "enunciation" to specific curriculum policies expressed in specific textbooks (understood as "partial closings of meanings"), in other teacher materials, and in records of observations and interviews of those participants in the "everyday life of schools." In conducting empirical research, Macedo and her colleagues and students search for "associations among groups, struggles for hegemonizing positions, and calculated retrocessions." The "agency of subjects" becomes central, expressed in "decisions" enacted "in the undecidable space of displaced structure," which, one imagines, replaces as it reconfigures such structure. In so doing, this research (she is referencing a specific study of curriculum in Rio de Janeiro) contests conceptions of policy as only top-down ("landing on the heads of teachers," in Macedo's imagistic phrasing), conceptions of curriculum as "salads of theoretical options," of resistance as "non-implementation," dissolving any sharp distinction between "socially accumulated knowledges and cultures of students."

Regarding "culture," Hoadley asks about the relation between curriculum studies and "minority voices" in schools and society. Macedo replies that these have not been "the most relevant motor of preoccupation with culture in curriculum theory in Brazil." Curriculum became politicized after "redemocratization," marked by elections in 1989 at the end of the 1964–1985 dictatorship. Influenced by Marxism focused on culture (especially as inspired by Freire) and socially organized knowledge, political curriculum theory was "one of the key notes" of curriculum studies in Brazil. By the 1990s, the "new sociology of education" had been incorporated as well. There was, however, growing interest in post-structuralism, which "broke" into disciplinary visibility by the mid-1990s, altering the discursive landscape of the field.

Then "politics" meant gender and racial politics, Foucault[4] became an important reference, and it was no longer possible to write about curriculum without referencing postmodernity. These shifts became detached from minority political movements in Brazil. Accompanying these developments in post-structuralism and identity politics were studies in curriculum policy influenced by Marxism and, later, by constructivism. All of these were marked by developments in North America and Europe, in part because a generation of theorists had completed their graduate degrees there. The South African case was rather different, Hoadley rejoined, "we did had no equivalent to Freire—an indigenous theoretical project." She acknowledges "difficulty" reading the Brazilian chapters, recalling Macedo's acknowledgment to Baker regarding the "difficulty" engendered when not sharing the same "space-time." I would add that the difficulty scholars experience trying to understand each other does not disappear when they do share the same "space-time." Certainly it seems intensified when they do not.

Regarding Hoadley's question concerning the "formal contents of scientific subjects," Macedo reports that what "we are going through in Brazil is…a certain conservatism," expressed not only as a privileging of content, but also as a skepticism concerning methods, an insistence that knowledge is prerequisite not only to education but also to upward social and economic mobility. This "conservatism" is, she continues, Marxist in nature, as it claims that social transformation is contingent upon the equitable distribution of cultural capital.[5] Whose knowledge is key? Macedo contests what she views as an "overvaluation of nativist narratives," as "most [of these] sustained local hegemonies." Like Spivak, Macedo opposes not the reason associated with the European Enlightenment but its political use to occlude the Other. Much of what in Brazil is called "formal contents" is associated with colonial discourses that sought to fix "the ideological construction of alterity." Through preoccupation with epistemological procedures, such discourses promoted their particularized knowledge as universal. Macedo references Fanon to specify her critique of the internalization of self-alienating knowledge construed as universal.[6] What Macedo endorses is a curriculum in which colonial and nativist cultures are juxtaposed in order to renegotiate the terms of their coexistence, "creating a zone of ambivalence between repetition and performativity, in which it is possible to consider the existence of the other as a real other."

This Marxist-inspired argument concerning "the mastery of knowledge for social justice" has some traction in South Africa at the present time, Hoadley replies. Indeed, it represents "a major cleavage in South African curriculum theory." What predominated after Apartheid was a constructivist emphasis on "the enacted curriculum" and "the autonomy of the teacher in creating curriculum in conversation with learners," rendering the curriculum "underspecified," as "underqualified teachers" lacked an adequate "knowledge base" to take advantage of such autonomy. How, Hoadley asks, are these curricular politics played out in Brazil?

Complicating curriculum politics in Brazil, Macedo replies, is the differentiated management of the curriculum. There is a national curriculum, produced by Brazil's Ministry of Education, that coexists with "different municipal" or "state" curricula. The national curriculum is not obligatory, although there are indirect efforts (through distribution of federal funds) to instantiate elements of it. Since the end of the dictatorship, municipal and state curricula are obligatory, enforced by the political power of municipal and state governments. Due to these conflicting spheres of influence curricular uniformity is not possible in Brazil. In the 1980s, Macedo continues, the main theoretical debate occurred between those who endorsed the primacy of students' culture (inspired by Freire) and those who endorsed the primacy of universal knowledge. Constructivism was not yet a player. When it appeared (in the early 1990s), constructivism became mixed with both perspectives, thereby failing to alter the basic terms of the debate. In recent years the "universal" or "accumulated" knowledge argument has gained ground. Unlike the South African arrangement, however, the "top-down" model is vitiated by municipal and state authority. For Macedo, the question of organizational structure is less interesting than the understanding "beyond" the distinction between "formal" and "enacted" curriculum.

Autio asks Macedo about the influence of globalization on her formulation of "enunciation." Macedo replies that she has attempted to think beyond the polarity by considering the curriculum as "a process of localization of the global" through its "enunciation." By this term Macedo is emphasizing "action in the creation of the unexpected." What destabilizes the local is the global, as that "constitutive exterior" maintains a certain undecidability in the local. The curriculum constructs locality as it "articulates differential demands...creating cultural hybrids [through] plural knowledges." Autio then asks whether the Brazilian emphasis upon the quotidian incorporates the "post" claim that "practice is theory"?[7] Macedo acknowledges that a preference for the quotidian comprises "one of the motors of preoccupation with binaries that I deconstruct." Characterizing the quotidian "as a place of the new bothers me," she explains, especially as this "affirmation contains an expectation of liberation." Moreover, this emphasis challenges Macedo's privileging of the history of school subjects and her study of curricular documents, as these become positioned as secondary to everyday life.[8] Macedo formulated the concept of "curriculum as enunciation" to overcome the binary between formal and lived curriculum. In this concept the agency of teachers is "always" on the "horizon," although not with the naive faith evident (in her view) in "everyday life" research. Before this encounter, Macedo acknowledges, agency had been "dependent on a kind of illumination." In the theory-practice binary, education is valorized as "practice," although critical pedagogy has attempted to incorporate theory in practice through its embrace of "praxis." Rather than accepting the quotidian approach (in which practice is theory), Macedo judges these as "supplements" with "different operational qualities." In particular, Macedo wishes to "guarantee the place of the theoretical...as reflection, but especially as a possible place of the political."

Replying to Autio's concern over the "terminological replacement of education with the discourses of learning," Macedo underlines the "educative project of modernity" as a way of opposing the postmodern preference for "learning." That project privileged "subjectivation," reminiscent, perhaps, of self-cultivation associated with *Bildung* and *Didaktik* (Macedo references Kant and Hegel), in contrast to other discourses focused on the "worker" and the "citizen," both of which focus on the reproduction of society. The educative project of the Enlightenment involved the cultivation of autonomy, freedom, and emancipation, a humanist project that privileged reason and knowledge. The assumption that knowledge of human nature was possible led to the substitution of socialization for subjectivation, casting doubt on the possibility of autonomy, freedom, and emancipation. In postmodernity, subjectivity becomes identity. Although opposed to the effacement of subjectivity, the essentialization of identity, and the severance of History from the subject, Macedo wants to think beyond the private/public binary to emphasize "what cannot be foreseen in the order of things as they are or should be." As the "locus" of decision making in the "undecidable space of displaced structure," subjectivity reorganizes hegemony as it reconstitutes itself and the structures it inhabits.

Inês Barbosa de Oliveira

In response to Hoadley's question concerning the primacy of the quotidian, Oliveira asserts the vastness and invisibility of much social practice. Models cannot capture the specificity of the everyday, she contends, including those practices that subvert the hegemonic. Only through daily study of "what is said and done by teachers and students in classrooms" can we discern the "subtleties and wealth of daily life." Structural analyses cannot convey this complexity, nor can they honor how daily life reconstructs society in general.

Hoadley registers her skepticism that structuralism is superficial. She then asks what Oliveira means by the "the common heritage" of humanity. The phrase is Santos's, Oliveira replies, specifying that which can be protected globally, such as the environment. It denotes a more different political logic than, say, the struggle against inequality. "Common heritage" implies solidarity across culture and nation for the sake of the sustainability of the planet. Oliveira reminds, "so far, there is no such thing as a common heritage!"

Regarding Hoadley's question concerning methodology, Oliveira points to the effects of certain forms of research: the invisibility of realities they fail to discern or communicate. "Curricular creativity in the school quotidian," she continues, "is thus excluded from the majority of curricular studies." In Oliveira's research this plurality of practice is sometimes "emancipatory," as it contributes to horizontal relations between academic and lived knowledge, between high and popular culture, hierarchies Oliveira associates with a "scientistic" Eurocentrism. While supervisory personnel may see only the transmission of knowledge and skills, Oliveira and her colleagues perceive multiple supplements. And these supplements do not always coincide with official directives. On occasion, they move outside their logic altogether. Hoadley wonders whether "science" and "Europe" are being "caricatured," asking, too, whether differentially distributed cultural capital does not provide middle-class students with advantages that studies of the privileging of everyday knowledge accentuates.

Reiterating the "emancipatory" moments of the quotidian, Oliveira decries totalization, as it obliterates the particularity of the everyday, the domain wherein the futures emerges. She then critiques the notions of "linear time" that disregard "errors, accidents," and those other "transformations of reality" that our "ecstatic expectations" may disavow. Oliveira questions the "imprisoning" of the future by insisting on its continuity with the present. It is through the plural and the concrete that the future becomes no longer the predictable continuation of an undemocratic present, that it becomes a surprising transformation, a materialization of what is "not yet." "Concrete possibilities and capacity," Oliveira continues, "will re-determine all they touch, modifying and, therefore, placing all previous determinations in question." There can be no certainty, of course; while the "potential is recognizable," its "result" is not. "All of this," she concludes, "makes the future scary and doubtful and [characterized] by an element of chance and danger." But the future is in the present, thereby challenging us to seize the moment.

Regarding Autio's question concerning globalization, Oliveira affirms its totalizing tendencies, but she emphasizes the local's capacity to resist eclipse. Scholarly fascination with globalization distracts us from the urgency of the local, Oliveira worries, including needs associated with specific realities, as well as the possibilities of curricular redress. Regarding Autio's question concerning shifts in the field's vocabulary after two decades of postmodernism, Oliveira reports that Brazilian scholars too have debated the various prefixes, "post" prominent among them, one consequence of which, she offers, is a "hyper-disciplinarizing" of the discipline around its own formulations. Although such "enrichment of vocabulary" contributes to the "deepening of debate" and leads to "new forms of understanding curricula," Oliveira believes that this "terminological multiplication" has blurred the distinction between "rhetorical dispute" and "conceptual construction."

Replying to Autio's question concerning interdisciplinarity, Oliveira acknowledges a tension between disciplinarity and school-focused research. In school-based research, she notes, there is "knowledge in a network," but it is not necessarily a disciplinary network but a social and even emotional one. This preference for the lived and the local reassigns value from the academic discipline to the specificity of the setting.

Responding to Autio's question concerning the internationalization of curriculum studies, Oliveira affirms the "incompleteness of all cultures" as she asserts the primacy of "learning with the South" and calls for the "recovery of [that] global experience" obliterated by "metonymic reason." Acknowledging the radical diversity of curriculum studies worldwide, she welcomes an intensifying conversation among scholars, in particular between European scholars and scholars in the Americas, between scholars working in countries or regions with histories of oral and other "non-graphocentric" traditions. Understandings of education can be multiplied and complicated by only such "interlocution." The primacy of particular remains; even "the notion of Brazil sounds to me like an abstraction," perhaps "too ambitious" for thinking curriculum in situation.[9] Regarding Autio's question concerning internationality of intellectual influences, Oliveira references Dewey's emphasis upon democracy, Piaget's ("today abandoned") concern for children's development, Foucault, Gramsci, Marx, Leffort, and "above all" Habermas. Working on her doctorate in France, she was influenced by Bourdieu, de Certeau, Goffman, Pais, Morin, and, especially, Boaventura de Sousa Santos. Other influences include Negri, Bhabha, Stuart Hall, and Canclini. Against the limits of Marxism, Oliveira juxtaposed psychoanalysis, with its acknowledgment of the erotic and the unconscious, its questioning the hegemony of reason and rationality, and the ambivalent contributions of both to progress. Of "significant relevance to studies on the quotidian" was Bourdieu's notion of "habitus."

Autio asks about the "quotidian," specifically, those vocabularies employed to specify its particularities, its subtleties. Oliveira reiterates her (and her colleagues') commitment to surpass the simplifications that the "parsimony" (Autio's word) of science enforces, in part, by paying attention to the complexity of action (its multiple influences on it, in it, from it) and researcher's presence within it. Research is, thereby, "in-dissociable" from theory. To Autio's question concerning the non-equivalence of cultural diversity and democratic equality, Oliveira asserts (after Santos) that "we have a right to be equal when difference makes us inferior, and the right [to] be different when equality denies our specificity." With this right affirmed, study of the specific discloses struggles that are underway even at the edge of the private sphere. How to portray these so as to encourage progressive political action is not self-evident, Oliveira notes, as the play of "plurality" in "democratic interaction" assumes ever-changing forms.

In response to Baker's question concerning globalization, Oliveira reasserts that the scope of her attention is the quotidian: "globalized localisms."

Answering Baker's question concerning capitalism, Oliveira assigns it a background status, indeed severing the "emancipatory" from the economic. Accepting that capitalism disallows democracy, Oliveira has no faith, however, that the end of capitalism portends democracy. A necessary but insufficient condition, the prospect of capitalism's demise does not animate studies of the quotidian. Social equality that is supportive of a "dignified existence" is not associated with capitalist values—in particular with "individualism" and "competitiveness"—and it must be worked out within daily life, not through restructuring the economy. Rather than formulating an alternative economic model, then, Oliveira and her colleagues focus upon those social practices that exhibit "the potential to contribute to the democratization of society," especially those educational practices that disclose "the plurality of the world, of the knowledge and cultures that inhabit it." Such practices are "less hierarchical, more ecological."

During the second round of exchanges, Baker explained that her questions concerning "capitalism" had less to do with "capitalism" and more to do with "the tensions, interplay and paradoxes I perceived in the moving back and forth between foundationalist and post-foundationalist reasoning." How the concept functions in the text—"as a causal and constitutive location in terms of the problems discussed"—was Baker's focus. Oliveira disputes that "capitalism" carries "the weight that has been given to it," but that acknowledgment of it is "inevitable," as it "establishes a founding inequality between social groups." Her "discomfort over the question" is that it contradicts what Oliveira takes as one of her central points, namely that "different forms of domination require different forms of social struggle," and "that the economic model cannot explain always all the questions we have in relation to emancipatory struggles." Capitalism is "something more than merely an economic system, and when I refer to it, I am considering a social model."

Regarding Baker's questions concerning normalization and resistance, Oliveira assumes "a degree of autonomy" that enables "social participants" to remake the "rules, without necessarily resisting them." Baker asks whether education apart from normalization is, in fact, possible, wondering whether the embrace of a new discourse system represents only a new rhetoric of normalization. Oliveira eschews social narratives that forefront "opposition to others" by searching those strata of daily life that are "beyond" or "to the side of social structure and control." Here one finds "curricular and social practices, multiple knowledge and activities that bring to light the complexity of life...all of which can help us to understand the paths of a possible emancipation towards a democratic society." Oliveira rejects the association of democracy with modernity, in which it becomes subsumed alongside rationalization, capitalism, and nationalism (as Baker notes, referencing Delanty and O'Mahoney). Oliveira points out that democracy must be dissociated from modernity, the former being more ancient than the latter.

Replying to Baker's question concerning the distinction between "experience" and "understanding," Oliveira invokes Larossa's expansive definition of the former as "everything that goes through us, affects us, changes us." Understanding emerges retrospectively, in reflection, as experience is "re-valued." Referencing Santos, Oliveira separates "understanding" from scientific knowing.

Baker's question concerning the modernity of temporality, spatiality, and visuality does not resonate with Oliveira who separates temporality from modernity and fails to see the relevance of visuality to the exchange. Concerning Baker's question on "other possibilities for thinking in terms of appearances and emergences," Oliveira acknowledges that her own research program is not "inevitable." Other formulations could prove fruitful. Regarding Baker's question concerning the *telos* of studies of quotidian, the possibilities of "less egalitarian outcomes," Oliveira affirms the unfinished character of such studies, indeed that they do not produce "truths" but, rather, "open doors." Oliveira declines any reparative (in the religious sense, as Baker asks) agenda, separating the "fight for more happiness" from religiosity. What animates the fight—"strong desires"—provide happiness, not frustration, as the "ambiguity, precariousness, and limitations" of the quotidian project characterize human existence itself.

"I understand from your response to others how you oriented to the global/local as problematic or a false forced choice, that globalization is in a sense over-exposed and too accumulative as a discourse," Baker begins her second set of questions. But "how ideas-practices such as globalization...are invoked at the outset will matter." Baker asks, "Can your arguments about globalization and [its] history of effects...be more directly marshaled to the notion of the quotidian? How might these vectors change the very nature of the quotidian in different locales, regions, and/or groups, and thus change what constitutes an emancipatory possibility?"

The point is not to change the nature of the quotidian, Oliveira replies, "which is always woven into the fabric of the global reality that influences it." The point is to understand how "different subjects, both individual and collective, weave their networks of social practices...that are specific to them." Discernible, then, is "the autonomy of populations in relation to norms and hegemonic thinking...and it is along these lines that we seek to attribute emancipation...to some of the social practices that have development within different spaces and times." The question of "emancipation," Oliveira continues, is not one of "great movements or narratives aimed at 'structural' transformation of society...but rather an understanding of the complexity of quotidian life and of the small-scale events that modify relations and behavior." What we find is the "horizontalizing" of relations "that are historically unequal and hierarchical." These, Oliveira continues, "I classify as emancipating." Just as the quotidian is always marked by difference, "globalization" is likewise dynamic and complex, with "different forms of influence in different contexts." Oliveira concludes, "From my point of view, I believe that...the ways in which social subjects implant themselves within the social sphere, reinventing sociability, knowledge and social practices, creatively incorporating that which is imposed on them, modifying products and rules with which they interact...capture the complex articulation I perceive between global and local."

Baker cautions Oliveira that terms such as "empowerment, emancipation, and democracy" can operate "as catchalls, remaining within surface deployment rather than engaging...their invocation as moral high grounds within a salvific discourse of the redemptive, the paternal, and the pastoral." Oliveira replies, "I will try to improve the text along these lines and am grateful to you for the warning....In my final reformulation of the text, I will try to minimize the weight of foundational categories." Regarding Baker's skepticism toward a "pluralist logic," Oliveira substitutes "the difficult question...of establishing intercultural dialogue," emphasizing "dialogue that could ensure a mutual intelligibility," not the totalizing logics of social incorporation sometimes implied by formulations of "pluralism." Regarding Baker's invocation of "governmentality" to denote forms of "surveillance, regulation, and rationality that may equally inhabit quotidian research techniques and strategies of reflexivity," Oliveira acknowledges that "processes of control and vigilance...almost certainly are presenting quotidian life, where everything that is exists." She further acknowledges that "the research methodology that we have been developing is immersed in this world and woven into networks into which are incorporated hegemonic learning and convictions as well as those that...oppose them." Oliveira emphasizes that being embedded in social reality does not preclude participation in "democratizing transformation." Although positioning oneself outside hegemony is in principle impossible, it does not consign one to complicity, as "one must fight on and stay on the battlefield, adapting struggles, procedures and mechanism to battle against that which makes our present-day world so unequal."

A Postcolonial Cosmopolitan Curriculum Studies

Like Bernadette Baker, Tero Autio began with general questions for every scholar-participant, followed by questions addressed specifically to each. (Only Antonio Carlos Amorim replied likewise, offering comments not only to the panel members but to his Brazilian colleagues as well.) Rather than constructing bridges between individuals, these general questions created an "outside" to the Brazilian situation. Autio's first question concerned globalization and localization, suggesting that the former phenomenon constituted a "sucking black hole without a real power of explanation." Left to its own devices, globalization inflates itself into an abstract totalization without concrete referents. Coupled with—juxtaposed to—localization, these general questions also pointed to an "inside": Autio then asked about intellectual movements within the field, from the importation of the British "new sociology of education" that "continued to work within the traditional confinements of the modern society, the modern self, and the nation-state as its universalistic and theoretical guidelines." From the "outside" it is clear that something singular is occurring "inside." Simultaneously self-absorbed and preoccupied with the world (specifically with intellectual developments abroad), curriculum studies in Brazil exhibits a cosmopolitanism conspicuously absent elsewhere.

Both inner- and outer-directed, this "dual consciousness" (de)structures the distinctiveness of the field, (de)forming its singularity not only as a duality but also as a multiplicity. Focusing on the internationalization[10] of curriculum studies, Autio asked, "what would be...the most urgent lessons (e.g., theory/practice, history, ethics, aesthetics, ecological concerns) scholars from Europe or other geographical or intellectual territories could learn from your experience and expertise in the (Brazilian) educational field?" Shifting from outside to inside, he asked what ideas from abroad had been most influential. Still emphasizing the "inside" of curriculum studies in Brazil, Autio acknowledges the montage-like phrases ("doing-knowing", "experimenting-problematizing") that provide "an index of exhaustible limitations of the conventional scholarly discourse." This implies, Autio suggests,

> a deep ontological trust in human potential, in *concretum*, here and now, without a further need for teleological projections of human future in advance. This attitude, as it seems to me, creates a "hidden curriculum" in all your papers and manifest their explicit or implicit separation from main western narratives of modernity.... This kind of optimism, invested persistently in the present, compressing the future while expanding the present, still conscious of history, deviates decisively or at least alternatively, I suppose, from these two main narratives of modernity, for example, the Enlightenment, Marxist/socialism and capitalism specifically.

Autio designates this distinctiveness as "the space of postcolonial." He then supplements these general questions with specific ones, referencing the matter of vocabulary when asking Oliveira about representing "the quotidian in education." This represents no simple one-to-one exchange of one concept for another, but a dissatisfaction with "the scientific canons of parsimony, the complexities of practice to the simplicities of empiricism." He then links conceptual complexity to cultural complexity, referencing "cosmopolitan rationality" as embodying an "emancipative subjectivity formation," wondering about the coexistence of "cultural diversity and democratic equality." No reinstantiation of hegemonic power relations, internationalization becomes (as Autio's questions imply) simultaneously self-knowledge and knowledge of alterity.

Not only a project promising a cosmopolitan postcolonial future, internationalization is also a fact of the past, as influences from the United States and France (as well as elsewhere) have long been crucial in the intellectual history and present circumstances of curriculum studies in Brazil. Not all imports originate in the North; Oliveira especially welcomes scholarly exchanges not routed through the metropole. The hybridity of the Brazilian field is derived (in part) from its international sources, Lopes notes, including "the acceleration of cultural exchanges" due to the "new technologies." Autio emphasizes the "global archive of knowledge" and, in fact, "decenters" European and North American influence, "thereby implying not only a hybridized curriculum theory." Macedo links internationalization and interdisciplinarity through the complexities of translation. No straightforward matter of mimesis, the Brazilian field reinvents what it imports. "What stands out," Amorim asserts, "in the invention of language in our researches... [is] resistance to colonization."

Elba Siqueira de Sá Barretto notes that "the most representative line of curriculum studies is probably centered on school knowledge." Perhaps this focus on "the school"—simultaneously an abstraction and a series of concrete everyday realities—pulls our attention away from the field as an ongoing complicated conversation, for, as is apparently the case in South Africa (Pinar 2010, 3), Brazilian researchers (Macedo suggests) "pay little attention to the work of colleagues." Although that may be the case, I must say I was struck by the rigor and candor of the exchanges, by what one must acknowledge was an exemplary willingness to accept challenge and criticism. Consider the exchange between Baker and Oliveira over the concept of "emancipation," a term Baker worried reiterated discredited discourses of redemption. Oliveira expresses *gratitude* for the warning. This was no act of capitulation—Oliveira held her ground firmly during the exchanges—and so her openness and generosity are all the more laudable. And these qualities were evident throughout the exchanges.

What concepts did the exchanges (and chapters) emphasize? These I will discuss in chapter 10; here I note that they resonated with the concepts I associated with curriculum studies in South Africa. That alerted my (and no doubt your) suspicion that I am projecting my own theoretical agenda. Surely that agenda and my "domain assumptions" (Gouldner 1970, 31ff.) are always in play, but for "projection" to occur, they must remain free of dialogical encounter. I invited my Brazilian colleagues to comment on this issue in the epilogue, "The Final Word." For now, I offer my sense of curriculum studies in Brazil as evident in four concepts.

NOTES

1. Recall that the exchanges occurred via the Internet over a two-year period. Because Professor Alves' reply to the panel's questions was general and reiterated the main points of her chapter, it goes unremarked here. Due to ill health, Professor Ferraço was unable to participate in the exchanges.

2. At one point Baker questions Amorim's usage of "social," wondering whether the concept also references the non-human. Does it, she asks, include "discourses" and "forces"? Amorim replies that the social is not limited to conceptions of "man" or "humanization" but, rather, forefronts "the violence of disfiguration." There is no "melancholy" or "nostalgia" here, however, but a dystopic affirmation of "degradation ... disillusioned with modern processes of constituting nations, civil rights, citizenship" and connected with a "micropolitics of desire." Amorim reports he is supervising doctoral dissertation research linking the social with the virtual, a concept in which "the idea of an organic body is not so much required."

3. For me, this is a point of inestimable importance: see Pinar 2009, 155, n. 14.

4. It is not only in Brazil that Foucault has assumed canonical significance, of course. In the United States too referencing his work has become obligatory, if only rarely employed with sophistication, as it is in Baker's (2001) stunning study. More commonly that work has functioned to efface subjectivity, and with it, agency, despite Foucault's recuperation of those concepts (see Paras 2006, 147). The general point that Anderson and Valente (2002, 8–9) make proves instructive, I think, for U.S. curriculum theorists: "At this historical moment, of course, disciplinary studies, like its more famous relative, cultural studies, is dominated by the figure of Michel Foucault. . . . In key respects, the present volume looks to a post-Foucauldian dispensation, keeping its distance from approaches that too easily assimilate bodies of knowledge to techniques of management—whether of the social body, the intellectual field, or the individual person. Nevertheless, the effort to show how disciplinary developments have affected both theories and practices of modern selfhood remains central to the project of rethinking the human sciences. This effort can also be adapted to the end of dislodging some of the comfortable pessimism of Foucauldian scholars, who do not sufficiently register the very struggles with questions of human agency that has characterized the project of the human

sciences since its inception." Fashionable Foucauldian pessimism (see, for instance, Popkewitz 2008) is nowhere to be found in this collection; agency is everywhere.

5. In the United States this argument—that knowledge is prerequisite to equality of opportunity—is made not by Marxists: see Hirsch (1999, 12).

6. Crain Soudien seeks to "provincialize" Europe, so that its African and Asian elements—present even at the "high moment of the Enlightenment"—are acknowledged, enabling a decoupling of educational achievement from whiteness (see Pinar 2010, 222). Soudien makes this point regarding the universalization of the particular that accented Eurocentrism in an exchange with Elizabeth Macedo, a member of the international panel that questioned South African scholars (Pinar 2010).

7. Oliveira will assert the intertwined relation between theory and practice in studies of the quotidian.

8. Macedo reports that her research was criticized by some as "modern" (in contrast to "postmodern"), even as "conservative."

9. Recall that Baker too is skeptical of "Brazil" as a meaningful modifier of curriculum studies. See introduction (this volume), note 6.

10. Hongyu Wang (2002) reports that the term "internationalization" translates into Chinese as "between/country/change (process)." "Globalization," she continues, translates as "whole/world (planet)/change (process)." For Wang "it is the inter-space that is more interesting." For Wang, "internationalization," in this Chinese sense, represents a challenge to the centralizing control and power of nationalism, due to its tendencies toward the realignment and destabilization of traditional, now ever-shifting, borders.

REFERENCES

Anderson, Amanda and Valente, Joseph (Eds.) (2002). *Disciplinarity at the fin de siècle.* Princeton, NJ: Princeton University Press.

Egan, Kieran. 1990. *Romantic Understanding: The Development of Rationality and Imagination, Ages 8–15.* New York: Routledge.

Fuller, Steve. 1993. "Disciplinary Boundaries and the Rhetoric of the Social Sciences." In *Knowledges: Historical and Critical Studies in Disciplinarity,* ed. Ellen Messer-Davidow, David R. Shumway and David J. Sylvan (pp. 125–149). Charlottesville: University Press of Virginia.

Gouldner, Alvin W. 1970. *The Coming Crisis of Western Sociology.* New York: Basic Books.

Hirsch, Jr., E. D. 1999. *The Schools We Need.* New York: Anchor Books.

Paras, Eric. 2006. *Foucault 2.0: Beyond Power and Knowledge.* New York: Other Press.

Pinar, William F. 2004. *What Is Curriculum Theory?* Mahwah, NJ: Lawrence Erlbaum.

Pinar, William F. 2009. *The Worldliness of a Cosmopolitan Education: Passionate Lives in Public Service.* New York: Routledge.

Pinar, William F., ed. 2010. *Curriculum Studies in South Africa.* New York: Palgrave Macmillan.

Pinar, William F., William M. Reynolds, Patrick Slattery, and Peter M. Taubman. 1995. *Understanding Curriculum: An Introduction to Historical and Contemporary Curriculum Discourses.* New York: Peter Lang.

Popkewitz, Thomas S. 2008. *Cosmopolitanism and the Age of School Reform: Science, Education, and Making Society by Making the Child.* New York: Routledge.

Wang, Hongyu. 2004. *The Call from the Stranger on a Journey Home: Curriculum in a Third Space.* New York: Peter Lang.

Chapter 10

Curriculum Studies in Brazil: Four Concepts

William F. Pinar

*Living with the uncertainty of the political game seems to be what remains
for us.*

(Lopes's chapter 6 of this volume)

Acknowledging what Bernadette Baker characterizes as the "incommensurability" among the chapters, I will attempt to articulate their "synergy"
(also her term). I share Baker's view that there is "no consistent *a priori* that
would enable them to be considered a range or variation of the same normative themes." She reports that "reading the papers in a sequence point to
aporias that are important to affirm." Understanding these "aporias" as a
"productive incommensurability" (Baker's phrase) enables us to appreciate
how these aporias (Baker does not specify them) comprise (if indirectly)
the chapters' "synergy."

I hope to point to both as I disaggregate the concepts comprising it.
Baker might express skepticism with this undertaking, given her observation that at least one concept—hegemony—"is vastly different across the
texts." That difference is simultaneously definitional and functional, as
Baker emphasizes: "The weight the term is given in the argument, the role
and its location—the pivotal point at which it is invoked or deployed—
and the work that the term is meant to perform within the narrative, cannot be reduced to a common core conception." Although its usage varies
according to context and its meaning cannot be reduced to a "common

core," I point out that the term "hegemony" remains, signifying *something*, even if this "something" varies according to context. A "common language... [may be] impossible," as Alice Casimiro Lopes asserts (in an exchange with Ursula Hoadley), but she also points out that "we act as if translation were possible," provisionally fixing meanings in order to "communicate" and "understand." Lopes emphasizes that this is a "precarious and limited process."

Like the concepts of "nation" and "hegemony," the four concepts I identify here are, yes, "precarious" (and, as you will see, inextricably interrelated) but also, I would emphasize, precious, as they are prerequisites to our efforts to communicate and understand within and across (not only national) difference. After completing this chapter I shared it with participants, inviting their critique and comment, registering these in revision or—when there is non-negotiable disagreement—in the epilogue. The Brazilian scholars have the "last word."

In my study of curriculum studies in South Africa, I identified four concepts around which "discursive movements"[1] were organized: disciplinarity, dialogue, agency, and translation (Pinar 2010a, 232). Although unique to curriculum studies in South Africa, these concepts were not permanent residents there, as they also circulate in curriculum studies in Brazil, as Elizabeth Macedo's comments on disciplinarity (Pinar 2010a, 232) make explicit. (Macedo served both as a member of the international panel questioning the participating South African scholars and as a participating Brazilian scholar in the study documented in the present volume.) As in the South African project, I emphasized particularity, not comparison. There may be no a priori unifying these chapters, but their specificities are clearly interwoven, crafting an unmistakable sense of shared difference. Although these concepts may neither reflect an "a priori" nor add up to a "totality," they do denote the distinctiveness that is curriculum studies in Brazil.

As in South Africa, these concepts are refracted through my own situated subjectivity, reflecting—but not reducible to—my ongoing preoccupations[2] with disciplinarity, dialogue, agency, and translation. In curriculum studies in Brazil those concepts were also audible, if subsumed in different terms. I am not suggesting that the concepts in the two countries convey the same a priori; they do not. Nor do they circulate in the same ways; present circumstances differ in the two countries. In Brazilian curriculum studies I choose different concepts to convey these nationally distinctive realities. In Brazil the field—as reflected in these chapters and exchanges—seems preoccupied with (1) enunciation, (2) eventfulness, (3) the quotidian, and (4) hybridity. While each is significant in itself, their interrelatedness (including their dissonance) accents their synergy.

Too tersely, one could express this interrelatedness as a syllogism: Agency structures (and is structured by) eventfulness, animated by processes of enunciation, structuring as it destructures hybrid (dis)figurations in the vast immanent expanse that is the quotidian.[3] Dialogue and translation are agency's media, disciplinarity and its discontents comprise their structure and precipitate their disfiguration. Hybridity characterizes its precondition and consequence.

In South African curriculum studies, agency was inflected racially and politically, echoing a long history of struggle from slavery through Apartheid into the post-Apartheid present. In Brazil the concept, although hardly severed from History, seems more specific to efforts to understand curriculum, what Steve Fuller (1993) terms the "internal approach."[4] In "enunciation," the agency of teachers is "always" on the "horizon" as "political reinvention" through "signification." Its discursive status underscores the symbolic sphere in which the curriculum can be reconstructed. As discursive, "agency" implies "translation."[5] These concepts stand separate from and, indeed, become subsumed in others, forming a "knowledge network" (the quoted concepts are from Macedo) wherein the "agency of subjects" becomes central, expressed in "decisions" enacted "in the undecidable space of displaced structure."

Agency becomes almost inevitable as the "creative tensionality" (this phrase I import from Ted T. Aoki [2005 (1991), 383]) demands decisions, an interpretation supported by Elba Siqueira de Sá Barretto's emphasis upon representation as a space of "in-between" straddled by the social and the personal. For Nilda Alves, agency appears through the "everyday lives of educative networks" that engage emotion and fantasy in creating classroom realities other than those prescribed officially. This notion of "in-between" or "third space" (see Wang 2004) has a prominent position, and not only in curriculum studies in Brazil; it recalls still another key concept: hybridity. In such an "in-between" space, moments are opportunities for "action" and "creations of new meaning." Recall, too, Tero Autio's praise of Ferraço's employment of hybridism as "an interstice" between "official" and "practiced" curricula, providing a space of "overcom[ing]...power in their reproductive and resistant forms." This location of agency is also evident in conceptions of disciplinarity.

In curriculum studies in South Africa, disciplinarity is associated with post-Apartheid state-directed curriculum reform, specifically its blurring of disciplinary boundaries between the school subjects through curriculum integration. Although curriculum integration is prominent in Brazil as well, disciplinarity is less associated with racialized social structures and state-directed curriculum reform than it is with multiple positioned knowledge-power relations. In chapter 6, Lopes references disciplinarity as risking "a pathology of knowledge" associated with its pretense of social disinterestedness while in the service of capital accumulation. Lopes links disciplinarity with libraries, self-encased collections of knowledge produced (and reproduced) by "methods" and "common thinking devices." In her reply to Autio's question concerning the contributions of information technologies to a "global archive of knowledge," Lopes expresses her skepticism that this "acceleration" of knowledge flows jeopardizes the disciplines even if they blur their boundaries. Hoadley questions postmodernism's preference for the political over the epistemological, threatening presentism and relativism, stripping us of knowledge that could strengthen the field both politically and epistemologically. In her reply, Lopes emphasizes interdisciplinarity, asserting that the hybridity of curriculum studies renders the field "more dense and mature." Disciplinarity, Lopes continues, acknowledges that epistemology is encoded politically, and it is this fact that obligates us to study the history of the field. Hoadley remains unconvinced, concerned that hybridity means the "loss of a common language... [and thereby] cumulative understandings."

Both Hoadley and Lopes are right, it seems to me. There is embedded in some celebrations of interdisciplinarity "a deep distrust" of the academic disciplines (Anderson and Valente 2002, 1), in part due to North American misappropriations of the Foucauldian association of disciplinarity with power. Studying the intellectual histories and present circumstances of nationally distinctive fields disables expansive if reductionist applications of Foucauldian governmentality while acknowledging the vexed interrelations between epistemology and politics. Anderson and Valente's (2002, 2) point seems to me pertinent here:

> If the tendency is now to associate interdisciplinarity with freedom, and disciplinarity with constraint, a closer look at the history of these disciplines shows that the dialectic of agency and determinism, currently distributed across the disciplinary/interdisciplinary divide, was at the heart of disciplinary formation itself.

In the Brazilian case, the emphasis upon agency—enacted also through the associated concepts of enunciation, eventfulness, and the hybridity of the quotidian—instantiates creativity and contestation at the core of curriculum studies.

Hybridity characterizes the discourse of disciplinarity. Regarding Autio's question concerning shifts in the Brazilian field's vocabulary after two decades of postmodernism, Inês Barbosa de Oliveira reports that her colleagues have indeed debated the various prefixes, "post" prominent among them, the consequence of which, she offers, is a "hyper-disciplinarizing" of the discipline around its own formulations. While such "enrichment of vocabulary" contributes to the "deepening of debate" and leads to "new forms of understanding curricula," Oliveira worries that this "terminological multiplication" also blurs the distinction between "rhetorical dispute" and "conceptual construction." This is a point well taken.

Others (such as Lopes) endorse "polysemy," especially due to "cross-cultural borrowings" through the historic importation of concepts from France and the United States. Those "borrowings" and "grafts" result in the "hybridism" of the field, a state intensified by its already interdisciplinary character, informed, as it is, by multiple (and conflicting) intellectual traditions, prominent among them Marxism and post-structuralism. Hybridity also occurs through the juxtaposition of European and nativist knowledge in the school curriculum (as Macedo endorses), "creating a zone of ambivalence" wherein the enunciation of hybridity can be undertaken.

Such a "zone" enables the translation of the academic disciplines in the everyday life of schools. Even subjects closest to the academic disciplines (Lopes points out) become reinvented in schools. It is not only the intersecting spheres of the epistemological and the political that become performed in schools, so do cultural differences.[6] The curriculum is the site of translation among these different vocabularies and the realities they represent and reconstruct. Translation becomes a paradigmatic instance of enunciation, when agency is enacted, representing and creating moments of hybridity.

Always relational, discourse is (Lopes emphasizes) never static or complete but always "susceptible to subversion." Emphasizing the point, Lopes declares, "There is always a polysemy, a multiplicity of meanings." Hybridity (or hybridism, emphasizing the process not the product), she continues, is both the "denial and affirmation of particularity." Macedo states the matter in these terms: the curriculum constructs locality as it "articulates differential demands...creating cultural hybrids [through] plural knowledges." We can glimpse this "locality" through four concepts that distinguish curriculum studies in Brazil. Animating each, it seems to me, is the concept of enunciation.

Enunciation

Macedo invokes "enunciation" to "discuss the thematics of difference." Referencing her earlier interests in "dialogue" and "negotiation"—she acknowledges these as "fundamental to curriculum and democratic practice"—Macedo also recalls her move from a Habermasian concern for consensus to the forefronting of difference. She likens curriculum to a Pollock painting[7] wherein "successive deferments...open like 'islands spawning islands'," recalling an epigraph by Pessoa in her chapter. "Like Pollock's painting," Macedo explains, "the textual structure is decentered, without limits, but is momentarily fixed around a provisional center," always "open to new possibilities of meaning." She continues: "every enunciation is hybrid because it is obliged to negotiate, antagonistically and incompletely, its meanings with the other." In dialogue, Macedo summarizes, meaning becomes politicized, hegemonies form, and power becomes structured and achieves force. Macedo characterizes the subject as the "agency of enunciation." She notes, "The discussion about hegemony is, therefore, also a discussion about the constitution of the subject and of its agency." She acknowledges her intellectual life history: "I think that here I am admitting my Enlightenment heritage—which only allows me to think of education as symbolic self-construction of the subject—but aware...[there can be no] free and conscious subject, but that that impossibility does not eliminate its necessity."

Curriculum as *enunciation* endorses the unexpected in the classrooms, thereby locating agency at the core of everyday life in schools. Registering her disagreement with studies of the quotidian, however, Macedo reports that she devised the concept of "curriculum as enunciation" to "overcome the binary between formal and lived curriculum." Recall that in her conception of enunciation, the agency of teachers is "always" on the "horizon," although not with what Macedo regards as the naive faith sometimes evident in "everyday life" research. Enunciation emphasizes "signification of the world" (Lopes' phrase[8]), linking discourse and material reality through meaning, a hybridized conception incorporating post-structuralism, hermeneutics, and cultural studies. In Macedo's formulation, "culture" becomes a "signification," an "*enunciation*," a "production, irregular and incomplete, with meaning and value." Thus understood, culture is no static inheritance to be preserved or contested, as both movements are evident when students and teachers articulate what is hybrid in their "political reinvention" of academic knowledge. In Amorim's terms, curriculum becomes disfigured. It is through the "destructured structure" of articulatory practice that the "agency of subjects" is performed. Enunciation recasts curriculum implementation as "translation."

For Macedo, hybridity becomes the "condition" in which enunciation occurs. As such, hybridity denotes both the site and structure wherein agency takes form. Macedo emphasizes the "destructured" character of structure to make unmistakable its negotiable character. Such a conception enables (again in my terms) reconstruction, through enunciation, as in "the talking cure,"[9] as through pedagogical interventions in the ongoing "complicated conversation" that is the curriculum. Through enunciation, the agency of teachers is "always" (not only) on the "horizon." Through enunciation the horizon, that edge or limit of the situation in which one dwells, becomes visible, becomes negotiable. For some, Macedo notes, agency is "dependent on a kind of illumination." Indeed, in the theory-practice binary, education was valorized as "practice," although critical pedagogy had attempted to incorporate theory in practice through its embrace of the concept of "praxis." In enunciation, the eventfulness of the quotidian becomes enacted in agency, and everyday reality becomes reconstructed.

In the postmodern era, subjectivity disappears into identity, and agency evaporates into governmentality. Opposed to the effacement of subjectivity, the essentialization of identity, and the severance of history from the subject, Macedo theorizes beyond private/public binaries to emphasize "what cannot be foreseen in the order of things as they are or should be." As the "locus" of decision making in the "undecidable space of displaced structure," subjectivity reconstructs hegemony as it reconfigures itself and those structures it inhabits. By "enunciation" Macedo emphasizes action in the everyday creation of the unexpected. There is no effort to force the future to become like the present by linking outcomes to objectives.[10]

Addressing Macedo's "highly sophisticated and locally instantiated theory of curriculum as enunciation," Autio asks Macedo about the influence of globalization on her formulation of "enunciation." Macedo replies that she has attempted to think beyond this polarity by considering curriculum as "a process of localization of the global" through its "enunciation." What destabilizes the local is the global, she continues, as that "constitutive exterior" guarantees a certain "undecidability" in the local. The curriculum constructs locality as it "articulates differential demands...creating cultural hybrids [through] plural knowledges." Here we discern a productive tension between the two imbricated domains, and within that tension—what could be construed as a "third space"—the "composition" of curriculum (a concept employed by Amorim) converts this tension into animated encounter with the everyday, the local. Here we glimpse the reciprocal relations among enunciation, eventfulness, and hybridity in/through the quotidian.

Eventfulness

Among the questions that structure contemporary curriculum studies in Brazil (as Ashwani Kumar points out in chapter 1) are processes of negotiation, translation, mimicry, and uses. These I embed in the concept of *eventfulness*, itself something of a hybrid term that forefronts (in my terms) the immanence of education, not its fragmentation into static binaries: process/product, subject/object, goal/outcome. This is evident in Antonio Carlos Amorim's aspiration to free curriculum theory from its subsumption in critique and politics, threading it instead through difference in the world. Such an embrace of intellectual independence and creativity underscores the agency of enunciation. Using neither term, Amorim nonetheless speaks of movement[11] and action, if in different terms (without the subject), among these "differing" and "singularization."

For Oliveira, the eventfulness of education is associated with the concept of "emergence,"[12] which she defines as "emancipating the potential...in quotidian practices." Such emancipating practice is articulated by means of a "cosmopolitan rationality" that "transforms absences into presences." The future is thereby built from "plural and concrete possibilities discernible in the present," constructed "through individual and/ or collective action." Although the terms are linked they are not interchangeable. Indeed, each accents reality distinctively, but each—again it seems to me, reading from a distance—emphasizes movement, action, and agency, what I might summarize (after Dewey) as " subjective and social reconstruction." Curriculum may remain a complicated conversation, but underscored in Brazilian studies of the quotidian are its turbulence and intensity.

Carlos Eduardo Ferraço links two gerunds—experimenting-problematizing—to invoke the eventfulness of everyday life in schools. Through this linkage teachers and students become, in his terminology, "protagonists of the educational scene," enacting transgressions of the official curriculum, often in "powerful and inventive ways." Even those subjects that might seem closest to the academic disciplines—chemistry, for instance—are, Lopes notes, reinvented in schools. In postmodernity, rationalization becomes questioned, she suggests, leaving us with "legitimation through performance," rendering the political and the epistemological intertwined. But Nilda Alves emphasizes that narrative and event are not simultaneous or coincident: eventfulness always exceeds our capacity to narrate it. Alves employs the gerund[13] "happenings" to underscore the eventfulness of everyday educational life.

Time itself is variable, as Lopes suggests: "the past of one place is the present of another." Duration destructures eventfulness—the latter term surfaces in Amorim's linking of image and memory, sensation and movement; it is also evident in Alves' "fifth movement," expressed in the question "why didn't I see this before?" and in her linking of "space-times," specifying the interrelation between time and place. Despite working from different intellectual traditions, both Alves and Amorim link place and time through duration. Eventfulness, then, not only expresses temporality but also occurs in location, in the specificity and complexity of place. The enunciation of eventfulness requires translation across national borders and within academic disciplines. Replying to Baker, Macedo acknowledges the "difficulty of translation" in both "internationalization" and in "interdisciplinarization." By these concepts Macedo is referencing issues of "translation" between "academic cultures...marked by national bias." It is not only national location that complicates communication/translation, but also the bricolage that interdisciplinarity invites. "I agree with you," Lopes writes, referencing Baker's emphasis upon the distinctiveness—sometimes incommensurability—of various intellectual traditions and the specific texts we use to construct our "translations." Eventfulness follows from difference, even incommensurability, juxtaposed temporally and locationally, enacted through translation.

Duration emphasizes not only "what is" and "what is not yet," but also what has disappeared. Baker emphasizes the concept of "disappearance," noting that in her specialization (curriculum history: see Baker 2009) the phenomenon is an ongoing source of debate. Does disappearance constitute "change" or "secret continuity"? Is it "rupture" or "something lesser," like "(dis)continuity"? Baker relocates her question from historiography to internationalization, wondering about "the difficulty of translating the term 'curriculum' into many languages," especially when it does not exist in local language. How does the term's importation "force" us to "think differently" about knowledge, cosmology, and subjectivity? In her reply, Lopes links the "difficulty of translating" to the "antagonism" of "social relations," their even provisional totalization blocked by antagonism. For totality, antagonism is both its "condition of possibility" and its "condition of impossibility." Social processes are, then, constructed by incommensurable differences that structure translation, rendering it always "precarious, contingent, political." Baker and Lopes agree that the meanings of "disappearance" are multiple and always open to revision, contestation, and resignification.

Translation structures the eventfulness of curriculum policy in Brazil. Recall that Elba Siqueira de Sá Barretto, replying to Hoadley's question regarding curriculum integration, provides a historical account, linking curricular integration with national integration. States became responsible for providing curriculum guidelines, but in "better developed" municipalities additional guidance was provided. Barretto judges that there has been, historically, alignment between state and municipal guidelines. Like similar reforms across Latin America and in accordance with UNESCO recommendations, the National Curricular Parameters (PCN) supplemented (but hardly eliminated) state and municipal guidelines. They left undisturbed the disciplinary structure of the curriculum while introducing "transversal themes" such as "preservation of the environment, respect for differences, and education for health." Recently, studies of African history as well as Afro-Brazilian and indigenous cultures have also been incorporated into the curriculum. It would seem that Brazil bucks the worldwide trend toward neoliberalism as it grapples with the eventfulness of curriculum, stimulated in part by multiple sites of power, multiple cultures, and multiple social demands upon the curriculum, all of which become translated through enunciation in the quotidian.

The Quotidian

Emphasizing "absence" and "emergence," Oliveira's conception of the quotidian provides the site of enunciation, translation, and hybridity. The quotidian is the sphere of the singular, denoting (simultaneously) site, time, and action, what Oliveira summarizes as "makings/doings." Despite the phraseology, the intellectual debt here is as much to Marxism as it is to phenomenology, as Oliveira implies: "we understand each reality as a product of the singularities and specificities of subjects and circumstances that define them, constituting potential for social emancipation." That potential can be realized pedagogically, Oliveira asserts, as "apprentices of the quotidian" become "holders of possible formal education contributions to the society's democratization."

I am struck by the association of emancipation with particularity, by the tacit acknowledgment that speech—in Macedo's formulation, enunciation—becomes the medium of movement. The singularity of the situation becomes the portal to its reconstruction, to, in Oliveira's terms, the "emergence" of what is "not yet." This is no radical particularism, however, as Oliveira also acknowledges the "common heritage of humanity" as inhering in the singularity of the quotidian. Baker seems skeptical, asking what it can mean to find "convergences in the middle of differences." Does this conception reinstall the "identity-difference schemata indicative of the modern episteme"? In the unlinking of democracy from modernity and capitalism, Baker questions the status of "agency." Is it possible to think of education without the "agent"[14] who acts to improve the self and world?

Also a researcher of daily life, Ferraço looks to the "interstices," neither "fixed or immutable," for what is "not yet." Ferraço forefronts the everyday as the site of "enunciation." Oliveira's "apprentices of the quotidian" become, in Ferraço's terms, "practitioners of daily life," themselves the "protagonists of their *history* and *experience.*" For him, enunciation underscores the translation of official policy through local networks into reinvented practices, on the "frontier of cultural differences." Even "mimicry" discloses "difference, slippage, excess." Quoting Silva, Ferraço locates the hybrid in difference, as it carries the "marks of power... as well as resistance."

Ferraço focuses on "narrative-images of teachers" engaged in "action-knowledge," concepts not often paired in U.S. curriculum discourse, let alone hyphenated. Ferraço also fastens together what are often (in North America) two separate, even antagonistic concepts: "the *individual-collective* subject." In everyday life research there seems solidarity between researchers and the researched. "With them," Alves reports, referencing her informants, "we began to understand, in individual and collective processes, the ways how knowledges and meanings are created in everyday lives, seeking to understand the different logics with which they are articulated."

In reply to Hoadley's question concerning the quotidian, Oliveira affirms the vastness of what is, in particular how invisible much everyday social practice is.[15] Models cannot capture the specificity of the everyday, including those ever-changing practices that subvert the hegemonic. Only through study of "what is said and done by teachers and students in classrooms," Oliveira cautions, can we discern the "subtleties and wealth of daily life." Structural analyses cannot convey this complexity, nor can they honor how daily life reconstructs society more generally.

Macedo cites the quotidian as "one of the motors of preoccupation with binaries that I deconstruct." Depicting the quotidian "as a place of the new bothers me," she explains, as this "affirmation contains an expectation of liberation." Moreover, this emphasis challenges Macedo's privileging of the history of school subjects and her study of curricular documents, as these are positioned as secondary in studies of everyday life. They are, simply, among the particulars whose articulation from absence to emergence enacts emancipation. Is it, then, the facility implied by this faith that bothers Macedo? Does enunciation rest upon resistance?

Autio also asks about the "quotidian," specifically, vocabularies employed to specify its particularities, its subtleties. Oliveira reiterates her (and her colleagues') commitment to surpass the oversimplifications that the "parsimony" (Autio's word) science enforces. They do so by attending to the complexity of action (its multiple influences: on it, in it, from it), including researchers' presence within it as students of the everyday. Regarding Autio's question concerning globalization, Oliveira acknowledges its totalizing tendencies but emphasizes the local's capacity to resist it. Scholarly fascination with globalization distracts us from the urgency of the local, Oliveira asserts, including needs associated with specific realities, and the possibilities of curricular redress. In response to Baker's question concerning globalization, Oliveira reasserts that the scope of her attention is the quotidian, for example, "globalized localisms."

Reaffirming the "emancipatory" potential of the quotidian, Oliveira decries totalization; it obliterates the particularity of the everyday, the domain wherein the future emerges. She then critiques notions of "linear time" that disregard "errors, accidents," and those other "transformations of reality" that our "ecstatic expectations" may disavow. Oliveira questions the "imprisoning" of the future by institutionalized insistence on its continuity with the present. It is through the plural and the concrete that the future becomes no longer a predictable continuation of an undemocratic present, but a surprising materialization of what is "not yet."[16] "Concrete possibilities and capacity," Oliveira continues, "will re-determine all they touch, modifying and, therefore, placing all previous determinations in question." In this conception of everyday life, instrumentalism—with its demand that outcomes coincide with objectives—fades into the simultaneity of eventfulness. In everyday life Oliveira finds "knowledge in networks"—not only disciplinary networks, but social and emotional networks as well.

Replying to Baker's skepticism regarding the "emancipatory" intent of everyday life research (specifically, its Marxist antecedents), Oliveira asserts that the social equality prerequisite to a "dignified existence" is not associated with capitalist values—in particular with "individualism" and "competitiveness"—and it must be worked out within daily life, not through economic structures. Rather than formulating an alternative economic model, Oliveira and her colleagues focus upon those social practices that exhibit "the potential to contribute to the democratization of society," especially those practices that disclose "the plurality of the world, of the knowledge and cultures that inhabit it." Such practices are "less hierarchical, more ecological."

Baker is not persuaded. She asks, "Is 'experience' already laced with the 'understanding' that gives rise to 'its' noticeability in the first place?" What would constitute the "emergence" of "experience"? How does such a notion "exceed...conceptions of instrumentality"? Baker underscores the contested character of "globalization," specifically, its utility as a category of attribution or causality. She wonders what its relationship to the quotidian might be, and whether that relationship—indeed whether the very concept of the quotidian itself ("what is *not* daily life?" she asks)—might be different in different locales, regions, and among different groups. Baker does not find capitalism and socialism to be "exclusively politico-economic systems or models, nor necessarily oppositions. [They] have taken multiple forms...of organization, regulation, and subjectification." Likewise, the quotidian itself takes multiple forms and cannot be free of surveillance and regulation. In fact, rendering the quotidian visible may enable surveillance and regulation of it. Baker asks, "In a world of cruelty and violence, how can one imagine a less hierarchal, more ecological world?"

The *quotidian* is indeed a key concept in curriculum studies in Brazil (see Lopes and Macedo 2003, 194). Against totalization, against abstraction absent its concrete referents, invisible to quantitative research, studies of the quotidian emphasize the creative contestatory curriculum wherein students and teachers reinvent what they are obligated to study. "In each quotidian reality," Oliveira asserts, "the struggle happens in different forms.... [T]o know the circumstance is fundamental." It is within the sphere of the everyday where "transformations of reality" occur. In this turbulent—in Amorim's term "violent"—mélange hybridity seems almost inevitable.

Hybridity

Amorim defines hybridity as "difference without identity," emphasizing the movement and instability of reality, its resistance to totalization. Recall that he trades concepts implying stasis, even coherence, for those accenting motion and duration, for example, "differing" and "singularization." Such concepts construct an "immanent relationship with the event." For Amorim such eventfulness has no "subject," but for Macedo one remains. "The notion of hybridism," she notes, "has enabled me to treat curricular texts—always permeated by the *différance* of the writing—like ambivalent enunciations because they are marked by the separation between the enunciated 'I' and the 'I' of the enunciation." Here hybridity structures enunciation, demarcated spatially by the differential locations of the "I." Perhaps this "differing" produces, in Amorim's term, "singularization."

For Amorim, research occurs in space emptied of structure. It is, he asserts provocatively, a space of "disfiguration," a plane of "sensation." Simultaneously imagistic, auditory, and virtual, these planes are accented by "intensities." These forms of disfiguration constitute the "events" of "curriculum creation." A "metamorphosis machine," he asserts, "the curriculum is no repetition of the same but the production of something altogether different." That "something altogether different" is specified by "concepts like hybridism, in-between, trace, and boundaries." Spatial figuration locates this conception, and Deleuze's notion of "becoming" emphasizes its duration, as "time" splinters the subject into multiple spaces.

"To think with the connective *what if* is to constitute a thought without a subject," Amorim writes, "a thought of time and spatial effectuation." He adds, "And, then, it opens gaps to the creation of senses, to inventions, to fabulations, to intensities." This emphasis upon the eventfulness of hybridity—spatially and temporally disfigured and dispersed—reminds me of Macedo's insistence that accumulated knowledge is never narrowly disciplinary but always "also hybrid" in its constitution, never a "controllable entity." This same hybrid sense of eventfulness seems implied in Amorim's theorization of curriculum as a plane of sensation.

Lopes examines how signification, especially school knowledge, becomes "hegemonized." To denote hierarchy,[17] Lopes invokes the concept of "library," defined as "the mechanism that organizes and ranks symbolic assets," differentiating them according to organizational logic. Lopes underlines the Internet's role in "deterritorializations [that] accelerate the de-collection of libraries." Associated with globalization, this "threat" is not only to our "libraries" but to our very "identities." Lopes adds, "It seems to me that the hybridism category can help us to understand these de-collections, deterritorializations and impure genres." Indeed, hybridity enables Lopes "to rethink the...stability with which we construct history."

The concept of "subject" is for Lopes simultaneously the academic discipline, the school subject, and the "members of a disciplinary community" who are always positioned politically. To be focused on power and the present, however, does not mean scholars can ignore their intellectual histories. Furthermore, for a field to advance we must not treat its hybridity as a "loss." Referencing Laclau, Lopes suggests we return to our "libraries" and to the "valorization of canons...without essentialisms or fixing identities." Disciplinarity is, then, without certainty: its hybridity "corresponds to those alterations in which the differential identities 'waive' their particularities on behalf of a common project." The very articulation of projects requires hybridity, "the simultaneous negation and affirmation of a particularity."

Barretto points to the adoption of Lefebvre's formulation of representation as in-between the social and the personal, enabling researchers to emphasize the moment between the "lived" and the "conceived." In this "in-between" moment are opportunities for "action" and "creations of new meaning." Within mediation we encounter both blockages and ruptures. Barretto seeks to identify both as they inhere in daily teaching practice, thereby exposing hybrid genealogies of teacher agency and creativity. Such hybridity seems implied in Alves' "movements," among them "turning upside down" and "drinking from all fountains." In these images I hear echoes of Lopes's de-collection and Macedo's "enunciation" occurring on Amorim's plane of "sensation."

That last sentence summarizes but in so doing obscures significant differences among the concepts. Like Freire's pedagogy of the oppressed, everyday life research contains traces of Marxism and phenomenology, if accented in post-structuralist terms. In enunciation, eventfulness, and hybridity, the influence of post-structuralism and postcolonialism is conspicuous. I discern traces of Marxist teleology in everyday life research, as Baker noticed as well. Although there may be no historical inevitability, there is in everyday life research, if not a certainty, at least a confidence that the future can be threaded through the everyday. Although deferred, the future is not split-off in some abstract universal domain no one can influence. It is present in the concreteness and particularity of everyday life, in (recalling Amorim) "forces unknown before, forces which surpass imagination and experience."

I am struck by an echo of early twentieth-century U.S. progressivism and its faith in social democracy: Addams's Hull-House and Dewey's Laboratory School, both emphasizing the simultaneity and eventfulness of social and subjective reconstruction. Separated by a century (not to mention a continent), these movements are not the same, as everyday life research seems to lack any hint of the proceduralism latent in pragmatism, a lack that would become horrifyingly explicit in Tyler's "rationale." Moreover, the tendency toward cultural separatism evident in North American identity politics seems absent in curriculum studies in Brazil. Culture is key but it is its evocative potential, not its polarizing fragmentation into essentialized and mythologized identities, that is emphasized. No ritualistic reification of what is already past, culture becomes the medium through which we pronounce the present and thereby foreshadow the future.

Missing, then, in curriculum studies in Brazil (as we glimpse the field here) is the pervasive instrumentalism shredding especially U.S. educational discourse, always emphasizing how we get from here to there. Missing too is the theoretical shredding of educational experience, demands to choose between structuralism or subjectivism, class or culture, gender or race. Also missing is the demand that schools restructure society and that teachers be accountable for student learning. Missing are those misappropriations of postmodern concepts—such as governmentality, surveillance, biopower—that totalize reality and render not only individuals but also collectivities mute, despite self-righteous demands that we "talk back to power." Cursed by objectives and outcomes, we Americans miss the potential of the present, of the everyday, realizable through enunciation in hybrid forms we cannot know at the outset. The excitement that was evident in the United States a century ago (in Jane Addams, in John Dewey) seems palpable in Brazil today; in these chapters and exchanges one senses the dynamism of U.S. educational discourse felt during that period.

Differences seem sharper in proximity than from a distance. Although present and no doubt magnified within Brazil itself, these differences strike me—writing from not only geographical distance—as interrelated. Despite the differences in intellectual traditions that inform them, despite differences in focus and emphasis, it seems to me that each of the concepts I have identified addresses the others. Indeed, each depends upon the others, while differences ensure that boundaries (however porous) remain. In my reconstruction of curriculum studies in Brazil, enunciation becomes the "engine" of the everyday, as its articulation of what is and what is not yet marks the movement—the eventfulness—that everyday life portends. And because enunciation is not only the pronouncements of policymakers and administrators, but also (especially) the actions of teachers and students (and the pressure of parents), located in the everyday world of the school, inflected by the world outside the school, the mélange that is social reality becomes restructured—and de-structured as both Macedo and Lopes emphasize—in endlessly hybrid forms. This ongoing composition of curriculum—spatial and, as Amorim emphasizes, durational, a plane of sensation—promises no utopia, but it does fracture the hegemony of homogeneity. Is this intensity the aporia that synthesis signifies?

Notes

1. There were similarities in the discursive movements of the exchanges between the Brazilian scholars and the international panel and those characterizing the exchanges among South African scholars and that panel (see Pinar 2010a, 231–232), for example, situating the self (usually by reference to one's country of residence or employment), explanation, expressions of understanding and appreciation. The exchanges between participating Brazilian scholars and the international panel members were marked by challenges to concepts and conceptions to which the Brazilian scholars replied diplomatically but firmly.

2. It *almost* goes without saying that intellectual preoccupations are always already inflected by history, culture, and society, including the now tiresome triumvirate: race-class-gender. I emphasize "inflected," but not "reducible to," as these concepts are not my projections onto alterity, but rather the refracting of alterity through my subjectivity.

3. In Canada, the quotidian became an "object" of curriculum inquiry through phenomenology. As Chambers (2003, 227, emphasis added) suggests, "What might be the substantial interest that phenomenology holds for curriculum in Canada? Perhaps phenomenology's focus on lived experience—the particulars of life lived in a *specific place* in relation to others—enabled scholars to at once be critical of the *abstract* discourses dominating curriculum and the violence they do the earth and children, and to see, hear and feel the 'stubborn particulars of grace' (to quote Jardine quoting the now-deceased Canadian poet Bronwen

Davies) of *everyday life wherever it is lived.*" Tero Autio (2003, 307) suggests that one opening to the quotidian occurs through, of all people, Ralph Tyler: "While preferring contemporary life to ethics or metaphysics Tyler is actually affirming everyday life as a source of morality like Descartes and Locke at the dawn of modernity. This emphasis on everyday practice might prove to be anything but unproblematic: it instantly brings the question of social and political power and control to the forefront." Alves and Oliveira and their colleagues have forefronted that question, answering it within studies of the quotidian.

4. In studies of the history of science, Fuller (1993, 126) distinguishes between "the *internal* approach, devoted to charting the growth of knowledge in terms of the extension of rational methods to an ever-larger domain of objects, and the *external* approach, devoted to charting the adaptability of knowledge to science's ever-changing social arrangements."

5. The U.S. scholar Susan Edgerton (1996, 53) endorses "translation" to underscore that the curriculum is comprised of reconstructions of what others have studied in other times, in other places, for other purposes, for present purposes. This key curriculum concept reverberates with historiographical debates concerning the reconstruction of the past (see Roberts 1995, 163, 183, 200).

6. Carlos Eduardo Ferraço, too, seeks to overcome binaries, writing, "I also search to overcome, as much as possible, the dichotomy between 'school knowledge' and 'scientific knowledge,' having in mind that in the weaving of the daily knowledge, action and power networks, many processes of use, translation, negotiation and hybridism are performed. These processes imprint in themselves the mark of complexity of everything being weaved together and simultaneously.... In fact, in those fights on the frontiers of cultural differences, many movements of translation are performed." This observation resonates with Lopes's emphasis on translation, for example, how knowledge production in schools requires not only epistemological but also historical and social reconstruction. Hoadley finds "fascinating" this question of "translation," not only its internal features (structure) but also the conditions of its production, including its ideological conditions.

7. The paintings of the abstract expressionist Jackson Pollock have been referenced in U.S. curriculum studies as well (see Pinar 1972; Slattery 2006).

8. Lopes's conception "culture" as "signification of the world," involving always, of course, politics, recalls the simultaneity and reciprocity of the subjective and the social (my terms). Lopes acknowledges the centrality of culture in curriculum studies without succumbing to its memorialization, as in identity politics.

9. Anticipating the agency of enunciation, Freud valorized the ongoing free associative self-disclosure of "repressed memory," thereby earning the process—psychoanalysis—the characterization "talking cure" (see Zaretsky 2004, 28).

10. These are two of what Tyler (1949) later theorized as "basic principles" of curriculum and instruction. Linking them to instrumentalized even progressive curriculum reform (see Pinar 2010b).

11. Everyday life research also studies "movement," which Alves (2009) characterizes as a "theoretical-methodological process." There are several montage-like movements, among them (1) "the feeling of the world" (a tribute to the Brazilian poet Carlos Drummond de Andrade), a phrase specifying the researcher's commitment to "dive" into everyday life; (2) "turned upside down" (from the title of the English historian Christopher Hill's study of the sixteenth century); (3) "to drink from all sources," indicating the importance of incorporating multiple and diverse sources, including the "most impure" memories and narratives (including images and sounds, the so-called—after Deleuze—concept-personages); (4) "narrate life and literature science," underscoring the importance of not only writing for academic peers but also engaging school practitioners in dialogue; and (5) "*ecce femina*" (after Foucault), which acknowledges that everyday life research cannot proceed without the contributions of practitioners in each of these moments, marking it "feminine" with "all its nuances and all its history."

12. "Emergence" is also a key concept in complexity theory (see Doll 2005, 53).

13. These gerunds not only underline the eventfulness of education, they also link dichotomies as creatively connected. Moreover, gerunds are often pluralized (to dispute self-same identity) and inverted (to contest hierarchy): *spaces/times, practices/theories/practices, inside/out* (of the school), *local/global*, and *learning/ teaching*. These "movements" are also "forms" that structure research into everyday life. These are hardly desubjectified forms, however, as they ascribe significance to "memory" expressed through "narrative" (not only verbal and written, but also imagistic and musical), focused on the "tactics" of practitioners, employing "cultural artifacts" (often made available by the "producing power") and "strategies" to supplement their intended usage. Central to the research is the concept of "conversation" (after the film director Eduardo Coutinho). (Quoted concepts from Alves 2009.)

14. At one point Amorim suggests that curricular concepts are the result of "verbal actions," casting curriculum "onto the plane of thought wherein French poststructuralists are juxtaposed with Brazilian curriculum theorists Croazza, Tadeu, and Veiga-Neto," thereby proposing a "plane of sensation and composition to curriculum." The constitution of such a plane is the challenge of "thinking without representing," for example, engaging the "power of words, images and objects" as "political commitment." Here "agency" is no product of a unitary (or collectivized) "agent"—the legacy to Enlightenment rationality is stretched thin—but a fluidity discursively disfigured. This post-structuralist reconstruction of "agency" is evident as well in the work of the Australian theorist Bronwyn Davies (2000, 68): "Agency is spoken into existence at any one moment. It is fragmented, transitory, a discursive position that can be occupied within one discourse simultaneously with its non-occupation in another."

15. Siegfried Kracauer, that great commentator of Weimar Germany, also focused on the quotidian in the service of understanding history, nation, and politics (see Kracauer 1995; Weitz 2007, 322).

16. In North America, Maxine Greene has made this phrase famous (see Pinar 1998; Miller 2005).
17. For that concept's elaboration in South African curriculum studies, see Hugo (2010).

REFERENCES

Alves, Nilda. 2009, June 8. Email communication.
Aoki, Ted T. 2005. 1991. "Taiko Drums and Sushi, Perogies and Sauerkraut: Mirroring a Half-life in Multicultural Curriculum." In. *Curriculum in a New Key: The Collected Works of Ted T. Aoki*, ed. William F. Pinar and Rita L. Irwin (pp. 377–387). Mahwah, NJ: Lawrence Erlbaum.
Anderson, Amanda, and Joseph Valente, eds. 2002. *Disciplinarity at the Fin de Siècle*. Princeton, NJ: Princeton University Press.
Autio, Tero. 2003. "Postmodern Paradoxes in Finland: The Confinements of Rationality in Curriculum Studies." In *International Handbook of Curriculum Research*, ed. William F. Pinar (pp. 301–328). Mahwah, NJ: Lawrence Erlbaum.
Baker, Bernadette, ed. 2009. *New Curriculum History*. Rotterdam, Boston and Tapei: Sense Publishers.
Chambers, Cynthia. 2003. " 'As Canadian As Possible Under the Circumstances': A View of Contemporary Curriculum Discourses in Canada." In *International Handbook of Curriculum Research*, ed. William F. Pinar (pp. 221–252). Mahwah, NJ: Lawrence Erlbaum.
Davies, Bronwyn. 2000. *A Body of Writing 1990–1999*. Walnut Creek, CA: AltaMira.
Doll, Jr., William E. 2005. "The Culture of Method." In *Chaos, Complexity, Curriculum, and Culture*, ed. William E. Doll, Jr., M. Jayne Fleener, Donna Trueit, and John St. Julien (pp. 21–75). New York: Peter Lang.
Edgerton, Susan Huddleston. 1996. *Translating the Curriculum: Multiculturalism into Cultural Studies*. New York: Routledge.
Fuller, Steve. 1993. "Disciplinary Boundaries and the Rhetoric of the Social Sciences." In *Knowledges: Historical and Critical Studies in Disciplinarity*, ed. Ellen Messer-Davidow, David R. Shumway, and David J. Sylvan (pp. 125–149). Charlottesville: University Press of Virginia.
Hugo, Wayne. 2010. "Drawing the Line in Post-Apartheid Curriculum Studies." In *Curriculum Studies in South Africa: Intellectual Histories and Present Circumstances*, ed. William F. Pinar (pp. 51–105). New York: Palgrave Macmillan.
Kracauer, Siegfried. 1995. *The Mass Ornament: Weimar Essays*. [Translated, edited, and with an introduction by Thomas Y. Levin.] Cambridge, MA: Harvard University Press.

Lopes, Alice Casimiro, and Elizabeth Fernandes de Macedo. 2003. "The Curriculum Field in Brazil in the 1990s." In *International Handbook of Curriculum Research*, ed. William F. Pinar (pp. 185–203). Mahwah, NJ: Lawrence Erlbaum.

Miller, Janet L. 2005. *The Sound of Silence Breaking and Other Essays: Working the Tension in Curriculum Theory*. New York: Peter Lang.

Pinar, William F. 1972. "Working From Within." *Educational Leadership* 29 (4): 329–331. [Reprinted in *Autobiography, Politics, and Sexuality*, Peter Lang Publishing, Inc., 1994, 7–11.]

Pinar, William F., ed. 1998. *The Passionate Mind of Maxine Greene: "I am not Yet."* London: Falmer.

Pinar, William F., ed. 2010a. *Curriculum Studies in South Africa*. New York: Palgrave Macmillan.

Pinar, William F. 2010b. "The Eight-Year Study." *Curriculum Inquiry* 40 (2): 295–316.

Roberts, David D. 1995. *Nothing but History: Reconstruction and Extremity after Metaphysics*. Berkeley and Los Angeles: University of California Press.

Slattery, Patrick. 2006. *Curriculum Development in the Postmodern Era*. 2nd ed. New York: Routledge.

Wang, Hongyu. 2004. *The Call From the Stranger on a Journey Home: Curriculum in a Third Space*. New York: Peter Lang.

Weitz, Eric D. 2007. *Weimar Germany: Promise and Tragedy*. Princeton, NJ: Princeton University Press.

Zaretsky, Eli. 2004. *Secrets of the Soul: A Social and Cultural History of Psychoanalysis*. New York: Alfred A. Knopf.

Epilogue: The Final Word

Last Words..., or the Beginning of Difference

Antonio Carlos Amorim

I would like to remind readers that my text does not insist on the freedom of the subject, reasserting the category of the "human," or, better yet, of "man" and of humanization. After choosing Brazilian films that "represent" the identities of Brazilians, I wanted, in my text, to approach the field of curriculum in Brazil in which concepts of "culture" and "identity" are almost fundamental. I approached these concepts so as to deconstruct them in their interior, retaining several of their intensities as a tendency to some kind of essentialism. As I, analytically, faced some inevitable effects of my dialogue choices, I sought to stress the continuity of thinking with certain concepts: for example, utopia and freedom, both evocative of a life present historical-socio-cultural circumstances prohibit.

When I inserted the question about dystopia, following Lúcia Nagib, what I wanted to bring to curriculum studies—a field organized around the figure of a subject (human, preferably)—was a series of questions underscoring that such an identification occurs out of the force of violence: a *disfiguration*. This is no bet on irony or melancholy or nostalgia, as we find in other types of peripheral cinemas. Dystopia is a category that politically affirms cultural identifications in a field of degradation, disfocusing, and "malformation." Such concepts are tantamount to disillusionment with the modern processes of constituting nations, including civil rights, citizenship, and so on. But what catches my attention are the connections that dystopia might have with micropolitics of desire (referencing Suely Rolnik and Félix Guattari), forcing us to think of subjectivities whose cultural identities (even if hybrid) are no more than tenuous moving anchorages.

Especially regarding *enunciation*, as one of the key concepts of Brazilian curriculum field (as William Pinar suggests in this volume), one can observe that it is a concept, like *imagination*, that I have faced while working with images articulated with language and structure that, as in phenomenology or studies of representation, "ground" images in historical and ideological contexts. There are several researchers who, in analyzing Gilles Deleuze's

(a)

PELA JANELA DO ÔNIBUS VOCÊ
PODE VER DIVERSOS LUGARES
PASSANDO MUITO RÁPIDO OU
NÃO. EM GERAL, O QUADRO É
FORMADO POR MUITO VERDE,
ALGUNS ANIMAIS E CARROS.
FAÇA DE SEUS OLHOS UMA
CÂMERA E TIRE FOTOS DO QUE
VÊ. O QUE VÊ? UM BELO CON-
TRASTE INTENSO E TOCANTE
GERADO PELA MISTURA DO AS-
FALTO, DO VERDE, DOS CARROS,
DO CÉU.

HTTP://BIOUNICAMP08N.BLOGSPOT.COM/

POLARÓIDES (IN)VISÍVEIS POR RAABE MOREIRA GABRIEL

(b)

Figure 11.1a and b   Imageless Visualities[1]

Translation of the Polaroid snap text: Through the bus window you can see several places passing very fast or not. In general, the scenery is made up of a lot of green, some animals and cars. Turn your eyes into a camera and take pictures of what you see. What do you see? A beautiful, intensive, touching contrast created by the mixture of the asphalt, the green, the cars, and the sky.

thoughts on images, seek to articulate them with the idea of imagination—although Deleuze himself has withdrawn from this undertaking. In this way, connections to Bachelard and Merleau-Ponty are made. I have noticed a certain detachment of imagination in various cinema studies (conducted in the departments of cinema studies and literature). In this varied set, it is commonplace to relate image with thought structures, that is, to articulate image with language that corresponds to the thought expression: therefore, it becomes possible to articulate what the image can represent, including with what was thought. Imagination (or *enunciation*) would thus become, contradictorily, both freedom *and* the imprisonment of significations.

I question the coherence of enunciation with my experimentations with images and words, presenting a reflexive record of my practice as a professor in which I propose to work with the concept of *fabulation* rather than enunciation. Art (including literature and images) and writing are my wager on alternatives, to a curriculum, wherein the liberty of life can appear.

Before the intervention of (in)visible Polaroid snaps (2005), one of the features of my photographic research was immobility. And I do not mean the inherent immobility of the photograph, but of my creative process. The images themselves came to me, through either television or newspaper pages; these images were captured, reworked, and enlarged on photographic paper.

In (in)visible Polaroid snaps this process appears inverted: its execution comes as a result of a ride I take around the city, it is not necessary to use a camera to record what I see and the image production is transferred to those who read the text on the Polaroid snaps. In this sense, *displacement* appears

Figure 11.2   The (In)visible Polaroid Snaps and Their Movements
Source: A. C. Amorim.

to be an important word in this intervention: the artist, from the viewer's perspective, from the photographic making, and from the often stationary sense of visibility we have of the place we inhabit (LISBOA, Tom. http://www.sintomnizado.com.br/ polaroides_sobreaspolaroides.htm).

Through invisible Polaroid snaps, do we find the educative? What is this educative image that is on the bus window, at the bus stop, or what does the writing on the paper glued to the wall or the glass incite us to imagine? Writings without light, superficial on white paper, with guidelines printed in dark ink. When asked about education, the students were only surprised at the answer that the pedagogy *represents*, and it is exactly there that its policy is actualized. And it represents without images, creating visuality without imagetic corporeity. The possibility of educating through imaginative writing is powerful.

The Polaroid snaps open a path from teaching to *fabulation*, a radical displacement of reality represented as true. It can be told, understood, and not located. The fabulation—translation of the language established as foreign (that is, the Polaroid as an imageless visuality, a photograph transferred by writing, an eyeless image)—can become an openness to think of education beyond the powers of representation, as articulated with forces that fly on and in the real. The impersonal and incorporeal of the fabulation and the event are Polaroid snap writings.

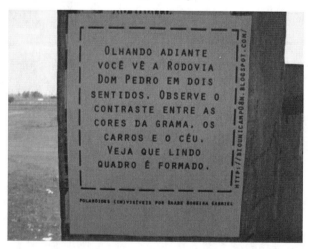

Figure 11.3   Two-Way Traffic
Source: A. C. Amorim.

Translation of the Polaroid snap text: Looking ahead, you can see Dom Pedro Highway two-way traffic. Observe the contrast between the colors of the grass, the cars, and the sky. See what a beautiful picture it forms.

Simply Words

Elizabeth Macedo

Unlike Pinar in the introduction, I do not intend here to say any "final word," even between quotes. I just want to share some of my feelings during the project. From the initial invitation to participate in a project for internationalizing curriculum studies to reading Pinar's comments, a little over two years passed in which I lived an experience of being with the other, of translating the untranslatable, and of pretending that I shared a common space impossible and necessary at the same time. That is internationalizing in Pinar's definition: "to institutionalize the endless effort to communicate across difference."

The first task of the research was to tell about myself, my country, and the local field of the curriculum. Part of that task I had already done countless times in texts about the field of curriculum in Brazil, one of them was published in the *International Handbook of Curriculum Research,* edited by William F. Pinar himself, in an initial stage of the internationalization project. The difference now was to reflect on my intellectual preoccupations and research agenda, relating them as much to the development of the curriculum field as to the social and political history of the country and to "worldization" processes. My interlocutor, like all of us, is a singular person for whom I needed to aggregate various events into a story with a sense that might enable me to say, borrowing from the Brazilian poetess Cecília Meireles (1983, 316), "here is my life:/ this sand so clear/ with drawing that walk/ dedicated to the wind." Thus, I emerged for myself (and in English). In the same movement in which I emerged, I was diluted in the field, in the history of the country, in the world from where I emerged again as a subject.

The second task, familiar and easy, which was to write a text to be read by the curriculum tribe, turned out to be a surprise. Not that I did not know how varied that tribe can be from the experiences of opinions that accept or reject, at times, the same texts. Internationalization as "communication across difference" or as difference that emerges from intersubjective contact was more evident. My initial attempt was to return to the text and bring to it all the polyphony of those conversations, but I realized the impossibility of something like an incorporation or recontextualization of those debates without exploding the text. I did not want to explode it because, after all, it was an interesting piece for the debate. So I am using this opportunity to pick out some explosions that those complicated conversations brought to my research agenda and that, certainly, will be present in future texts as well.

It is interesting how Hoadley's questions clearly indicate a need that had already been transpiring from the reading of other colleagues of other texts related to my research. My concern about dialoguing with aspects of curricular theory that I consider problematical—such as insistence on accumulated knowledge as being central in curricular theory—may be strengthening the oppositions that I would like to deconstruct. I am constructing, without wanting to, an opposition that I maintain is present in curricular theory in Brazil to then try deconstructing it. I perceive, nonetheless, that the tradition I call curricular theory is an invention that perhaps may not be shared by everyone—obvious, perhaps, but (for that reason) hard to perceive when constructing my texts.

Autio's kind provocations had a harshness that he, certainly, could not realize. The harshness of a personal dialogue, mediated by his questions, between what I do today and my enlightened inheritances related to the Frankfurt theoreticians. Inheritances that made me believe in education as a project that defends the function of subjectivation in comparison with the idea of socialization predominant in discourses associated with qualification. With Autio's questions I felt obliged to ask why I had abandoned (if I did) the idea that the educational project should seek to educate the human subject for autonomy, freedom, and emancipation. Although those doubts still resound, I feel I have not actually withdrawn from the project but continue to work on it from the assumption that it is possible to know human nature defined by the autonomy of reason. The definition of a rational basis for the human led, I guess, the function of subjectivization to be substituted, in the humanist educational project of Enlightenment, by socialization in that form of rational life. It is important to point out, however, that I do not question the subjectivity (or the subject), but the definition of subjectivity prevalent in the Enlightened humanism, a subjectivity in which invention itself became impossible because the standards of humanity were already predetermined.

From the extensive discussion with Bernadette Baker, many resonances obliged me to explore the notion of destructured structure, the concept of episteme with which I do not operate directly, the approximations and withdrawals among the authors with whom I dialogue, among other instigating topics. I am mentioning, however, the question of the subject that is, doubtless, one of the most difficult questions with which I have been dealing. In this volume, I tried to avoid that discussion, a sidestepping that did not escape Baker's watchful eye and certainly would not be overlooked by future readers. I have continued to look for post-structural discussions in which the subject assumes centrality, that talk about agency, inheritances from which I do not want (yet) to free myself. Homi Bhabha and Stuart Hall have been companions in that journey, as were, more recently, Ernesto Laclau and Chantal Mouffe. The latter two, although strongly influenced by Jacques Derrida, have associated with subject-agency-decision, minimizing what Baker called (in the e-mail exchange with the author on November 12, 2008) "the risks that Derrida has been willing to take."

Certainly, for the moment, this is what I am desperately looking for. It is not a case of a full and conscious subject capable of acting with total clarity of his/her positions (like in the philosophy of the subject), but of a "subject of lacking." A subject whose contingent intervention, the decision taken in the undecidable space of the structure, supplements it and guarantees it, momentarily, with the systematicity that it does not have. It is a subject produced by identification processes that, for Derrida, are no solution because, if subjectivation is only identification, there is no decision, which would also call for disidentification. I am still, therefore, dealing with the question that emerged from the debate with Baker.

Lastly, I would like to look at one more reading of my text, now together with those of my colleagues and integrating all that was produced in the project—an analysis of part of the curriculum field in Brazil made by a colleague who was, at the same time, like we all are, a tribe companion and a foreigner. As a colleague, Pinar is one of those experts who knows curricular thinking like no one else. As a foreigner, he is a watchful reader, concerned with the cultural nuances that make us, also, local subjects. Pinar's synthesis was based on four concepts—enunciation, eventfulness, the quotidian, and hybridity—that "interwove" the texts in their specialties. My first feeling was of surprise when perceiving concepts such as enunciation and hybridity, with which I have worked, used together with others such as "eventfulness" and the "quotidian." Like Baker, I have become accustomed to seeing these in their incommensurability, not exactly by the meanings that they articulate in the field of the humanities, but by the meanings they are assuming in the field of curriculum of Brazil. Coming close to the unfamiliar was, then, the last exercise. What was perhaps harder was feeling ill at ease with my own customs in order to be able to accompany the movement of Pinar's reading and perceive the synergies he indicated. Another vision of the field emerges from that dual exercise, quite different from that which I mentioned at the start of the project and which I have emphasized in my text. I is an "internationalized" story that recovers something of the difference that we have been excluding.

The synergy that Pinar perceives between the texts and articulates as the four concepts points toward a transitory curriculum, impossible to be entirely grasped. Whether as quotidian practice, as enunciation, or as eventfulness, the curriculum is not fixed but is being formed in movement. Communicated across difference, the centrality of the curriculum as a moment of creation was intensified. A creation that emphasizes, in many of the texts, the subject and the agency, the teacher and the epistemic communities as producers of the curriculum. Although the field of curriculum in Brazil is much more plural—including colleagues who could not or did not want to participate in the project—Pinar's reading leads us to read our research preoccupations in another way. On my agenda is the aspiration to understand how, during recent decades, we constructed that centrality of the curriculum as movement and how we failed (or I failed) to perceive it.

Before dedicating myself more effectively to that agenda, I want to mention some ideas that require more consistent research work. First, the perception that this synergy may point toward a greater influence from Paulo Freire, whose reduced impact on curricular theorization in Brazil has always intrigued me. That supposed greater influence reminds us of the debates of the 1970s—among followers of Freire with his preoccupation with the culture of the different groups and more universalist currents—when seeking to understand the insistence of the curricular discussion, especially in the form of curricular guidelines, in the centrality of knowledge, of scientific knowledge, or of knowledge accumulated by humanity for the curriculum. A second idea refers to the place of the tradition of didactics in that synergy. The coexistence in Brazil of studies in didactics and in curriculum always instigated us to look for differences between those fields, without our having been able to differentiate them from the epistemological point of view. Inverting the exercise of differentiation, we could ask ourselves how the tradition of didactics, before the existence of curriculum as an area of studies in Brazil, nurtured our understanding of the curriculum. If we consider research on training teachers—one of the most developed areas in the country in which all curricularists in some way have passed—as part of the tradition of didactics, perhaps we may understand how the agency of teaching became an important marker of the theory of curriculum in Brazil.

These questions continue as does, for me, the curiosity to understand how we naturalize, to the point of no longer perceiving, our clashes over eventfulness, enunciation, and practice that share the common ground of curriculum as movement. I joined the field not so long ago, but long enough to remember that at the annual meetings of our Postgraduation and Research Association there was a session dedicated to studies of quotidian practice, headed by researchers who worked around references produced by Nilda Alves. At other sessions, we had discussions about post-structural studies, knowledge, and the history of the curriculum. That division was also what we—Alice Casimiro Lopes and I—used in the text published in the *Handbook* organized by Pinar. Recalling other studies that I made in the field of the history of curricular thinking in Brazil also reminds me that there has been a recent displacement of meanings of curriculum by the idea of movement. On the research agenda is the determination to understand how the field produced that displacement and how, in order to guarantee that rearticulation, the idea of practice began assuming meanings so fluctuating that it became inappropriate as a meaning of movement in the curriculum. What my local vision saw in those texts was the path of differentiation, and what internationalization presented to me was a displacement of approximation.

If I consider it relevant to study that approximation, I also want to maintain the differentiation that the texts contain. As Pinar himself says when pointing out their synergy, the interrelatedness of these concepts includes dissonance. The greater dissonance perhaps refers to the place of the extra-discursive in the curriculum. Although it cannot be said that the theory of curriculum in Brazil is primordially post-structural, it is undeniable that some preoccupations of post-structuralism (and even of structuralism) are shared by the great majority of curricularists. The idea that language is not transparent was very well received in a field that struggled against positivism. Although we may have accepted with some ease that the extra-discursive can be related only by means of language, we are capable of wagering that the world exists, even if it cannot be controlled in its totality. There was the incorporation, by the field, of the crisis of representation, but we have not escaped from the idea that knowledge needs to be related to the multiple facets of the real. In that sense, the idea of enunciation (and the hybridity that it contains) differs from the notion of quotidian practice because it rejects the idea of representations that presumes the realism and defines the practice of that which exists, for example, as quotidian. It understands that realism sustains the distinction between theory and practice and, in a more dangerous way, associates the latter with political action, disqualifying the theoretical as the place of the political. As for the idea of eventfulness, certainly the approximations seem greater, especially concerning their non-realist nature. I am not, however, so certain that, as in Pinar's syllogism, agency structures (as it is structured by) eventfulness. It seems to me that the idea of eventfulness presupposes language without subject and, more surprising for me, without enunciation. If the abandonment of the subject is, as I described, a movement that I am reluctant to undertake, I cannot imagine, not even as an initial work hypothesis, the idea of language without enunciation. But that is not a final word.

NOTE

1. As one visits the site http://www.sintomnizado.com.br/polaroides_sobreaspolaroides.htm students read the news Estudantes de graduação da

Unicamp, de cursos de licenciatura, fazem workshop a partir da idéia das polaroides (in)visíveis, whose link will lead to the blog page of the bio_unicamp class 08, one of the classes I worked with in the subject School and Culture, which is part of the Teacher Education Undergraduate Program at the University of Campinas, durng the second semester of 2008. Besides biology students, there were also students of languages, sociology, music and the Physics-Chemistry Integrated Teacher Education Undergraduate Program.

References

Meireles, Cecília. 1983. *Obra Poética*. Rio de Janeiro: Nova Aguilar.
Pinar, William F. ed. 2003. *International Handbook of Curriculum Research*. Mahwah, NJ: Lawrence Erlbaum.

Notes on Contributors

Nilda Alves teaches curriculum studies at the State University of Rio de Janeiro. From 1983 to 1995, Alves taught at Federal Fluminense University. She is the recipient of the Medal of Educative Merit from the federal government of Brazil in acknowledgment of her work developing curriculum for undergraduate education. She was the President of Brazilian Association for Teacher Education from 1996 to 1997 and of Brazilian Educational Association for Research and Graduate Studies from 1999 to 2003. Alves is the author of many books and articles. She coordinates a laboratory dedicated to education and image (http://www.lab-eduimagem.pro.br).

Antonio Carlos Amorim is Professor in the Faculty of Education at the University of Campinas, Brazil, and Researcher in its Laboratory of Audiovisual Studies and in the Philosophy Studium at the University of Porto, Portugal. He has been acknowledged for research productivity by the National Advisory Board for Scientific and Technological Development (CNPq/Brasil). He was the Coordinator of Curriculum Division of the Brazilian Educational Association for Research and Graduate Studies during 2006–2007. Amorim is the author of many articles and book chapters in Portuguese. In English he published "Non-Figurative Narratives, or Life without Subjects," a chapter in the British collection *Exploring Selfhood: Finding Ourselves, Finding Our Stories in Life Narr*atives. His articles have also appeared in the *Journal of Reflexive Practice* and the *Educational Action Research Journal*. He serves on several editorial boards for national and international journals of research in education.

Elba Siqueira de Sá Barretto has been teaching curriculum studies at the University of São Paulo since 1989. She is a Senior Researcher at the Carlos Chagas Foundation and Editor of its scientific journal, *Cadernos de Pesquisa*. At the moment, she is also engaged with the Brazilian Ministry of Education as a member of the Curriculum in Movement Program Committee and as a consultant to the Brazilian National Board of Education for the revision of the National Curriculum Guidelines for Basic Education.

Carlos Eduardo Ferraço is a Professor in the Graduate Studies Program in Education at the Federal University of Espírito Santo, working in the Culture, Curriculum, and Teacher Education research groups. He started his career as an educator in 1977. Since 1985, he has conducted studies on curricula in the public elementary schools. He has published widely, served as a CNPq researcher, and is coordinator of the Curricula, Routines, Cultures and Knowledge Networks Research Group.

Ashwani Kumar is a PhD student at the University of British Columbia where he has studied curriculum studies in South Africa, Brazil, and Mexico. He has published in the *Journal of the American Association for the Advancement of Curriculum Studies, Education Review*, and *Journal of Critical Education Policy Studies* and presented his research at meetings of the American Educational Research Association, American Association for the Advancement of Curriculum Studies, National Council for the Social Studies, and Canadian Society for the Study of Education. His dissertation research articulates the relationship between the nature of consciousness and self-inquiry in the educational theories of Krishnamurti.

Alice Casimiro Lopes is the Coordinator of the Graduate Program of Education of the State University of Rio de Janeiro in Brazil. She is also the Coordinator of the research group Curriculum: Subjects, Knowledge and Culture. Lopes is the Representative of Brazil in the General Assembly of the International Association for the Advancement of Curriculum Studies. She has published many books, chapters, and papers in Portuguese and Spanish. In English, she has published in the *Curriculum Inquiry, Journal of Iranian Curriculum Studies Association, Journal of the American Association for the Advancement of the Curriculum* and the *Journal of Curriculum and Pedagogy*, and in the books *International Conversations on Curriculum Studies: Subject, Society and Curriculum*, edited by Tero Autio and Eero Ropo, and the *International Handbook of Curriculum Research*, edited by William F. Pinar.

Elizabeth Macedo teaches curriculum theory and politics at the State University of Rio de Janeiro. She was the Coordinator of the curriculum division at the Brazilian Educational Association for Research and Graduate Studies from 2008 to 2009. She is the Vice-Coordinator of Education Area at the Brazilian Federal Funding Agency (CAPES). Macedo is the author of many books and articles in Portuguese. She wrote a chapter in English for the *International Handbook of Curriculum Research* as well as articles for journals such as *Curriculum Inquiry* (Journal of the American Association for the Advancement of Curriculum Studies) and the *Journal of Curriculum and Pedagogy*.

Inês Barbosa de Oliveira teaches courses on curriculum, culture, and everyday life in schools at the State University of Rio de Janeiro, where she coordinates the research group focused on knowledge networks and emancipatory practices. Among the subjects of her published academic papers are studies of the epistemological and political issues associated with her research.

William F. Pinar teaches international studies in education at the University of British Columbia, where he holds a Canada Research Chair. He is the author of *The Worldliness of a Cosmopolitan Education* (2009) and the editor of *Curriculum Studies in South Africa* (2010).

Index